Hotspur

HENRY PERCY: MEDIEVAL REBEL

A.W. BOARDMAN

SUTTON PUBLISHING

First published in the United Kingdom in 2003 by
Sutton Publishing Limited · Phoenix Mill
Thrupp · Stroud · Gloucestershire · GL5 2BU

British Library Cataloguing in Publication Data
A catalogue record for this book is available from the British Library.

ISBN 0-7509-2878-6

Typeset in 11/14.5 pt Sabon.
Typesetting and origination by
Sutton Publishing Limited.
Printed and bound in England by
J.H. Haynes & Co. Ltd, Sparkford.

Contents

Acknowledgements

This book began life as a re-appraisal of three important medieval battles – Otterburn, Homildon Hill and Shrewsbury – but quickly developed into a more personal search for one of the most enigmatic and elusive figures of British history – Henry Percy, nicknamed Hotspur. The work was also prompted by a fascination with Shakespeare's history plays, an affinity with the north-east of England, and a more immediate and long-lasting passion for the varied historic tapestry of my home county – Yorkshire.

Standing under the rugged walls of Bamburgh and Alnwick castles or walking and exploring the now peaceful battlefields of Otterburn and Shrewsbury is to catch the faded glimpse of an England largely forgotten in the modern consciousness. Henry Percy, Shakespeare's most beloved anti-hero and rebel, knew this bygone England intimately, but even he shares the fate of most historical characters – that of being depicted as only a shadow of his former self. And since Hotspur rode across the pages of recorded history at breakneck speed, it is even more surprising that his name has stood the test of time and memory. However, in much the same way as the legend of Robin Hood has survived many ages and interpretations mainly through tradition and word of mouth, the persistence of Hotspur's fame owes more to allegory than to fact.

That Hotspur's historical sobriquet conjures up an image of a man of speed and daring is perhaps self-evident and we may wonder how he earned such a lucid and fiery description. That he was badly misinterpreted by many writers after his death is chiefly due to his failed rebellion; that he was remembered as something of a unstable 'loose cannon' is mainly down to how Shakespeare characterised him in his history plays. As the high-spirited, impetuous, and outspoken youth of Elizabethan drama, Hotspur unfolds before us like an breath of fresh air in an altogether more homogeneous cast. However, the evidence for the real Hotspur, the one his

Acknowledgements

enemies chose to immortalise in a name, is far removed from a performance of *Richard II* or *Henry IV* at the Globe or the Old Vic. In particular, Henry Percy's many rash actions have been attributed to an inexplicably hyperactive nature, and therefore no heed has been paid to the deep and meaningful semi-religious chivalric standards that he and many of his creed came to hold so dear. His rebellious character must also be measured against a more sobering will to survive amid increasing personal and military pressure not only at court but also within the confines of his own immediate family. To summarise, the reader must synthesise all these deeper meanings from the evidence presented here in order to form a balanced opinion about the character of Henry Percy and the age he knew so well.

Battles of any era have long been my greatest fascination, and the fact that this year marks the 600th anniversary of one of the most interesting and unusual makes this work all the more poignant and timely. The battle of Shrewsbury, fought on 21 July 1403, heralded in a new era of warfare that saw Englishmen fighting their battles at home using similar weapons and military conventions. Hence, for me at least, this military biography of Hotspur completes a circle with a re-assessment of a battle that has much in common with that sanguinary conflict known later as the Wars of the Roses. My own lifelong interest in the wars between York and Lancaster was certainly put to the test on several occasions in the quiet meadows surrounding Battlefield Church and resulted in a healthy scepticism about what actually occurred there in 1403. However, the real uniqueness of the field known ever since as Battlefield is nothing short of astonishing. In short, all the evidence surrounding Hotspur's last fight points to an exact acreage of land where the two contending armies finally clashed – a fascinating prospect to the battlefield detective and historian considering that most medieval battles have alternative sites attributed to them.

That the dead still remain buried in Battlefield is a measured certainty and a testament to what terrible events took place there in 1403. Therefore we must honour that certainty and always view any battlefield as a war grave, not to mention a lasting personal memorial to those that fought and died there so long ago.

In the course of fleshing out the historical Hotspur and his times I am indebted to a number of people who, apart from their enthusiastic support, have helped me with various technical and historical aspects of this work.

Acknowledgements

Wakefield Library Headquarters (Balne Lane) has been particularly helpful in tracing some of the primary source works, especially E.B. de Fonblanque's very rare book *Annals of the House of Percy*. I am also indebted to Shrewsbury Reference and Research Library for locating some of the original material on the battle of Shrewsbury and Battlefield Church. I would also like to thank all the staff at Leeds Central Library for their help, not forgetting Kevin Bullimore at the British Library for his interest, and particularly his information on the Percy family.

Simon Stanley in particular has shared a great deal of his expert technical knowledge and data on the medieval bow and arrow with me a subject that continues to fascinate, not to mention confound so-called specialists by presenting an image of the great weapon that scuttles all 'accepted' theories with a sound measure of practical proof. His work is ongoing, and his drawing of the most powerful bows legendary – long may it continue.

As ever, I am thankful to Robert Hardy CBE, who continues to encourage me with all my projects while at the same time correcting me on the fact that Shakespeare was not all wrong in his assumptions regarding Hotspur's impetuous character.

Once again I would like to thank Geoff Wheeler for providing most of the pictures in the book and especially for rooting out a hoard of obscure data relating to the Percy story that otherwise I may never have come across, especially in connection with the history of the Douglas 'Cavers' Standard.

On a more personal note, I would like to thank my father for reading the manuscript and for correcting it, my family and friends for their invaluable support, and especially my wife Sheree for her patience, her interest, and her unfailing faith in me which has led to many memorable days exploring castles, battlefields and museums all over the country. This work is dedicated to my beautiful daughter Maisie, who was born when this book was nearing its completion.

Preface
Battlefield: 8.30 p.m.

> . . . After him came a man spurring hard
> A gentleman almost forspent with speed,
> That stopp'd by me to breathe his bloodied horse.
> He ask'd the way to Chester; and of him
> I did demand, what news from Shrewsbury.
> He told me, that rebellion had ill luck,
> And that young Harry Percy's spur was cold.
>
> *Henry IV Part 2*, Act 1, Scene 1,
> William Shakespeare

In a field near Shrewsbury there had been a battle. A battle fought by Englishmen against Englishmen for the prize of the crown of England.

Several thousand dead bodies lay in scattered heaps at the base of a gently rising slope. Flattened crops, which had suddenly yielded to a rushing tide of men and horses, now tangled with thousands of arrow shafts angled obliquely into anything that had halted their deadly path. It was as if a wooden harvest had been spirited out of the ground to greet the knots of men-at-arms and shire levies that had tried to stand firm against some of the best archers in the land. Volley upon volley had rained down from the heavens in dreadful repetition. Needle-sharp and deadly thick, the relentless arrow storm had hit their partially armoured bodies several times over. Like lifeless porcupines, shocked and bloody faces now frozen in mute agony stared blindly skyward, while countless severed limbs and shattered body parts denoted the place where the two armies had finally closed in bloody hand-to-hand combat. The kingdom had not seen a battle like it since Simon de Montfort had rebelled in 1265. And never had longbow been used against longbow to such deadly effect on English soil.

A famous northern hero had died at Shrewsbury that day. Opposing his king to the very last, he had been cut down somewhere amid the metallic, manic disorder that was glorified as the epitome of medieval chivalry. Littering the once-quiet meadows flanking the Whitchurch road, the conflict could literally be traced by the human wreckage that he had caused, but as yet it was impossible for anyone to remember where the rebel leader had fallen, such had been the ferocity and uncertainty of the final moments of battle.

Flocks of scavengers from nearby Shropshire villages were already picking greedily at the dead like carrion crows on a freshly harrowed field. Wounded men screamed as victorious royalist soldiers in search of loot finished them off with whatever weapons they could lay their hands on. Riderless horses, darting back and forth between the ghastly heaps of death, reared and bucked savagely, eager to be free of their wagging arrow wounds and of the carnage that had stained the battlefield copper-red with their masters' blood. Their frantic whinnying and the constant lament of dying men were sounds to send a man mad, that is if a man were not mad enough already from witnessing the many horrors of war.

Confusion and uncertainty reigned supreme in every living soldier's scarred mind and blood-shot eyes. Only the gaudily attired heralds and their pursuivants, nervously roaming the field in search of the noble and highborn, showed any kind of order and restraint amid the terrible slaughter. Their place was to record the glorious dead and to supervise the teams of gravediggers that would later clear the field of its mortal refuse as soon as it was safe to do so. Having lost their lives for king and country, those men fortunate enough to have fought and died on the winning side would be noted and buried with full battle honours, their dependants cared for with generous annuities paid by the crown. As for the rebel leaders, their heads, and what remained of their battered bodies, would soon adorn the gates of many an English town and city as a warning to others who might dare rebel against the king's high estate.

Those soldiers who had survived the terrible ordeal without injury were extremely lucky to be alive. Some of the wounded would be scarred for life, while others who had been lacerated by soiled weapons would die slowly from infected wounds some weeks later. Yet others would be scarred mentally for years to come by the horror of medieval combat. Both winners and losers would venerate the battle in old age, while those who were predestined to remain on the field later known as Bateleyfield would soon be heaped into communal grave pits near the patch of ground they had so gallantly defended with their lives on St Mary Magdalene's Eve.

In later years a chantry chapel and secular college would be built on the exact site where the rebellion had been crushed and where its ambitious young leader had met his fateful end. Some of his faithful supporters had failed him at the last, but a select few had followed him blindly into the pages of medieval legend without a second thought. Those unfortunate enough to have fallen into enemy hands were already branded traitors by their king. Bound to their horses, and with heads bent low in captive despair, they too would soon meet their deaths in the nearby town of Shrewsbury or be attainted for high treason, their lands and titles forfeited to the crown.

But he had died a death worthy of his illustrious ancestors' warlike reputation.

His blue lion rampant banner of Louvain, Fitzalan and Lucy, now ripped to shreds in a last desperate attempt to slay the king, was spattered with the blood of his enemies. Covering his armoured body like a death shroud, the heraldic symbolism of his forebears had cleverly concealed his identity from his adversaries, while the arrow wound that had suddenly pierced his brain had masked his famous features in a welter of crimson blood.

The king's men were still looking for him in the jaded half-light of what had been a total eclipse of the moon. Soon wild dogs would be roaming the field in search of meat, and then no one would believe that the rebellion had been crushed and that the famous Harry Percy, known as 'Hotspur', was dead.

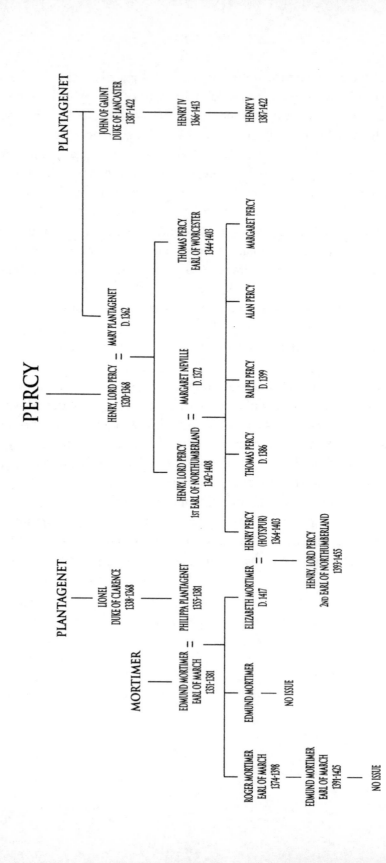

ONE

Spofforth: 1364

Henry Percy, better known to history as 'Hotspur', was born on 13 June 1364 at the now ruined but still impressive Spofforth Castle, a manor house situated midway between Wetherby and Harrogate in what is now North Yorkshire.[1] Built on the foundations of a much earlier castle that stood on the same site in the eleventh century, Hotspur's birthplace was refashioned by his grandfather, another Henry Percy, who obtained a licence to crenellate the building in 1308.[2] Battlements, however, were not to be added to Spofforth's high imposing walls. Being situated a relatively 'safe' distance away from the Scottish border, and protected by the great defensive chain of northern castles that extended from the Pennines at Richmond to the royal castle at Scarborough on the east coast, it was thought that Spofforth could be afforded a little luxury in comparison.

Today the great hall is a quiet ruin, but with imagination it is easy to visualise 'Spawford's'[3] grandeur in Hotspur's day, with its hanging tapestries, sumptuous apartments and roaring log fires providing every possible luxury to so great a northern family. However, in 1364 the 'castle' and its large estate was but a small part of the Percy inheritance, an inheritance that at first commanded only a portion of Yorkshire then later spread over several other English counties to become one of the most formidable concerns in the land.

At the time of Hotspur's birth the Percy family held substantial manors in what was then the old West Riding, most notably at Healaugh, Leathley, Linton and Tadcaster. In the north of the county they were lords of Asenby, Gristhwaite, Kirk Leavington, Seamer, Throxenby and Topcliffe, and in East Yorkshire their possessions comprised Arras, Catton, Gembling, Leconfield, Nafferton, Pocklington, Scorborough, Wansford, Wasplington and Wressle. In addition to this impressive list of Yorkshire 'lowland' manors, Percy influence also extended even further north, into parts of Craven, Ribblesdale and Langstrothdale, south to their manor at Petworth in West Sussex, east into Lincolnshire, and across the River Tyne to their great castles of Alnwick and Warkworth, from which the Percy earldom of Northumberland later originated. In short, by 1364 the Percy family were the major landowners in the north after the Duchy of Lancaster. By the end of the century, due to their successive appointments as the king's 'seigneurs marchers del north',[4] or northern marcher lords, it was perhaps inevitable that the Percys had also become one of the leading noble families in England.

Fourteenth-century Yorkshire was a vastly different region, both in importance and character, than might at first be imagined. Contrary to popular belief, it was the actual geographical location of the county that was partly responsible for moulding its inhabitants into extremely resourceful individuals who possessed an in-built ability to survive against great adversity. Some fifteenth-century medieval historians who sought to distinguish the military aptitude of the north over the south noted this resilience in their chronicles during the Wars of the Roses. However, the substance of their philosophy undoubtedly stemmed from an earlier age and centred on the important role played by Yorkshire in Anglo-Scottish border warfare.

The distinction between life in fourteenth-century Yorkshire and in the border region cannot be clearly defined with any degree of accuracy, other than to say that the lowland areas of Yorkshire had much in common with southern England. York was a booming city and a centre for international trade, while Berwick-upon-Tweed was primarily a garrisoned outpost threatened by sporadic Scottish invasion. Newcastle, situated between the two, was a walled town, a port, and something of a blend of both places, populated by a highly sophisticated merchant class that was occasionally disturbed by the intrusion of Scottish raiding.

When men aged between sixteen and sixty were called upon by Commissions of Array to help defend northern England against the threat of Scottish invasion, it was crucial that the ruling English monarch could rely upon his northern lords to spring into action at any given moment with as many men as possible to protect the border. However, the population of the six northern shires as a whole posed inherent military problems for the king and his official, or officials, responsible for defending the marches towards

Scotland. The historian R.L. Storey aptly demonstrated the fact that, 'The influence of the north was disproportionate to its wealth and population. The six northern counties occupy a quarter of the total area of England, but their adult population was only 15 per cent of the total recorded in the poll tax of 1377. The particulars for Yorkshire distinguish it from the five other counties. Its size is not quite equal to the total area of the others, but it accounted for two-thirds of the northern population. In other words, one-tenth of the English population in 1377 were Yorkshiremen.'[5]

Strong personal ties had been forged between Yorkshire and the lands bordering Scotland during the fourteenth century, and Storey's 'disproportionate northern population' meant that English armies had to be gathered in depth. Taking the above statistics as proof of population, this gives us ample reason to believe that Scottish invasion and raiding was consequently not only a northern border problem, but also a Yorkshire problem in late medieval England.

Also, the character of Hotspur's Yorkshire, or more precisely that of its people, differed from the rest of England to such an extent that from the twelfth to the sixteenth century some of the most dangerous rebellions had their origins in the north. Several complicated political and social events caused these rebellions to reoccur in England during the medieval period; underlying any such short-term causes, however, were more basic long-term traditions. It was these 'hidden factors' that helped distinguish northerners from the rest of the medieval population of England by assigning them a dual reputation for being hardy warriors on the one hand, and belligerent individuals on the other.

To understand this northern duality it is important to remember that the six northern shires were extremely isolated from central medieval government. Being 200 to 300 miles from London, this was one reason why Yorkshire and the border counties came under the jurisdiction of an independent, trusted and powerful officer of the king. A journey of several days to possibly two weeks on badly maintained medieval roads made southern control of northern England virtually impossible on a day-to-day basis – so much so that English kings had to delegate command and responsibility for these highly militarised areas to their most powerful lords, some of whose ancestors had held sway over the north since the Norman Conquest.

What the medieval northerner experienced of border life also explains why he was such a difficult subject to control. Constant exposure to the likelihood of Scottish invasion and indiscriminate raiding, coupled with the everyday medieval hazards of robbery, arson and manslaughter, made each borderer skilful in the use of arms, a vital prerequisite for every landowner and tenant farmer who had to defend his property in order to survive. In short, to recover what was rightfully his from an invader there was only one option open to him – he had to fight back.

A great northern lord faced with such difficulties might call upon his local tenantry to help him recover his property by force of arms, even at the expense of breaking formal treaties imposed by the all-powerful wardens of the marches. If influential enough, the noble in question might petition his king to advance his claim on Scottish-held land that he felt was 'lawfully' his. However, for a simple smallholder living on the absolute margin of subsistence there was no such political alternative. Existing on a constant knife-edge of adversity was an age-old and inbred fact of life in the marchlands, and its reddened blade had accounted for the lives of many men, women and children on both sides of the border by the end of the fourteenth century. Thus for the common people of Yorkshire, but more particularly for all those who lived within striking distance of Scottish raiding parties, respect for law and order was a hard pill to swallow compared with a life of poverty and slavery; therefore they had to seek help from elsewhere.

For great magnates like the Percys, who held the majority of northern power in the fourteenth century, it was much the same story; they too had lands to defend, some of which had been acquired over many generations of hardship, cost and great personal risk. But what better individuals could a noble wish to recruit into his following against a common foe than those smallholders who were on the receiving end of Scottish raiding? As paid guardians of the north, here was the strength in numbers that ensured a noble's survival, reinforced his garrisons and bolstered his esteem. As for the retained borderer, the lucrative aspects of such northern employment are self-evident, the structure of man and master extending from the lowliest vassal to his supreme master, the king of England. With this kind of military 'structure' in place it was not only possible for the Percys to raise armies to defend the border, but also it was far easier for men like Hotspur and his father to achieve independent control of the northern marches.

There were, however, inherent problems for these all-powerful guardians of the north in peacetime. Faced with such a volatile northern population bent on avenging the last pillaging raid into England, treaties were difficult to maintain for long periods of time. The close proximity of farmland and estates to ever-shifting borders made it virtually impossible for northern marcher lords to control their 'subjects'. Thus an unpredictable factor was introduced into the equation, creating a formidable barrier against any lasting peace settlement with the 'old enemy'. Violence, in the form of cross-border raiding and feuding, meant that wardens like the Percys were often forced into turning a blind eye to private warring. As a result, sympathetic royal efforts to improve relations with Scotland came as unwelcome news not only to their long-suffering tenants but also to nobles who were determined to control at least a major share of the northern defences.

Ever since Edward I, the redoubtable Hammer of the Scots, had tried to impose his will on Scotland at the beginning of the thirteenth century, northern England had known no peace. It was a legacy of unfinished business, and a quarrel that had never been fully settled. Full-scale wars were infrequent, but raids and the indiscriminate burning and pillaging of crops, border towns and farmland were commonplace activities on both sides of the divide. Add to this the violent aspects of everyday medieval northern life, and it was no accident that borderers made good soldiers, violence being a deeply seated living memory that demanded immediate retaliation by those who suffered the direct results of it.

J.A. Tuck shared this view in his *War and Society in the Medieval North*. Giving credence to the unseen mental effect that sporadic border raiding had on northern populations, he reiterates that 'it was easier for inhabitants to recover from the damage done by raiders than for them to come to believe that it would not happen again'.[6] In fact, the fear of Scottish invasion was more compelling than the actuality and it was for this reason that fortified houses and 'peel' towers were built, not just along the border with Scotland, but also in parts of Richmondshire, Craven and North Yorkshire, in order to combat this lingering threat of invasion.

Hotspur's family, and also a host of other northern lords who shared control of this highly unstable and militarised area, habitually closed ranks against royal authority when their own interests were threatened. By protecting their own tenantry from both the fear and actuality of Scottish invasion and raiding they were in effect ensuring their own survival. But they had to be careful not to upset the northern equilibrium, or disturb the ties that existed between other northern nobles and the ruling monarch, as both evils could spell disaster if the same favours they enjoyed were monopolised by another. Therefore a balance of power had to be maintained by the king, and men like the Percys were acutely aware of this when it came to governing the north with their own private forces.

At the time of Hotspur's birth the ambitions of the Percy family were, like those of any other English noble household, fixed on protecting their own territorial interests by mediation and tolerance. However, in the next century, when the Neville family finally squashed Percy ambitions in the north, personal greed was to open the political and military floodgates of private warring and blood-feuding to such an extent that civil war was the result. It perhaps comes as no surprise that the aforementioned nobles' ever-loyal northern 'subjects' followed both families into battle in what later became known as the Wars of the Roses – in essence, they had very little choice. The devotion of these 'unruly' northerners was unbounded and selfish. They helped the Percys and their kind win power in the north for as long as the threat of Scottish invasion existed. Consequently, their loyalties rested chiefly with their northern masters and not with their king. As the biased Percy chronicler, John Hardyng, informs us of his first patron Henry Percy: '. . . For trust it true there is no lorde in Englande that may defende you agayn Scotlande so well as he, for they [the Percys] have the hertes of the people by North, and ever had: and doute it not, the North parte bee your trewe legemen.'[7]

Hotspur's father, Henry Percy, 1st Earl of Northumberland, was the leading player in this remarkable show of northern dominance. In both local and national politics, by the end of the fourteenth century, his territorial power in Yorkshire, Northumberland and Cumberland was almost complete. In short, for a brief period of time, he was the only true northern magnate who could claim to 'strut the northern shires like a king'.[8]

How is it then that Hotspur's name is better known to history than that of the man who made all this possible? The simple answer is that Northumberland's impetuous offspring was a larger-than-life historical character whose renown provided a fascinating subject for later writers. Thus Shakespeare, by creating a highly dramatic anti-hero out of an extremely elusive historical character, was responsible for giving 'Harry Hotspur' legendary status; Percy's enigmatic nickname, even in Shakespeare's England, became synonymous with all the more sublime and eccentric charms of youthful impetuosity that, even today, make him so appealing to audiences throughout the world. In his famous plays *Richard II* and *Henry IV Part 1*, Shakespeare succeeds admirably in portraying the extremely 'juvenile' Hotspur as the impetuous knight, outspoken to the point of foolishness, who dares to rebel against authority in a moment of classic madness. Much like his counterpart Prince Hal, although not as successful, it could be said that Hotspur, like most noble 'sons' of his age, was deprived of real power until it was too late. Shakespeare goes on to cast Hotspur as the quintessential medieval rebel seeking glory on the field of battle at the expense of his own safety.

However, contemporary chroniclers such as Thomas Walsingham tell of a different Hotspur, who gained fame as easily as others of his age gained land or titles, of a knight who was constantly seeking to fulfil the chivalric ideal, but ultimately of a man who was a victim of others' greed for power. Focusing on his chivalric notoriety, rather than his impulsiveness, the legendary status of Hotspur is therefore cast aside by Walsingham for a more honourable one. The reality is difficult to trace, the appeal of Shakespeare's 'Mars in swaddling clothes' difficult to exorcise. But herein lies the appeal for this rather complex individual whose famous exploits have stood the test of time and whose death would later ensure that his nickname would become a byword for anyone with the same outspoken and hyperactive behaviour.

Of Hotspur's very early life little is known, but it is highly likely that from a very young age, like most of his contemporaries, he must have been aware of his own lineage and also of the Percy inheritance that might one day be his. John Leland, the great traveller and antiquary who wrote in the early sixteenth century, recalled in his *Itinerary* that one of the Percy manor houses had a special room for the purpose of studying genealogy: '[Leconfield] is a large house and stondith withyn a great mote yn one very spatius court. 3 partes of the house, saving the meane gate that is made of brike, is al of tymbre. The 4 parte is fair made of stone and sum brike. I saw in a litle studiying chaumber ther called Paradice the genealogie of the Percys.'[9]

In such a place as 'Paradice' it is highly likely that Hotspur would have been told tall tales of his illustrious ancestor William de Percy, the first baron, surnamed '*als gernons*' (with the whiskers) who probably arrived in England from Normandy sometime after 1067. However, lacking first-hand knowledge of Leconfield's more ancient genealogical roll, the prime source for any serious modern research into the Percy family derives chiefly from the pen of E.B. de Fonblanque in his very rare book, *Annals of the House of Percy*. First published in 1887, this important work, along with some other more recent studies of the Percy family, points our way back in time to a rather less hospitable north than even young Hotspur might have been used to, and to an England where Saxon resistance against Norman incursion had been systematically reduced to ashes in its beloved capital of York.

A supposed intimate friend of the Conqueror, Hotspur's great ancestor, William de Percy, is recorded in the Domesday Book as holding *in capite* eighty-six lordships in Yorkshire, thirty-two in Lincolnshire and a number of other manors in Essex and Hampshire. The Percy family had no connection with Northumberland until two centuries after their settlement in England, but their principal residences were built on sound and highly prized foundations 'in the cradle of their race – Yorkshire'.[10] Of William de Percy's Norman estates, such as the family seat of Perci in the valley of the River Dives, twenty-five miles south-east of Caen in France, there is very little mention after William's arrival north of the Humber, and it is highly likely that Als Gernons was from a younger branch of the family not destined to inherit a major share of Percy lands in upper Normandy. Fonblanque, our guide to this rather complex history of the Percy family, describes William as Comte de Caux and de Poitiers and asserts that the family owned the Chateau de Perci near Villedieu in the Department of La Manche. However, it is certain that with lands to be acquired in England Als Gernons was not slow in capitalising on the Conqueror's recent 'acquisitions' in Yorkshire. Soon after the Saxon rebellion of Gospatric in 1069, and the desolation of the north by Hugh Lupus, Earl of Chester, Percy obtained substantial parcels of land all over Yorkshire. Here he built a number of fortified manor houses, including the Percys' four most important seats of power at this time: Topcliffe, Spofforth, Sneaton and

Hackness. William de Percy also gained a great cluster of lands around the coastal port of Whitby, where he began to rebuild the monastery that had previously been destroyed by Danish invaders.

Although probably never the subject of much debate in Hotspur's day, it seems that Als Gernons Percy was a particularly headstrong and obstinate individual when it came to parting with any of his hard-won lands. Indeed, it seems that he even rebelled against the current Norman fashion of appearing clean-shaven, hence his 'hairy' nickname. This obstinacy and determination to be different can be best illustrated by briefly describing the events surrounding the famous ongoing different to control the Whitby Abbey estate, which raged on and off for almost twenty years.

After William's friend and cousin, Reinfeld, ceased to be abbot of Whitby in 1078, a monk named Stephen sought to question the charter under which the monastery held its lands from the Percys. Refusing to make the charter absolute in favour of the abbey, William de Percy drove Stephen and his monks away, and they in turn petitioned the king to resolve the dispute. The resulting attempts at mediation ended in deadlock and the monks sought refuge at nearby Lastingham, Abbot Reinfeld being reinstated at Whitby in Stephen's place in the interim. However, the dispute was far from over, and it now found new roots in a quarrel much closer to home when Reinfeld suddenly died, apparently while he was supervising the repair of a nearby bridge. After deciding to appoint his brother Serlo to the see of Whitby, William de Percy gifted a portion of its land to his armour-bearer, Ralph de Eversley, for services rendered. Inevitably, this opened old wounds, and Serlo also rebelled against his brother by petitioning the king (then William Rufus), who in turn threatened William with excommunication. Both Percys were ordered to keep the peace, and in harmony with this edict, Serlo and his monks were also ordered to move away until William came to his senses and agreed that the abbey lands should be held jointly.

Like so many of his contemporaries, Als Gernons Percy was insanely jealous of other men's territorial influence, and this stubborn trait seems to have so plagued Hotspur's family in later years that it is perhaps worth remembering that its origins had an early precedent. However, in the harsh realities of the medieval north it is perhaps also useful to note that there could be no compromise for a man like William de Percy when it came to landed power. As discussed previously, Yorkshire in particular had witnessed a degree of Norman devastation and rebirth, and leading nobles naturally became extremely protective of their hard-won estates, defending them to the last acre in some cases in order to survive. William de Percy was not unique in this 'stubbornness', nor was he exceptional in his decision to pay good service with land in the time-honoured fashion of feudalism.

Men like Ralph de Eversley took advantage of 'good lordship' in order to carve out power of their own and this inevitably was paid for in return, usually by military service. In the latter years of the eleventh century this service took Eversley overseas, and in about 1095 he followed his master to Palestine, where Percy joined Robert of Normandy on crusade. It was here, two years later, that Percy died, his body being buried at either Antioch or Montjoie within sight of Jerusalem. However, far from being wholly lost in an obscure grave, William's heart was removed from his body and brought back to England at his own request, and it is said that this task was performed by none other than Percy's faithful retainer, who survived the crusade and dutifully returned to England to bury Als Gernons' heart in the abbey that had caused William so much trouble.

Hotspur's famous ancestor left three sons by his Saxon wife, Emma de Port, and thereafter the eldest, Alan, succeeded to the Percy barony as the second of that name. In comparison to his father's notable landed achievements in the north, the career of '*Magnus Alanus*', despite his grand title, was undistinguished. However, when he died in 1120 Percy dominions in the north had multiplied tenfold, and had not only spread into parts of Cravenshire, but had also undergone a significant change of ownership. By the time Alan's son, a second William de Percy, succeeded to the title, most of the Percy lands acquired originally by his grandfather, Als Gernons, from the Earl of Chester were now held directly from the crown.

After the death of Alan's son, another William succeeded to the family title, becoming the fourth baron. This William de Percy fought for King Stephen and Thurstan, Archbishop of York, against the Scots at the battle of the Standard in 1138, the irony being that William's own uncle (an illegitimate son of Alan de Percy) fought on the losing side. Conflicting loyalties often caused many northern lords with lands in Scotland to side with the 'old enemy'; however, despite this fact, the Percys seem to have followed what appears to have been a family tradition of allegiance to English kings, never knowingly threatened until Hotspur rebelled against Henry IV in 1403. Later given the manor of Petworth and 10,000 acres of land in Sussex by Henry II for his devoted service to the crown, William, the fourth baron, left two daughters and four sons to succeed to a vast inheritance. Unfortunately, all four of these Percys left no male issue, and the barony passed equally to William's daughters Maud and Agnes Percy, who had each married into the nobility.

That young Hotspur's family historian would have glossed over the events relating to the next period of uncertainty faced by his family is highly likely. With the male line extinguished in one generation, not only was the actual name of 'Percy' in danger of disappearing, but also two of its family members found that they were plunged into a desperate quarrel to determine who would hold the moiety of the barony. The ensuing battle for power was not finally won without a great deal of family upheaval, however; the truth is perhaps a perpetual reminder of how influential and powerful wealthy landed women could be in the fourteenth century, especially when it came to the survival of a dynasty.

Maud Percy, the chief instigator of the resulting family litigation, was probably a very resourceful and single-minded woman. Nevertheless, when she married William de Newburgh, Earl of Warwick, she could hardly have foreseen that he, like her illustrious forebear Als Gernons, would also die on crusade, leaving no male issue to inherit the Percy title. With the harrowing prospect of her lands being contested by others less worthy to inherit, she promised that her youngest nephew Richard de Percy, second son of her sister Agnes and Joceline, Count of Louvain should inherit her half of the Percy estates at her death. It was this bequest that was to later cause a major family rift.

The marriage of Maud's sister into the family of Louvain was made on the condition that Count Joceline should adopt the Percy name. Claiming noble descent from none other than the Emperor Charlemagne, Louvain appears to have consented to this proviso despite his noble breeding, which at face value seems to have been a wholly inappropriate thing to do under the circumstances. However, it seems that the impoverished count held slender estates at the time and although he adopted the name of Percy as his own, he refused to forsake his own arms (*a field or a lion rampant azure*) in fear that he would be unable to inherit his father's estates when he died. Thereafter, the arms of Louvain became quartered with that of Percy (*azure, five fusils in a fess argent*), and the name of Percy, and the famous blue lion, lived on through two sons, Henry and Richard.

Despite the obvious problems facing the Percy family at this time, Maud's bequest to her nephew Richard seems to have been natural enough, given that a strong, adult male heir was clearly the best chance of family survival in such uncertain times. However, there was a major stumbling block. Richard's elder brother, Henry de Percy, who had died in 1198, had left a son to succeed him, and this in turn brought about another fierce family quarrel when this son, William, came of age.

Richard was not unlike most of his medieval contemporaries when it came to coveting landed power. Quick to seize his own inheritance on the death of his mother Agnes in 1205, Richard found no difficulty in usurping the entire administration of the Percys in addition to his own. William's remonstrations changed nothing with regard to the baronial title, and a long period of litigation ensued which finally concluded that Richard de Percy should hold the moiety of the estates bequeathed to him by his aunt, Maud, but that on his death the whole property was to revert to his nephew William.

Richard, technically 5th Baron Percy, was now lawfully secured in his inheritance, albeit a usurped one. However, there can hardly have been a day that passed when Richard was not haunted by his nephew's diminutive shadow. After joining the twenty-five barons who forced King John to sign Magna Carta in 1215, Richard de Percy must have been contemplating what might happen if the king ever took revenge on those responsible for his subjugation. The reprisals were not long in coming. Less than a year later, when Richard and other northern barons reduced Yorkshire to the obedience of Louis of France against King John, Percy's worst fears came to pass. Excommunicated by the pope for his treasonable actions, he had all his lands immediately confiscated and declared forfeit to the crown. A change of monarchy in 1216 changed nothing, and in 1217 Henry III added insult to injury by threatening to grant all this power to William, Richard's nephew, if he did not submit to the crown. However, Richard managed to maintain his independence and a slender control of the barony, despite several brushes with adversity, right up to his death in 1244, when William finally got what he wanted.

It is highly likely that William de Percy heaved a huge sigh of relief when he received news of his uncle's demise. But the postscript to this particular story ends on a less than happy note for William. Less than a year after his uncle was buried at Whitby Abbey, William de Percy, then aged fifty-two, also died, leaving several children by his first wife Eleanor Baliol, of whom the eldest, Henry, became 7th Baron Percy.

During the Barons' War of 1264 this Henry de Percy fought under the royal standard at the battle of Lewes where he was taken prisoner by Simon de Montfort, the founder of the first medieval parliament. However, in the following year he was free again and negotiating a treaty between Henry III and the barons, after which he had the good fortune to ally himself to the royal family by marrying Eleanor Plantagenet, the king's niece. When he died in 1272, Henry left a son, another Henry Percy, to succeed to the barony, a man with whom no doubt Hotspur would have identified, judging by his ancestor's varied military career.

Henry de Percy, 8th Baron, was summoned to parliament as Lord Percy in 1298, and at the age of twenty-six he fought in Gascony under Edward I. Earlier, in 1296, the Percy battle cry of 'Esperance!' was doubtless heard in the Scottish marches and in what was soon to become the Percys' more usual haunt of Northumberland. Here, before the gates of Berwick-upon-Tweed, Henry Percy was knighted by his cousin Edward I, after which he shared in the glowing English victory over the Scots at the battle of Dunbar. In 1297 Percy made Carlisle his headquarters and it was here that he and Robert de Clifford set about mustering a large force to invade Scotland. After capturing the Bishop of Glasgow, Robert de Bruce and several other Scottish notaries, Percy tried to reinforce Sir Hugh Cressingham at Stirling, but he was ordered to withdraw his troops, fortunately escaping the famous English defeat there by the forces of William Wallace.

For the remainder of his life Henry Percy served both Edward I and Edward II in Scotland on many occasions, most notably against Robert de Bruce at the battle of Bannockburn in 1314 when the English were utterly defeated. Before this, however, Percy had been allowed to purchase Alnwick Castle from Anthony Bek, the Bishop of Durham, and from then on this famous fortress was to become one of the most notable seats of the Percy family. In fact, Henry Percy, now created 1st Baron Percy of Alnwick, was

13

chiefly responsible for transplanting the family name from Yorkshire into the Northumbrian heartland. Captured after Bannockburn by his arch-rival Bruce, Percy was speedily ransomed, but died in 1315, allegedly of a broken heart because of the English defeat. He was buried at Alnwick, leaving two sons to succeed him by his wife Eleanor Fitzalan.

Hotspur's great-grandfather, a third Henry de Percy, was born in 1299 and continued where his father's exploits in Scotland had left off. Knighted in 1322, he accompanied Edward II into Scotland, but when Queen Isabella and Roger Mortimer formed an open league against their sovereign in 1326, his decision to join their ranks, then oppose them, probably gives some indication of how fickle the notion of strong kingship had become in England at this time. Summoned to the parliament of 1327, Henry de Percy was among those who deposed Edward II and acclaimed his fourteen-year-old son King of England. Later passing sentence of death on Mortimer, who had recently, along with Queen Isabella, relinquished all English claims on Scotland for the princely sum of £20,000, Percy played a prominent role in the border war that followed. He took part in the siege of Berwick in 1333, and was probably present at the battle of Halidon Hill where the English longbow caused great slaughter against the forces of Archibald Douglas.

The feud between the rival houses of Percy and Douglas forms a major part of our story, and its origins can be traced to about this time. Certainly by 1345 the two families had become pitted against each other in a fierce dispute over land rights, and this was to remain so for some time to come, especially along the border where Hotspur was later to gain his fame as a guerrilla fighter. Sir William Douglas had recovered vast territorial gains from the English by the middle of the fourteenth century and David Bruce, the son of Robert, strove to push his conquests even further while Edward III was otherwise occupied in France. In the absence of his king, Henry de Percy was made one of the Guardians of the Kingdom and, along with other northern barons, was chiefly responsible for halting the Scottish advance into England at Neville's Cross in 1346. The Lanercost Chronicle has a stirring account of the battle, not to mention a rather rare physical description of Hotspur's famous ancestor:

> They [the English] arranged themselves into three columns, of which Sir Henry de Percy commanded the first. . . . Sir Henry Percy like another

Judas Maccabeus, the son of Mattathias, was a fine fighter. This knight, small of stature but sagacious, encouraged all his men to take the field by putting himself in the forefront of the battle . . . then with trumpets blaring, shields clashing, arrows flying, lances thrusting, wounded men yelling, and troops shouting, the conflict ended about the hour of vespers, amid sundered armour, broken heads, and, sad to tell, many laid low in the field.[11]

After a fight which saved the north and probably the whole kingdom from Scottish invasion, it is said that Henry Percy received huge ransoms from those who were captured. Subsequently, he was able to rebuild parts of Bamburgh Castle and start work on a new tower at Alnwick, although he probably did not live long enough to see either completed. After campaigning with his kinsman Edward Baliol in Scotland, Percy suddenly died and was subsequently buried at Alnwick in 1352, leaving his son and namesake to succeed to the title.

Henry, 3rd Lord Percy of Alnwick, was Hotspur's grandfather, and while his father was busy fighting the Scots at Neville's Cross, this Henry Percy was serving his king in France, most notably at the battle of Crécy, where the huge army of Phillip VI came to grief against the deadly effects of the English longbow. Henry Percy continued to fight for Edward III in France, but was on several occasions also employed in the north of England against the Scots, most notoriously in Edward's disastrous campaign known as 'Burnt Candlemas' by reason of the devastation caused by English troops north of the border. However, Percy was recalled to France in 1359, where he took part in the exhaustive campaign that led to the Treaty of Bretigny, an agreement and temporary accord that ended the war and his military career overseas in a flurry of uncertain rhetoric that echoed well into the next century. In the course of his life Hotspur's grandfather married twice, leaving two sons by Mary Plantagenet, the daughter of Henry, Earl of Lancaster, and one daughter by his second wife Joan Orby. Henry's two sons by the Lancastrian heiress were Hotspur's father, another Henry Percy, and Hotspur's famous uncle, Thomas Percy. Born in 1364, Hotspur was only four years old when his grandfather died in 1368.

It is perhaps inevitable that young Hotspur's character – brave to the point of rashness, yet to a fallen foe chivalrous to the point of absurdity –

was moulded by the glowing exploits of his warlike ancestors from an early age. A rich tapestry of men and women had preceded him, and each one in their turn had cultivated and helped protect the often very fragile branches of his family tree against great political and military adversity. Moulded by the harsh realities of the north, both male and female had earned their place, first in Yorkshire and then in Northumberland, as one of its most prolific protectors. Many Englishmen must have felt the Percys' rough northern presence at court, their abrupt speech in parliament, as well as appreciating their uncompromising courage on the battlefield. Casting all thoughts of personal safety aside in favour of direct action was a family characteristic that was to help and also hinder their survival, and this was to become Hotspur's way when he came of age. Indeed, Hotspur was to become a living testament to his family's impetuous need to prove itself in a world of political and chivalric extremes.

Today, this cavalier image may be seen as a kind of abstract foolishness, a Baroque masterpiece perhaps, faded at the edges by time and memory – in short, the brightly burnished image of medieval chivalry that is illuminated in all the great chronicles of the period. It may also be observed that great skill in arms was an unnecessary evil aimed at perpetuating pointless violence in an age when peace and courtly love walked hand in hand with double-dealing and treachery. However, some aspects of the chivalrous life may be condoned when measured against the violent backdrop of Hotspur's world: a world in which the darker side of medieval chivalry is well documented for all to see in the many acts of blind stupidity, war crimes and downright barbarism that one might construe today as verging on the criminally insane.

Yet contrary to what we in the modern world may think abhorrent, to men like Hotspur the pursuit of a chivalrous life was never questioned for a moment. To the son of a great and illustrious fighting family, chivalry was the embodiment of all that was noble in life. It was a clear-cut case of 'how it was'. This was how a man of breeding had to conduct himself in time of war. It was also the surest route to fame and fortune, even to the point of individuals accepting death as a kind of living immortality. This was Hotspur's world. Even before his birth the north of England was a battleground, a place that had to be defended with both political and military might. Defeat in such an unpredictable environment spelt political and personal disaster for those responsible for its safety, and in an age when power reigned supreme, such an unnatural and lowly existence was unthinkable by those whose landed interest was built on firm ancestral foundations.

If nothing else, this brief chronology of Hotspur's family illustrates two important aspects of what it meant to be the son of a famous northern household. First, that geographically the position of Percy dominance dictated the family's political and martial involvement in English affairs; and second, that while Scotland warred with England there could be no other choice for a king but to relinquish northern military responsibility to a chosen military leader – primarily one who had everything to lose and gain from involvement in such a conflict.

Landed power in the north ensured the survival not only of the Percys, but also of all their retainers and tenants who lived there. It was much the same story for all other northern households that held land in Yorkshire and on the border, Scottish ones too. Rival claimants and cross-border feuding were necessary evils that had to be endured in order to survive, and it was in both kingdoms' interests that all forms of competition were pursued at every available opportunity. National politics, and even the fate of kings, could be determined by such territorial advantage, just as the appointment of a supreme military commander in the north could spawn local dissent among those who craved ultimate power.

Like the sons of all noble families before him, the young Hotspur was undoubtedly influenced and shaped by all these factors governing his northern upbringing. The responsibilities were great, the training ground hard, but as far as we know Henry Percy took to his charges naturally, knowing that one day these great duties would come to rest upon his shoulders. When he was young he could hardly have imagined where such responsibilities might lead, or to what extent the sacred mantle of kingship might influence his short life, but he did not have to wait for long to experience his first acidic taste of medieval warfare.

TWO

Berwick: 1378

The English chronicler John Hardyng was descended from a respectable northern family. He was born in 1378, and at the age of twelve was admitted into the Percy household to be instructed in religion, learning and the exercise of arms. It was the same in all 'gentle' families throughout England, although as will be seen from Hardyng's own evidence there was nothing 'gentle' about a medieval upbringing if a candidate was aiming at military fame:

> And as lordes sonnes bene sette, at foure yere age,
> To scole at lerne the doctryne of lettrure,
> And after at sex to have thayme in language,
> And sitte at mete semely in alle nurture;
> At ten and twelve to revelle is their cure,
> To daunse and synge, and speke of gentlenesse:
> At fourtene yere they shalle to felde I sure,
> At hunte the dere, and catch an hardynesse.
>
> For dere to hunte and slea, and se them blede,
> Ane hardyment gyffith to his corage,
> And also in his wytte he takyth hede
> Ymagynynge to take thaym at avauntage.
> At sextene yere, to werray and to wage,
> To juste and ryde, and castels to assayle,
> To scarmyse also, and make sykyr scurage,
> And sette his wache for perile nocturnayle;
>
> And every day his armure to assay
> In fete of armes with some of his meyne,

His might to prove, and what that he do may
If that he were in suche jupertee
Of werre by falle, that by neccessitie
He might algates with wapyns hym defende:
Thus shuld he lerne his priorite
His wapyns alle in armes to dispende.[12]

That Hotspur, like Hardyng, underwent this kind of tuition and military training is certain, although, unlike Hardyng, Hotspur probably first tasted military life earlier than most. In fact, according to de Fonblanque, it was thrust upon him when he was only nine years of age.[13]

As one might imagine, this must have been an awe-inspiring experience for any boy who was suddenly exposed to the many horrors of war. But for such young hopefuls this exposure to violence was common practice in an age when brutality and honour walked hand in hand with perfect kindness and mercy. John Hardyng's school of 'hard knocks' was one way for young men to prepare for a chivalrous life, but the real thing, incorporating all the 'darker' elements associated with the pursuit of arms, was an altogether different matter, especially when it came to witnessing the sights and sounds of medieval campaign life, not to mention the more adult mental trauma of bloody hand-to-hand combat.

It was for this reason, according to de Fonblanque, that the nine-year-old Hotspur accompanied his father to France as a page. Although not seen as a legitimate combatant on this occasion, it was here, during a typical English *chevauchee*, or ride across enemy territory, that Hotspur first witnessed a large-scale military campaign. It may also have been here that he was taught the merits and methods of channelling such violent action to a particular place and time in order to gain great personal renown at the expense of others, the surest road to fame and fortune for the budding medieval knight. Indeed, Hotspur would have had ample opportunity to talk to many English knights who had been through the same kind of military indoctrination many years before, the importance of which can only be appreciated if we try to enter the mind of the medieval knight and substitute seemingly 'normal' life for an often extremely violent existence.

A life of chivalry underpinned all the more noble elements of medieval society with a structured hierarchy that followed a specific code of conduct.

As Gardiner so aptly described it, 'Chivalry was to the medieval warrior very much what monasticism was to the medieval churchman. It placed before him his own mode of life in the best and highest light of which it was capable. The rough and often brutal warrior learned that self-restraint and respect for others was higher than prowess in the field.'[14]

It is uncertain whether Hotspur followed Gardiner's precept of medieval chivalry to the letter, but there is every reason to believe that many of his contemporaries thought him famous for it. Following a carefully specified convention of conduct, the medieval knight was, in Gardiner's words, bound by 'his own mode of life'; but what was this 'life' that he held in such esteem? One of virtue and honour? Possibly to himself. Was it perhaps that the chivalrous classes were expected to lead a life of adventure and good deeds? Certainly adventure came into it. However, clearly the real purpose of the medieval knight was to engage in military activity at the behest of his king or master. But if this was so, how could this code of conduct govern how he behaved in the heat of battle?

Because today we are so far removed from the milieu of medieval England, it is very difficult to understand what it was like to follow a chivalrous life. To live and breathe a code of conduct that condoned 'controlled' violence was one thing, but to put this into practice was altogether a different matter. It has been proved that the rules that controlled chivalrous activity were broken on many occasions, and this shows that chivalry could only operate when certain special conditions applied. In the heat of battle, for example, this problem was obviously greatly magnified, and thus the laws governing noble conduct in war could only apply to those with similar beliefs. This is precisely why the medieval knight sought out his contemporaries in battle while those lower classes that functioned under him were mere 'arrow fodder' to his aims. To gain honour and esteem from his contemporaries a knight had first to subdue his enemy, put him within an inch of his life, and then, after capturing him, treat him to a sumptuous dinner while he awaited his ransom – a contradiction in terms that certainly beggars belief by any modern standards of hospitality.

Such chivalrous niceties proved to all the nobility that the chivalric code was governed by a set of sacred laws that restrained the knight from committing war crimes. However, we know from history that this was far from the truth, especially with regard to how non-combatants were treated in their own country. So what was chivalry? Was it a cover-up to commit violence at the behest of a higher authority? Was it perhaps a deception that enabled the dual contradictions of virtue and brutality to coexist as part of the same double-edged sword? Whatever the concept settled on, the conclusion arrived at is the same, and thanks to his father, it seems that young Hotspur learned his lessons well – perhaps too well for his own good. Given the ideal opportunity to witness the most brutal side of medieval warfare in an English *chevauchee*, there is no doubt that Hotspur would have seen the workings of chivalry at first hand in a living hell of burnt-out farmsteads, rotting corpses, and homeless French peasants craving mercy from their attackers. That this indiscriminate slaughter was the great unavoidable tragedy of chivalry was probably admitted by Hotspur's father in a moment of weakness, but there is no doubt that Hotspur would have been affected by its workings as part of his upbringing in more ways than one.

Hotspur's father and namesake, Henry, 4th Baron Percy of Alnwick, later created Earl of Northumberland, is one of the central characters of our story. As the head of so great a northern family it was no accident that he had an immense effect on everyone associated with it. Judging by what is known of Percy's actions and what he accomplished in such a short space of time, he was a man of great political stature, well loved by the commons for a time, but with a blind and single-minded craving for power that almost caused the total destruction of his household in one fateful generation. Along with his younger brother Thomas (later Earl of Worcester), he was party to two of the most sweeping historical decisions of his time and so looms gigantically over young Hotspur's life, much like any great medieval father might do with an eager young son chafing at the ancestral bit.

Contemporary parallels of this 'overbearing' parental influence immediately spring to mind if we consider for a moment the plight of three other all-powerful fourteenth-century fathers and their famous sons. Of course, the governing parental influence is not damning in itself, but the evidence in Hotspur's case is such a feature of his short life that it cannot be dismissed out of hand. On one level, the successful but tragic story of Edward III and his warlike son, Edward, the Black Prince of Wales, provides us with a clear example of how extreme longevity can deprive a son of his royal expectations. This may not have affected the Black Prince in any noticeable way, but there is every reason to believe that Hotspur's actions were greatly influenced by his father's perpetuity and imperious northern reputation. The actions of John of Gaunt, Duke of Lancaster (the fourth son of Edward III), and his eldest son Henry Bolingbroke (later Henry IV) illustrate the fact that great wealth and power, once lost, could lead to a son championing his father's cause even at the expense of causing rebellion and usurpation to recover what was rightfully his. Hotspur's rebellious nature may have stemmed from the need to follow a similar course of action when his family interests were threatened in 1403. A generation later, Bolingbroke's son, 'Prince Hal' of Shakespearian fame (later Henry V), encountered the classic difficulties of a 'king in waiting', who as a result of medieval succession became noticeably estranged from his father, although the actual extent of Hotspur's remoteness is hard to pinpoint with any great degree of accuracy.

However, of all these famous sons who walked in the cooling light of their father's shadow, Harry Hotspur seems to have been the most tragic example, and in this respect the father-and-son influence was probably more damning than ever. Henry Percy senior survived Hotspur by five years, and his actions prove conclusively that not only should fathers never outlive their sons, but also that they should never betray them in favour of political ambition. In the following chapters the influences of all these father-and-son relationships are at work, causing, in Hotspur's case, a reaction that was more noticeable than in his contemporaries. Hotspur, by this rule, was forced into living a life of restraint that, in times of unbridled freedom, caused him to act impulsively. In short, Hotspur's overbearing father was not only responsible for his son's reckless nature, but also for him discharging a powder keg of emotion on several important occasions.

It is well known that even the slightest association with powerful men in any age can have fateful consequences for those party to their actions. However, in Hotspur's England this situation was altogether more protracted, making the Percy affiliation with the politically unstable John of Gaunt, Duke of Lancaster, a very risky undertaking. John of Gaunt was senior to Hotspur's father by two years and Gaunt's eldest son, Henry Bolingbroke, was two years younger than Hotspur, although in the fourteenth century no great trouble was taken to record the birthdays of even the most important members of the royal household. Henry Bolingbroke's son, the future King Henry V, figures much later in our story; however, one man – whose image hardly fits the father-and-son comparison alluded to above – was central to the needs and expectations of all these men, and this was the cunning and autocratic son of the Black Prince, Richard of Bordeaux (later Richard II), who was almost exactly the same age as his cousin Bolingbroke.

During the reign of Edward III, and for some time after his death, Bolingbroke's father, Gaunt, managed, and later easily manipulated, a set of circumstances that helped Henry Percy's rise to power at the expense of others. Exploited to the full during the minority of Richard II, and at the price of making many enemies along the way, this caused Gaunt and Percy to become inexorably linked together in both war and politics. However, despite this fateful association with Lancaster, Henry Percy's long-sought-after recognition and subsequent earldom did not come lightly or easily, although, as will be seen, it is certain that his title was a direct result of Gaunt's magnanimous influence over the young boy king, who in his minority was wholly dependent on the rule of others.

Also lingering behind this close association with Lancaster was a simple case of family heredity. The Percys were cousins of John of Gaunt by marriage. Henry Percy's father had married Mary Plantagenet, daughter of the Earl of Lancaster, in 1334 and thereafter a strong kinship had developed between the heirs of both houses, a friendship that would soon be tested to the full when Henry Percy achieved his ultimate accolade and Gaunt realised the dangers of contesting his cousin's power in the north of England. It also follows that because of these strong family ties it fell to the house of Lancaster to instruct young Hotspur in John Hardyng's more 'gentle' warlike pursuits, although on this occasion Hotspur was not alone. He was probably joined in his tuition by two other young hopefuls: Gaunt's eldest son Henry Bolingbroke and Richard of Bordeaux, the latter being the less military able of the two.

While young Hotspur was learning how to conduct himself as a worthy contender for knighthood, his ambitious father was beginning to enter the political arena in a big way. Henry Percy's rise to power was gradual, but in order to trace how his association with John of Gaunt led to political disaster, it is important to document what went before; only then can we grasp the importance of the relationship between the two houses of Percy and Lancaster and hence later judge Hotspur's association with Gaunt's son when they both came of age.

It is alleged by the Percy chronicler, E.B. de Fonblanque, that Hotspur's father fought at the battle of Poitiers with the Black Prince when he was only fourteen years old; however, it is more certain that Percy saw active service in France prior to his knighthood in October 1360 when he acted as one of the guarantors of the Treaty of Bretigny at Calais. Then aged eighteen, and with the war in France temporarily over, Percy swapped fronts for life in the northern marches where in 1362 he was appointed warden of the east march and ordered to treat with the Scottish king, David Bruce. When the conflict later known as the Hundred Years War finally broke out in 1369, the driving force behind the English war effort was John of Gaunt. The failing Edward III, and Gaunt's elder brother, the disease-ridden Black Prince, were both temporarily out of action, and the renewal of hostilities saw Henry Percy and his younger brother Thomas joining Gaunt's ranks, primarily with the aim of furthering their own very different political ambitions.

Henry Percy had been made a Knight of the Garter in 1366 and was probably aiming to excel himself in the presence of his royal cousin, with the ultimate goal of further extending his northern domains. However, Henry's brother, Thomas Percy, was probably looking to a more chivalrous ideal, and judging by his later royal appointments, succeeded to a greater extent than his brother at gaining royal confidence. Despite his fame as a soldier, Thomas Percy comes across as a far more politically astute man than his brother, who, always eager to seize the initiative without the slightest thought to its outcome, was governed primarily by motives of self-aggrandisement. Already a seasoned veteran of many French campaigns, Thomas Percy had previously fought with John of Gaunt in Spain at the battle of Najera in 1367, when English forces commanded by the Black Prince had totally routed the Castilian army of Henry of Trastamara in favour of Pedro 'the Cruel'. Thomas was later to serve in France under such notable captains as Sir John Chandos and the famous Captal de Buch, but in 1369 the great days of Crécy and Poitiers were over, the French had totally changed military tack by avoiding pitched battles with the English, and the time had come for the first of Gaunt's many aimless *chevauchees* across France at the expense of the long-suffering English taxpayer. Already associated, and no doubt indebted, to Lancaster for their rise to power, the Percy brothers had no option but to follow their cousin's lead.

A series of arduous and abortive military campaigns followed, and there must have been many English captains who wondered what glory could be achieved in such ignoble campaigns where the enemy refused to fight 'properly'. However, the cautious French strategy succeeded where so many of their endeavours had failed previously and it was left to men like Sir John Chandos and Thomas Percy to pick up the pieces when the disgruntled Gaunt was forced to return home in disgrace.

According to Chandos's herald, 'fortune frowned horribly on the English in Aquitaine',[15] and in the latter part of 1369 the situation became increasingly difficult for those who remained in France. One by one, English territories were gradually overrun by French troops and Chandos was given charge of defending Poitou, while Thomas Percy was appointed seneschal of the all-important English port of La Rochelle. It seemed only a matter of time before the last remaining English territories were taken back, but incredibly the English held on, primarily due to an enforced unwillingness by the French to face them in open battle. However, when events finally took a turn for the worse on the penultimate day of 1369, the forces of Chandos and Percy became separated, and after a confusing skirmish at the bridge at Lussac, the brave Chandos was unhorsed and killed.

This latest military debacle hit the English hard, but while the fortunes of Thomas Percy waned in France, those of his elder brother continued to flourish in the north of England. In just two years Henry Percy succeeded in obtaining the wardenship of both east and west marches towards Scotland, as well as the constableship of Jedburgh Castle, a fortress balanced precariously on the ever-shifting Anglo-Scottish border. With the death of his father in 1368, Percy had also secured his much-sought-after baronial title, which, as it had done for all his ancestors, made him a chief player in northern border politics. However, along with his newly acquired 'northern crown' came two major problems. The first of these was not wholly apparent during the fourteenth century, but it was nonetheless a dangerous undercurrent flowing deep beneath the topographical surface of Yorkshire in Hotspur's day. Only in the next century would rivalry and antagonism between the houses of Percy and Neville draw family blood, but the territorial influence of both families ensured that the acquisition of military appointments would always lead to a measure of resentment and jealousy for as long as the two coexisted. The fact that Henry Percy had married Margaret, daughter of Ralph Neville of Raby, in 1359 proves that there was no real outward antagonism between the two families during the mid-fourteenth century; after all, both houses had shared the wardenship of the marches on several occasions, and their ancestors had fought shoulder to shoulder in many important northern battles, most notably at Neville's Cross in 1346. However, there is evidence that an intense rivalry existed between the two families, primarily because the Nevilles were the principal heirs to the northern military complex and the only real first-choice alternative to the Percys if the latter ever fell out of favour with the reigning monarch. If the Neville family were secure in the fact that their 'powerful' neighbours had not yet overreached themselves, there was every reason to question what would happen if they ever did. Intrigue and self-interest would follow greed and personal ambition later in the next century, although it would be foolish to say that the threat of Neville ascendancy was never spoken of in Hotspur's day.

The second hazard to the Percy family at this time was more real and immediate, and involved an ongoing border dispute with the famous warlike Scottish family, the house of Douglas. It was this same feud that was to continue during Hotspur's lifetime, although, as will be seen, it had a most unusual outcome despite a long and bitter struggle that involved succeeding generations of both warring families. For as long as Scotland had contested those lowland territories that had fallen into English hands as a result of the battle of Neville's Cross, a member of the Douglas clan had been at the forefront of the Scottish *schiltrons*, wielding his great battleaxe. In border politics, too, the Douglas earls had mirrored Percy ascendancy on the opposite side of the divide, primarily because Robert I of Scotland had granted the huge estate of Jedburgh and its nearby forest to the Douglas earls shortly before his death in 1329. This territorial problem was aggravated even further after the great English victory at Halidon Hill in 1333 when the Percys were granted the same Jedburgh lands despite the threat of Douglas retaliation. Still hotly pursued by both parties in 1373, when Henry Percy was appointed constable of Jedburgh Castle, sporadic invasion and raiding was a predictable outcome of their cross-border rivalry.

Henry Percy's contentment with his new-found northern status was therefore in stark contrast to his brother's plight in France. In southern England the depressing news of Chandos's death was met with a great outpouring of patriotism. In fact, the calamity caused a storm of anger among the whole of the English nobility. Still gravely ill with dysentery, and with an ageing father more eager than ever to quarter his own arms with those of France, the Black Prince vowed revenge for the death of his friend, although it was obvious that neither he nor his father could stand the rigours of campaign life to the same extent as their comrades-in-arms. Nevertheless, a renewed war with France was declared, culminating in the siege and sack of Limoges in 1370 when the Black Prince, so determined to fulfil his duties as commander-in-chief, directed the English forces from a litter carried by his men.

Thomas Percy, who was by then seneschal of Poitou, was present at the six-day siege and was no doubt an eyewitness to the alleged burning and pillaging that went on in the town, much to the horror of the French chronicler Jean Froissart. However, apart from the alleged 'war crimes' committed by the English on this occasion, the capture of Limoges and its destructive aftermath had no direct impact on French resolve. The destruction caused in the name of chivalry had no real purpose, and the brief appearance of John of Gaunt and Henry Percy at this time, and their equally rapid return home with the ailing prince, only served to illustrate that the war was being lost on a grand scale. Left in sole charge of Poitou and Saintonge, the continued involvement of Thomas Percy meant that he was immediately put in an extremely vulnerable and unwinnable situation.

Attacked on a number of fronts by French troops, and with La Rochelle captured and Poitiers threatened by Bertrand du Guesclin, the sixty-year-old Edward III was forced yet again into raising another army of conquest. In a last-ditch attempt to win back his lost territories in France, the king mounted a great expedition to try to relieve the hard-pressed English garrisons. Henry Percy joined Edward's large fleet in an effort to rescue his brother, but after nine weeks at sea the mission was aborted due to unfavourable winds. It was the last gasp of the ageing king and his famous black-armoured son. That anyone had managed to hold on to English territories so long was nothing short of a miracle.

With all hope of relief now gone, Henry Percy must have feared for his brother's life. However, he could hardly have anticipated that Thomas Percy would play the perfect hero. Rather than desert his comrades he decided to stand and fight in true chivalrous style, and – in the company of Jean de Grailly, the famous Captal du Buch – Thomas proved his worth not only as a commander of men, but also as a man of principle when in 1372 the English went on the offensive and managed to defeat a French force near Soubise. The Percy family motto *Esperance en Dieu* (Hope in God) could not have been more appropriate in the circumstances, but the battle at Soubise was to be the last rally of the English, and the French soon captured Thomas Percy, who was taken to Paris to await his fate. Thomas was ransomed in 1373 by the surrender of yet another English possession, the castle of St Germain Leuroux, and when he finally returned home to England in 1374 he was made a Knight of the Garter, receiving two annuities of 100 marks each from the king and the Prince of Wales for his services in Guyenne.[16] Henceforth, Thomas's fortunes were bound up with those of his brother and his nephew Hotspur, although there is a great deal of evidence to suggest that during most of his life this lesser-known Percy followed his own path, despite being later heavily involved in the revolution of 1399 and also in the rebellion of 1403.

Politically it may be argued that Henry Percy was the prime mover of his family, but while the elder Percy was driven by ambition, Thomas's later appointments to office prove quite conclusively that he was the more politically mature of the two. Froissart recorded that Thomas Percy was 'right honourable and gracious'[17] to him when they met in England in 1395, and that diplomatically the kings of France and Spain accepted the word of Hotspur's uncle as better than a bond. However, after the fall of Richard II, and the usurpation of Henry Bolingbroke, there was to be a noticeable change in Percy's honourable intentions towards the established principles of kingship. Using the assistance of his own family in an effort to depose one king for another in 1399, Thomas was accused by chroniclers for bringing about the battle of Shrewsbury in 1403 although, as will be seen, this fact is clouded by the interference of a Shakespearian myth.

As regards the war with France, Percy involvement was to continue unabated. Henry and Thomas had proved their unquestionable loyalty to Edward III and the Duke of Lancaster on numerous occasions, but Gaunt's next continental venture was to prove a more disastrous defeat than ever, and hence it must be questioned whether, after this setback, the Percy brothers held their cousin in the same esteem as they had done previously.

The small part played by young Hotspur in this last-ditch assault on the French is significant only in that he witnessed the English debacle personally. As previously stated by the Percy historian, de Fonblanque, Hotspur was only nine years old at the time, no doubt extremely impressionable, and thanks to his illustrious forebears' varied military careers, eager to see what real soldiering was all about.

The Percy retinue, comprising a picked force of 12 knights, 47 esquires and 160 mounted archers, landed at Calais at the end of July 1373, and along with a well-equipped English force of some 12,000 men, Hotspur must have looked forward to an experience of a lifetime.[18] Disembarking in the summer sun amid veterans' talk of past victories in France must have been an event to stir any young heart aimed at a military career. However, contrary to Hotspur's dream of glory, failure loomed on the horizon. Gaunt had no plan, and had shown previously that he had no capacity as a general either. As a result, Shakespeare's 'time-honoured Lancaster' failed miserably in bringing the French to battle and this indecision and failure must have had some effect on the young Hotspur's mind, although how this manifested itself is open to question. As winter closed in, and Gaunt's army entered the sterile districts of Auvergne on the road to Bordeaux, the sickening results of military ineptitude unfolded right before Hotspur's eyes: men and horses dying by the wayside; the army's baggage being abandoned to French flank attacks and ambuscades; an unseen enemy continually harassing the rear of the English column; and widespread desertion in the ranks.

It was all over in a matter of months. By April 1374 Gaunt was back in England, leaving only Calais, Bordeaux and Bayonne in English hands. French forces easily captured the rest of Aquitaine, and it only remained for yet another fragile truce to increase popular discontent at home. Coupled with high taxation, King Edward's growing infirmities, the prince's mortal illness, and the fact that the next heir to the throne was still only a child, it was understandable that this increasing pressure was directed on those responsible for the disaster in France. It was unfortunate for Henry Percy senior that his association with John of Gaunt was so high profile. When Lancaster's growing unpopularity prompted the widespread suspicion that he was aiming at the crown, this naturally reflected on his chief supporters, of whom Percy was the most partisan.

The situation came to a head in the so-called 'Good Parliament' of April 1376, and the irony of it all was that Percy was chosen as one of several magnates called upon to advise the commons on a course of reform. The ailing Black Prince, who was by this time quite well aware that the root cause of all this mistrust stemmed from his own brother, supported the actions taken, and the appointment of Henry Percy as a champion for the common good had a retrograde effect on his relationship with Gaunt. Caught on the 'other side' of the argument, several of Gaunt's followers were immediately attacked and Percy was forced into an embarrassing corner with his former benefactor. However, luck still favoured the Lancastrian duke. While parliament was still pursuing its course of reform the unthinkable occurred: on Trinity Sunday the Black Prince died and within a month Gaunt was once more in power. When a second parliament met on 27 January 1377, it was almost entirely in the service of Lancaster and it included Henry Percy who, despite his brush with Gaunt, had been favoured with the marshal's staff previously bestowed upon Edmund Mortimer, Earl of March, who was by coincidence Lancaster's mortal enemy.

No doubt tempted by other lucrative appointments to office, and in deeper with Gaunt than ever, Henry Percy must have wondered how long it would be until he achieved the ultimate accolade he so badly coveted – the earldom of Northumberland. He didn't have to wait for long, although his path upward would be at the expense of extreme unpopularity with the commons due to his constant support of Lancaster. However, Henry Percy's first mistake was taking up the cause of John Wyclif, the religious reformer. Wyclif's doctrine suited John of Gaunt as a means to renew the old struggle between the feudal party and the clerical party, the latter of whom Gaunt had recently fallen foul. The circumstances surrounding Lancaster's hatred of the Church had of late found its roots in an accusation by the Bishop of Winchester that Gaunt was not the legitimate son of Edward III. Gaunt, feudal to the core, resented the official arrogance of the prelates and their power; thus Wyclif's doctrine to purify the Church suited his cause admirably. On 19 February 1477 Wyclif was summoned by convocation to answer for his heresy, although the bishops' real target was undoubtedly of Lancastrian origin. Caught up in this purely private quarrel, Henry Percy entered the lady chapel of St Paul's with the temper of both sides nearing breaking point. Wyclif, a theologian and philosopher who had the support of the Lollard movement, was caught up in the middle of the ensuing argument.

Percy's second mistake was in losing his famous temper. Prior to the trial, he acted as Wyclif's protector, walking armed in front of the priest to shield him from the fury of the crowd. Even in the supposed sanctuary of St Paul's, Percy used violence against the people and persisted in guarding Wyclif in defiance of several protests levelled at him by the Bishop of London. However, matters were rapidly brought to a head when Percy directed his anger against the bishops themselves. The chronicler Thomas Walsingham's dislike for John of Gaunt is a hallmark of his writings, but on this occasion it seems that Percy had overstepped the mark. In Walsingham's eyes Percy had crossed the Rubicon and had become one of Gaunt's 'many minions': 'Oh! Unhappy and unfortunate duke! Oh! Those whom you should lead in war you betray by your treachery and cowardice, and those whom you should lead in peace by example of good works, you lead astray, dragging them to ruin!'[19]

The next day an angry mob, instigated it is said by Lord Fitzwalter, attacked Percy's London house, then situated on the west side of Aldersgate. After they had ransacked it, the Savoy, Gaunt's palatial residence, was the rioters' next target. However, Gaunt and Percy managed to escape by water to Kennington, where they sought refuge with the Princess of Wales, who tried to mediate on their behalf. This royal intervention saved both their lives, although the storm of protest against them persisted for some time afterwards, with the result that Percy had to work extremely hard to win back support from the commons due to his continuing support of the unpopular duke.

Meanwhile, Hotspur, despite our brief glimpses of him during his youth, had not yet entered the annals of history. But at Windsor in April 1377 all this changed when along with Henry Bolingbroke and Richard of Bordeaux, his two young contemporaries under Lancaster, he was knighted by the white-haired Edward III. Hotspur was just thirteen years old. Also among those gathered to be knighted on the feast of St George were Hotspur's two younger brothers, Thomas and Ralph Percy, the latter becoming Hotspur's closest comrade-in-arms against the French and later against the Scots at Otterburn in 1388. Hotspur's investiture was also the last official duty of the old king; two months later he died, his grandson, Richard of Bordeaux, becoming his successor at only eleven years of age.

The death of Edward III changed everything for John of Gaunt and the house of Percy. The Duke of Lancaster immediately found that he could now use his nephew's minority as the means to fulfil those personal ambitions of grandeur that had been so recently dashed by his own incompetence, and in this crusade Henry Percy was right behind him. On 15 July 1377, taking advantage of his benefactor's new-found power at court, Percy was created Earl of Northumberland by the young Richard II and was recognised as such at the king's coronation, thereafter showing so much courtesy and forbearance to the crowd that it is said he regained some of his former popularity.

During the coronation ceremony the new earl acted as Marshal of England, an office that was vehemently contested by Margaret, elder daughter of the Earl of Norfolk (the natural contender for the title). Margaret threatened to claim the office by deputy during the actual crowning ceremony of the new king, and this forced Percy into another embarrassing corner, the title of marshal clearly not being his to usurp. Humiliated by this action, Percy pleaded ignorance and claimed that private and border affairs needed his most urgent attention in the north. Indeed, soon after he had resigned his marshal's staff, the Scots under George Dunbar, Earl of March saved Percy's political skin by their pillaging and burning of Roxburgh, an attack that was swiftly repaid north of the border.

No doubt glad to be back in his much-coveted northern 'realm', the Earl of Northumberland crossed into Scotland with a large private army and set about wasting Dunbar's lands, burning everything within three days' march. Later in the year Percy was once again appointed warden of the east and west marches, and along with Lord Neville, his chief competitor for the northern crown, Percy attempted several times to secure a permanent peace treaty with Scotland. However, like all treaties made with the Scots it failed to take effect and predictably, towards the end of November 1378, an intrepid band of moss-troopers decided to take matters into their own hands and launch a surprise attack on Berwick-upon-Tweed.

Medieval chroniclers described the border town of Berwick as 'a second Alexandria, whose riches were the sea and the water its walls'.[20] Militarily, when occupied by the English, the town was the key to Scottish invasion –

English armies being supplied from its port – and thus its importance as a garrison town long outlived the medieval period. Strategically, however, Berwick was always vulnerable to attack, its town and adjoining castle being on the north bank of the River Tweed facing the exposed lowland territorial influence of the earls of Douglas and March. A veritable jewel in the crown of both contending kingdoms, Berwick had changed hands several times in the past. Captured by Edward I in 1296, lost in 1318, and recaptured by Edward III in 1333, the town was to remain in English hands (apart from brief intervals of occupation) until Margaret of Anjou surrendered it to Scotland in 1461 and the English took it back in 1482. Thinly garrisoned at the best of times because of its isolated location beside the River Tweed, Berwick was the responsibility of the English warden of the east march, being the administrative headquarters of English-occupied Scotland. Conversely, it was a matter of Scottish 'fay', or pride, that Berwick should be retaken at every possible opportunity, to such a degree that by 1357 English forces had been driven back to what is now the present border. Indeed, in Hotspur's day the English held little more than a chain of castles, chief among these being Lochmaben, Jedburgh, Roxburgh, Fast Castle and Berwick-upon-Tweed, to combat the ever-present Scottish 'menace'.

Unlike Newcastle and Carlisle, Berwick was not walled in the thirteenth century, but by Hotspur's day its castle had been substantially rebuilt and the town had received its first stone wall, of which the 'White Wall' is a modern survival. However, despite this rebuilding, in 1378 due to several successive sieges, raids and a measure of neglect, the odds against Berwick's capture had increased in favour of the Scots. Indeed, Berwick's defences were so badly in need of repair that the aforementioned band of wily Scottish march men, led, it is said, by John Hogg and Alexander Ramsay, had no trouble crawling inside. Thomas Walsingham recounts Hotspur's first taste of medieval siege warfare in the remote outlands of present-day Northumbria:

About the same time, namely the last Thursday before the feast of Saint Andrew the Apostle, raiders from the marches of Scotland secretly gained entry to the castle of Berwick by night through a hole in the tower. And the Constable appointed to the castle, Sir Robert Boynton, a good soldier, was surprised and killed; his good wife and sons, and the other members of his household were to be set free under condition that three-thousand marks were paid in seven days, otherwise they would be imprisoned. The next day, the same robbers came out of the castle, and taking sheep and oxen from the surrounding countryside, they drove them into the castle so that the occupiers might be well sustained in the event of a siege. Although they had few men, the Scots said that they did all this with the full agreement of their king. When he heard this, the courageous Earl of Northumberland hastened towards the town, and with four hundred men-at-arms surrounded the fortress and placed his siege engines accordingly. After setting his men in order, he himself, along with his first born son Henry, and all of his men with banners displayed attacked the large gate of the castle; Sir Alan Heaton, with his men, to one part, Sir Thomas Ilderton, with his men, to the other part, and the whole of the Heron household to the fourth part; thereby assisting each other in the assault. The defenders, not lacking courage either, strongly and vigilantly thrust back the English who opposed them for some two hours. At last, after a long fight, the castle was taken, and this was miraculous indeed, considering that the owners were surrounded and the English had tried to capture its walls simultaneously. There was much slaughter as a result. Two Englishmen were killed and very many were wounded, forty-eight Scots were put to the sword, only one life was spared.[21]

Like all his warlike ancestors before him, Hotspur had been finally baptised in the conventions of border warfare. Perhaps it was here at this little-known action that he killed for the first time in his life, although there is certainly no evidence to support this. Evidently he was only fourteen years old when he witnessed the stark realities of actual combat and no doubt savoured the sweet taste of revenge when Berwick's defences ultimately fell to the English. It must have been a veritable whirlwind of experience for a young teenager to take in, but one that would probably haunt Hotspur for the rest of his life given that a soothsayer's prediction would later state that one day he would die at Berwick.

Hotspur's teenage exploits certainly won the enthusiasm of later writers, including Thomas Walsingham, who was chiefly responsible for reporting Percy's lesser-known deeds, along with his more daring and chivalrous adventures when he came of age. Walsingham painted a contemporary picture of Hotspur that, even today, captures the essence of what it was like to be a medieval knight, while writers such as Shakespeare, for example, managed to inflate the 'infant' warrior's reputation at every possible opportunity, without paying the slightest heed to Hotspur's real historical age. Therefore, it is safe say that any story which has the young Hotspur leaping foremost into the breach, sword in hand at the head of his men, is apocryphal, given that young Harry Percy was probably very well protected by his father's household retainers on this and many other similar occasions while still 'in training'.

As for the siege of Berwick, it was no different from all the rest of the sieges that had preceded it. In short, the town's capture solved nothing with regard to Anglo-Scottish relations, and in the aftermath the Earl of Northumberland was forced into retreating across the border due to the implementation of a truce that was expected to last until the next 'March Day' – a mutually agreed gathering where both sides could 'in theory' attempt to iron out their differences without resorting to all-out violence.

Ironically, it is said that John of Gaunt had ordered the recall of Northumberland and his forces due to his own planned invasion of Scotland scheduled for the coming year. Cooperation with the Percys was to be an essential part of Gaunt's grand 'strategy', but this can hardly have been welcome news for the Earl of Northumberland, considering his new-found position of power. In fact, the subtle scheming of John of Gaunt was to be the shape of things to come, especially with regard to how he would later use the Neville family to counteract Percy authority in the north. Despite everything that had been achieved by Lancaster on behalf of his northern cousins, the eventual split between Gaunt and Henry Percy was perhaps inevitable considering that both men shared similar territorial ambitions. How this clash of personalities revealed itself in the Percy household is hard to fathom, but it is highly likely that all these political meanderings did not affect young Hotspur in the slightest. For the first time in his life he had proved himself worthy of his new spurs and although not yet heated to their accustomed temperature in the border haunts of his ancestors, militarily the son of the mighty Earl of Northumberland had finally come of age.

THREE

Windsor: 1388

Anti-hero is a difficult word and concept to come to terms with. In its simplistic form the perception of an anti-hero reflects the antonym of that which describes a hero – in other words, a coward or a villain. However, there is another meaning – albeit still a conceptual one – which describes a character purely for dramatic purposes, and in the works of Shakespeare this stereotype is demonstrated on more than one occasion. In his epic *Richard II* and *Henry IV Part 1*, the Bard's unique and rather unconventional portrayal of Hotspur is perhaps one of his most memorable offerings. However, fuelled by the equally dramatic histories of Edward Hall and Raphael Holinshed, Shakespeare made several Hotspurian mistakes and hence a union of Tudor and Elizabethan falsehoods has passed into modern times.

To begin with, Shakespeare's concept of heroism is, of course, a totally misleading description of anyone, let alone a *real* historical character. In fact, in the traditional sense of the word, 'hero' is hardly the right term to use for any medieval knight who, like Hotspur, followed the chivalric code to the letter. Considering that brutality and random destruction were by far the knight's greatest achievements, the opposite is perhaps more appropriate, especially if one considers what a medieval knight sought to do in order to enhance his reputation on the battlefield. The truth is that Shakespeare typecast Hotspur for the masses and hence the real Henry Percy has become more and more ambiguous with the passage of time. Even his well-known pseudonym has been applied and distorted to mean something completely different from that first intended.

Thousands of dead, pillaged lands, war crimes against civilian populations and a number of other 'unchivalrous' deeds give us cause to question the medieval knight's habitual need to prove himself through violent action; but this is exactly what it meant to live and breathe the code in a world where, like today, it was perfectly acceptable to destroy a country's infrastructure and dismiss civilian deaths as collateral damage. In the medieval world, this *was* chivalry in its purest form – no damsels in distress or dragons in sight. M.H. Keen expands on this point in his essay 'Chivalry, nobility and the man-at-arms' and gives us reason to believe that chivalry with all its idealisation of the freelance fighting man, could be a force effective in limiting the horrors of war: by prompting men to seek wars and praising those who did so, its tendency, for all its idealism and because of it, was rather to help make those horrors endemic'.[22]

Consequently, the theatrical labels of hero and anti-hero, in historical terms, are best discarded as products of romantic fiction, however appealing that fiction might be. The fact is that both these descriptions of Hotspur are chiefly tools of the trade, used by novelists and dramatists in order to heighten tension. They are devices that in no way describe anyone's real historical character at all unless they are compared with someone else who is perhaps more deserving of the title – and in this case the emerging character of Hotspur's even younger rival and nemesis at the battle of Shrewsbury, 'Prince Hal', provides a stark dramatic comparison.

As a useful military parallel to the budding Prince of Wales, Hotspur's erroneous 'anti' label is brilliantly fleshed out by Shakespeare in his well-loved propensity for playing one character off against the other. Indeed, on this occasion the difference between the two contenders for the heroic title could not be more marked. In *Henry IV Part 1*, the ever-glorious 'Prince Hal' is cast as the budding flower of a misspent and frivolous youth who opposes 'Harry Hotspur', the impetuous young firebrand who is rash to the point of extreme foolishness, rebellious to the core, and bold enough to win himself an early appointment with death at the hands of his adversary. Later emerging to lead his men 'unto the breach' in the Bard's most patriotic offering, *Henry V*, it is no accident that the Prince of Wales is considered the hero and Hotspur the anti-hero of the Hotspurian legend. However, yet again, both titles and descriptions contain numerous historical falsehoods, and the romantic imagery that pervades the lives of the two Henrys is perhaps best discarded for a far more intriguing concept of lost friendship played out to the ultimate point of no return.

In search of the real historical Hotspur, we therefore need to look no further into the mirror of Shakespearian myth. A much better line of enquiry is to explore a more contemporary avenue of investigation, namely the elusive character concealed within the pages of historical fact. Medieval chronicles and private letters point our way back in time, but first we must consider Henry Percy's cleverly contrived nickname which, in accordance with tradition, one would think might have originated from those who knew him best, namely the English. However, according to Thomas Walsingham, who wrote in the 1390s, it was not the English but Henry Percy's natural enemy who thought him worthy enough to receive immortality in a name: 'Unlike his father, who was the Guardian of the town of Berwick, Henry Percy was constantly active, more especially against the Scots, who he subdued with tireless courage at every outbreak of disorder. On account of this, they called him "Hatspore" [Haatspore] or "calidum calcar".'[23] Thus the ultimate accolade of 'hot spur', or more correctly in the Scottish tongue 'Haatspore', has quite literally passed from the pages of history into legend.

As early as 1386 the Scots were calling Henry Percy by his famous sobriquet, which if nothing else gives us some indication that his celebrated *nom de guerre* was a household word by the time he faced the Earl of Douglas at Otterburn in 1388. Hotspur's renown for striking hard and fast into Scotland along with a band of well-trained men-at-arms earned him nothing less than immortality in Scottish eyes, not to mention a reputation for valour in many English hearts. Evading capture time and time again, and travelling lightly armed with his band of trusted Percy retainers, the historical Hotspur can be visualised at his best and most effective. As a border fighter he knew the territory intimately, he had a traditional sense of loyalty and responsibility for the area, and, more importantly, he was impulsive and reckless enough to gamble everything on a calculated risk. Along with others of his breed, he was the epitome of a medieval knight in guerrilla's clothing. Not a champion of law and order by any means, but a brave and impetuous soldier with a rebellious heart, who risked his life over and over against incredible odds in the name of his beloved chivalric code.

There is no doubt that Hotspur sought fame, perhaps even kingship in the end (according to his followers' cry at Shrewsbury in 1403), using his military skill to achieve considerable renown. However, like all great historical characters before and after him, Hotspur had his failings and, contrary to his own belief about what chivalry stood for, he soon discovered that there was an increasingly complex and darker side to his beloved code that he had failed to take into account. In a world filled with intrigue and double-dealing, even among the members of his own family, a man of such honourable intentions was perhaps fated not to live long. This coupled with the fact that such recognition and exposure to danger were bound to court a posse of jealous enemies wishing to prove themselves in a similar fashion is all too apparently a recipe for disaster.

As mentioned, Hotspur's contact with northern border warfare came at an early age. However, this exposure to danger was not exclusive, and in part represented any medieval father's obligation to his son. Faced with a life of constant military pressure, there was no substitute for a harsh military apprenticeship in the northern marches and in this respect the Earl of Northumberland succeeded admirably – so well in fact that by 1388 his son had achieved great military repute both at home and abroad.

Sometime before 10 December 1379, Hotspur had also married into a very important family. His bride, Elizabeth Mortimer, was the eldest daughter of Edmund Mortimer, Earl of March, whose family was directly descended through the female line from Lionel, Duke of Clarence, the second surviving son of Edward III. Elizabeth was only nine years old at the time of her marriage, but given that most noble unions were matched in a melting pot of arranged alliances, ages were never seen as an insurmountable problem by those who craved great power. The Mortimer family would figure greatly – and as it turned out, fatally – in Hotspur's later life, but for the present the union of Percy and Mortimer could only have brought happiness to both families in that all Hotspur's children by Elizabeth would thereafter carry royal blood in their veins.

Titles and newly gained military accolades flooded Percy inventories in the 1380s, due to renewed hostilities with Scotland, and very soon it became possible for the Earl of Northumberland to hand over some of his more mundane border responsibilities to his fiery young son. These duties had small beginnings, but in 1381 Hotspur was fulfilling this role more and more, being first called upon to prove his knowledge in the laws of honour and chivalry in a little-known border dispute. As one of the judges of a solemn combat to be held at Liliot's Cross between John Chattowe, a Scots esquire, and William de Badby, an Englishman,[24] Hotspur was obviously thought experienced enough to officiate in matters that clearly required careful adjudication. He was only seventeen years old at the time, but very soon he was able to preside over more significant northern matters, again in place of his father who, it seems, had enough problems of his own. In the autumn of 1381 the Earl of Northumberland and his former mentor, John of Gaunt, had a serious quarrel that led indirectly to a variance between the Percys and their most famous Yorkshire neighbours, the Nevilles.

Sparked off by Gaunt's recent intrusions into the Percys' ever-expanding sphere of northern influence, the ensuing bid for power was to have far-reaching effects, and not wholly as a result of Gaunt's ambitious nature – it seems that Percy was also partly to blame. In the summer of 1381 the Earl of Northumberland had refused to give John of Gaunt shelter when the latter took alarm during the Peasants' Revolt. Fearing the political angle that had previously cornered him in 1377 and wrecked his London residence in the process, Percy's aloofness towards Gaunt was to cost him dear when his decision to spurn his former benefactor backfired, causing the fateful emergence of his chief rival in the north, John Neville of Raby.

John Neville was a very experienced soldier. He had fought in France and Spain on many occasions with Gaunt, and prior to 1383 he had also shared the wardenship of the marches along with Percy and other northern lords. However, now that the grand title of Earl of Northumberland had been bestowed upon his neighbours the Percys, John Neville's own sphere of influence had diminished somewhat and he set about using his position as one of Gaunt's many retainers to establish a powerful political bond with his master in order to bolster his own personal argument against Percy self-aggrandisement. As a result, the Lancastrian alliance worked both ways, and over the next few years the military offices that commanded the border region became ever more contested positions – a harbinger that climaxed some seventy years later in the bloody streets of St Albans when Percy and Neville became pitted against each other in the Wars of the Roses. The political power triangle was a familiar one, and its battlefield was the prized northern office of the warden of the marches, but no one could have foreseen what the outcome of Neville ascendancy might be or how the promise of sole wardenship might change the course of history during the revolution of 1399.

Both the east and west march wardenships had been in existence since the Scottish wars of Edward I, but it was not until the reign of Richard II

(1388 proper) that the important office of march warden first achieved the form that it was to retain for the next hundred years. March wardens were retained by contract of indenture, lasting for specific periods of time at agreed rates of pay (obviously more lucrative in times of war), and the northern bishops of Carlisle and Durham generally headed up both commissions. Under the clerical direction of these two important prelates, it became the principal duty of those nobles employed by them to preserve law and order using their own powers of indenture to summon local forces in defence of the realm. However, during the reign of Richard II, the management of this office changed somewhat.

When the young king succeeded to the throne in 1377, there existed a truce with Scotland that was not due to expire until February 1384. As with all Scottish truces there were lawbreakers, and the wardens, on their part, were responsible for maintaining law and order, sometimes punishing those who broke treaties and causing them to return their booty. However, in the summer of 1380 the Earl of Northumberland was actively raising a body of 120 men-at-arms and 200 archers against the Scots who had wasted part of his land. The raid had cost him more than 1,000 marks in damages and he was preparing to take vengeance for this intrusion when in September of the same year the king's council took the unusual step of appointing John of Gaunt as the king's lieutenant in the marches. Gaunt was granted extensive powers over the Percys, which included commanding the retinues of the Earl of Northumberland, a political affront to the earl that was to cause his rebuff of Gaunt when he fled into Scotland during the political crisis of 1381.

After the Peasants' Revolt of that year, and the total destruction of Gaunt's Savoy Palace by Wat Tyler's rebels, the king ordered Percy to accompany Lancaster back to London along with John Neville. Harsh words were exchanged between Henry Percy and the young king when Gaunt levelled a number of charges against his former ally in public. Percy replied with vehemence and the king immediately ordered Percy's arrest after he snatched up the Duke of Lancaster's gauntlet in expectation of single combat. Not surprisingly, soon after this, when Gaunt was reinstated to his former governmental position, his first task was to appoint his retainer Neville as sole warden of the east march – Percy's traditional sphere of influence.

Percy was not long in protesting against this slight to his pride, but after being saved from imprisonment (and combat) by those who had secured his bail, he was in no position to act decisively against his erstwhile friend. Placated by a new grant of the wardenship of a middle march – a part of Neville territory between the Newcastle–Roxburgh road and the boundary of the west march – Percy had no alternative but to swallow his pride. This appointment seems to have contented him, at least for the present, but thereafter the Earl of Northumberland attended meetings, and the next parliament, protected by an armed guard, in fear of his life.

In March 1382, Percy and Neville were appointed wardens of both marches jointly, but it was abundantly clear that Gaunt was vigorously working for Percy's exclusion from the office, and had been since 1381, advancing John Neville in his place. This personal vendetta reached another heated climax in 1383, when Neville was appointed warden of both marches for one year at a rate of 400 marks per annum. With the renewal of hostilities in Scotland imminent, Percy had very little choice but to work with his rival against the common enemy, both men being again appointed joint wardens, with Gaunt acting as England's principal representative in the north. However, when the official truce with Scotland ended in February 1384 and the Scots stormed Lochmaben Castle, it was not Percy or Neville who led the English counter-attack into Scotland. Instead, Gaunt took immediate control of the situation and led the assault personally. Characteristically, Lancaster's campaign was over in a fortnight, leaving a great yawning gap of responsibility in its wake, which Percy was ordered to fill single-handedly.

Immediately, Carlisle and the town of Berwick were given over to Henry Percy's charge and £4,000 was allowed for his expenses when Neville's term of office expired. As for Gaunt, the humiliating defeat in the north was short-lived due to his royal position. But realising that his own strength and territorial power in the north had been insufficient to punish the Scots, Gaunt must have been privately outraged when he was forced to confirm further orders relating to the guardianship of Roxburgh Castle, formerly a Neville stronghold. This royal appointment, and the confirmation of Henry Percy as sole warden of both marches, left Neville, once again, out in the cold. Hence the Earl of Northumberland managed to retain his dominant role over both his rivals and at least temporarily secured the rule of both marches, his son Hotspur eventually taking over the office of sole warden in May 1385.

But what had the young, impetuous Percy been doing all this time? The answer can be found in the writings of Jean Froissart, who reported in his chronicle that in 1383 Sir Henry Percy was quite literally looking for a fight. In fact he was on his way to Prussia hoping to fight alongside the Teutonic Knights in their crusade against Lithuania. Impetuous as ever, it seems that Hotspur had quit a relatively peaceful north, where open warfare was cancelled for at least a year, to pursue the chivalric ideal elsewhere in Europe. In point of fact Hotspur may well have been 'chasing' war, almost as if he needed the thrill of it in order to survive. So much so, that when he heard that fighting was expected in Flanders, due to the Bishop of Norwich's 'crusade', Hotspur rapidly changed direction and rode back to Calais hoping to fight there against the forces of the anti-pope, Clement VI.

It is not known whether Hotspur took part in the ensuing campaign against the Flemings, but there is every reason to believe that he arrived in Flanders too late to join the English near Dunkirk. However, if nothing else, Hotspur's rapid change of direction is more revealing of his character than any eloquent passage in Froissart or Walsingham. It betrays a side of him that expresses drive and ambition better than any dramatic label could ever hope to do. In short, his behaviour shows that, unlike any of his immediate family, Hotspur was something of an idealist. It is possible that he was in fact searching for a worthy cause to fight and possibly even die for at the behest of his beloved code. Not arriving in time to take part in the expected hostilities in Flanders is irrelevant here. What is more important is the way that Hotspur was drawn to warlike activity as if by a magnet, and the above incident provides a good illustration of this eager, almost hyperactive, side of Hotspur's character that his enemies, the Scots, knew all too well. In fact, Hotspur's insatiable need for action and the pursuit of all things chivalrous was so ravenously followed that by the end of 1383, with the onset of war with Scotland imminent, he was back in the north again, awaiting orders. He was appointed a commissioner, along with his father and John Neville, to receive the residue of the ransom for the King of Scotland, David Bruce. Associated with his father as warden of the marches in 1384, Hotspur next year became governor of the town he had so valiantly assaulted when he was fourteen – Berwick-upon-Tweed.

As might have been expected, it was not long before John Neville was reappointed joint warden of both marches, along with Roger, Lord Clifford – a lesson to all concerned that the office was still seen as a shared position and not privileged to any man regardless of birth or title. Yet, despite this long-standing tradition, on 20 May 1385, Henry Percy *le filz* was given the sole command of the east march in place of his father, an office that he held when he was called upon to accompany Richard II into Scotland during the invasion of August that year. Along with John of Gaunt and a little-known Welshman called Owain Glyndwr, who would later figure in his life, Hotspur witnessed the occupation of Edinburgh by English troops. However, the Scots could not be brought to battle, and the young king decided to call a halt to the enterprise after barely a fortnight of burning and pillaging. Gaunt, in keeping with his previous shows of military incompetence, wished to carry the invasion further north, but he was forced to admit defeat when the king declared that to enter such a barren wasteland would be foolish and might result in the destruction of his army. Thereafter, Hotspur held the wardenship of the east march until March 1386, at which time John Neville's son, Ralph, and Lord Clifford's son, Thomas, replaced their fathers in office, a fee of 8,000 marks per annum[25] counterbalancing the appointment of Hotspur in place of his father the previous year.

With all these sons of the northern nobility in the ascendant, it may seem that both John Neville and the Earl of Northumberland were finding their duties on the marches irksome, but this is far from the truth. It is more likely that each family head was threatening the other from a purely paternal standpoint. Indeed, it seems that their offspring were advanced for a particular reason – to be subordinates to their fathers, whose added bonus included being contracted and waged to come to their sons' assistance if required. Thereafter it became abundantly clear that if the government desired a border magnate to hold the all-important position of warden of the marches, then the choice was very limited – it had to be either a Neville or a Percy, both 'camps' now being split into two distinctive pairs of adherents, each following similar territorial northern ambitions.

In the late summer of 1385 no measured success had materialised from Richard's first abortive military campaign and he attempted to secure the northern border by indenture whereby the families of Percy, Neville, Clifford and others were once again forced into working together, Hotspur commanding 100 men-at-arms and 200 archers beyond his garrison of Berwick-upon-Tweed. However, these new appointments and periods of change failed to temper Hotspur's impatient nature. He soon became bored with garrison life, and decided that formal border politics did not fit in with his more vigorous disposition. In May 1386 the man 'whom the Scots call Haatspore'[26] was sent with a large force to Calais, where Thomas Walsingham, once again, recorded the details of Hotspur's frustrations and rapid movements at this time:

> This season there were incredible rumours relating how the King of France wanted to lay siege to the town of Calais, and to this purpose he prepared for a sustained attack; or rather to drive away, or starve out the English, amongst whom was the devoted, youthful and completely honest model of chivalry Sir Henry Percy junior, the son of Henry Percy, Earl of Northumberland. And after some considerable time at Calais laying idle Henry Percy deemed it unworthy not to go meet his enemies in the field. . . . Therefore he assembled his men and journeyed into Morinie and Picardy, carrying off booty and performing praiseworthy feats of arms. And when no more could be achieved, and alas, when there was no one else to oppose him, he determined to return home. The King of France, on hearing of this, decided against taking possession of the town of Calais, but thought it better to treat with England.[27]

This decision by the French king was, however, not carried out immediately and the persistent rumour of French invasion forces looming dark upon the horizon continued to haunt English coastal towns, to such an extent that Hotspur and his brother Ralph were ordered to Yarmouth with a force of 300 men-at-arms and 600 archers to repel an expected French landing there.[28]

Several weeks of inactivity followed this appointment; it was a carbon copy of what had occurred at Calais earlier in the year when Hotspur had become so frustrated by the lack of action that he had taken it upon himself to carry the war to the French. The situation at Yarmouth must have been even more unbearable when the promised invasion never came and Hotspur found that he was powerless to act against it. In the following year the

English Channel would not prove such a formidable barrier to Hotspur, but by taking part in yet another sphere of chivalric life he managed to escape from his duties on the coast and sample the sights and sounds of London. On 30 October, no doubt brooding over another missed opportunity to strike a blow at the French, he found himself in the dour confines of the refectory at Westminster Abbey. He had been summoned there by his father to give evidence at a rather unusual trial – the famous controversy, or lawsuit, between Lord Scrope, a kinsman of the Earl of Northumberland, and Sir Robert Grosvenor, a well-known Cheshire knight.

Although on the face of it it may seem somewhat insignificant to document a variance between two noblemen, the Scrope–Grosvenor trial is perhaps one of the best illustrations, if any were needed, of how important heraldic symbolism was to the medieval knight. In this case, Lord Scrope was trying to restrain the family of Grosvenor from duplicating his own heraldic arms of *azure a bend or*. Numerous witnesses were called to give evidence on different occasions during the trial, including John of Gaunt, Henry Bolingbroke (then Earl of Derby), Geoffrey Chaucer, the celebrated author, and even the Welsh soldier, Owain Glyndwr, who was at this point far from being at odds with his English neighbours.

It was the Earl of Northumberland's duty as judge to see that justice was served, even though his appointment to office on this occasion was considered somewhat biased on behalf of Lord Scrope, who was Northumberland's own retainer! Consequently, in the course of the trial the earl was accused several times by the adherents of Grosvenor of partiality towards Lord Scrope and this is perhaps why the trial was so protracted. However, in the minutes of the trial all witnesses were obliged to supply information about their status, and in Hotspur's case this provides a valuable, if suspect, piece of evidence regarding his date of birth. Indeed, the trial roll records that in 1386 Sir Henry Percy was, 'of Alnwick . . . born on 20 May 1366',[29] a strange disclaimer for Hotspur to make given that he was actually born two years earlier.

According to the evidence, however, the above declaration can be discredited on three counts. Firstly, that the *Chronicles of Alnwick Abbey* place Hotspur's birth on 13 June 1364 – a notable source given that the abbey had enjoyed a long association with the Percy family;[30] secondly, that in 1364 Spofforth Castle was in all probability a far safer place for

Hotspur's mother to be confined in the latter days of her pregnancy; and thirdly, that given Hotspur's new age, we must ask ourselves a rather obvious question – was an even younger 'infant' warrior present at the siege of Berwick in 1378, and was a seven-year-old Hotspur conveyed to war against the French in 1373? More likely, therefore, is the argument that Hotspur wanted to be known as 'of Alnwick' for a particular reason, and this can be best explained by the fact that the Percy family had quite noticeably 'moved on' since their Yorkshire baronial hall days. By placing his family roots firmly at Alnwick – the premier seat of Percy border authority, rather than Spofforth, by then a rural Yorkshire manor house – Hotspur was, in effect, positioning himself at the very heart of Anglo-Scottish border affairs. The two-year age difference cannot be proved either way, even taking into account Hotspur's own evidence, but the rationale is rather interesting, bearing in mind that birth dates, as previously explained, were very rarely known, or accorded any real prominence in medieval England.

Given the opportunity, Hotspur had every reason to publicise his Alnwick roots, but his appearance back on the south coast of England speaks volumes for his dislike of courtly affairs in London. In fact, he probably jumped at the chance of being awarded a commission by one of the king's favourites to raise ships in order to prevent French retaliation for the Earl of Arundel's recent naval exploits in the English Channel. Whether the commission was a genuine reward, or only a ploy to expose Hotspur, is open to debate. However, there is evidence that Percy was in all probability being conspired against at this time, which gives us reason to believe that his quest for notoriety was courting an array of jealous enemies who wanted him removed from office. These enemies are not named, but it is possible that after Hotspur had gathered every available boat in Yarmouth harbour there was an assassin on board his ship.

Soon he and his men were causing the same amount of damage that had so vexed the French in Morinie and Picardy the previous year, and after a few weeks of the same hit-and-run tactics so well practised on the northern border, it is said that the French 'never wished for a worse neighbour'.[31] Thereafter, Hotspur returned home with a fleet of ships loaded with plunder, not to mention a certain amount of water from a leak thought to have been sprung by his enemies.

Evidently, back in London, Hotspur's daring exploits soon became the talk of every tavern and meeting place in the city, to such an extent that when he arrived there in person he was acclaimed even louder than the king. His popularity rose to such heights that allegedly young knights at court began copying his personal defects. A certain hesitation of speech from which he suffered was eagerly imitated,[32] and many would-be admirers sought him out for the high honour of sporting the Percy 'manacle' badge or serving him as a page or squire. Acquitted with such wide, popular acclaim, Hotspur suddenly gained national renown as England's most lovable champion in much the same way as a successful sportsman might do through the media today. However, it was not long before he was resuming more martial duties in the north of England. After the death of John Neville of Raby in 1388, Hotspur was again appointed warden of the east march and keeper of Berwick for three years, with an annual income of £12,000 in time of war and £3,000 in time of peace or truce.

It was certainly a period of prosperity for the Percy family, and while Hotspur was predominantly in the public eye, his uncle, Thomas Percy, had also advanced himself rapidly to the forefront of national and international politics. Having taken no active part in the personal feud between his brother and John of Gaunt, Thomas had not only managed to steer clear of the kind of politics that might do him harm, but he had also been lavishly granted a number of lucrative royal appointments in the process, including the office of Admiral of the Northern Fleet. In 1380, Thomas had also returned briefly to France, and along with the Earl of Buckingham, he had marched to aid the Duke of Brittany against the French with a retinue of 400 men. Thereafter, Percy was employed between England and France most notably by helping to suppress the Essex rebellion led by Jack Straw, then returning to more diplomatic missions in France during the winter of 1384. Again, in the summer of 1386, Thomas Percy came into contact with John of Gaunt when he was ordered to convey him to Spain, but what caused Gaunt's sudden departure from England was very much a product of what the king thought of his uncle at this time.

In fact, as will be seen, Richard II was fast assessing his own royal prerogatives. Given his recognition that Lancaster's previous delusions of grandeur had caused both Richard and his father no end of trouble in the past, it was probably no accident that an unstable mixture was forming in the young king's autocratic mind: a fragile powder keg of mistrust that would ultimately explode into a storm of revenge years later when Gaunt died and his eldest son and heir, Henry Bolingbroke, succeeded to the Lancastrian title. This mixture had ample time to ferment, and although Richard was still ruled by others due to his long-enforced minority, he must have realised that it was primarily the bad governance of John of Gaunt that had caused the political crisis of 1381, through the levying of a scandalous poll tax at a flat rate regardless of wealth. Richard, then aged fourteen, came out of the crisis well enough to claim enhanced authority, but his second great ordeal in the year 1387 was a crushing personal humiliation and this caused him to act with venom against his enemies.

Richard was more a prince of the Renaissance than a Plantagenet warlord, and the cause of the 1387 crisis centred on the fact that he had managed to gather about him a number of councillors of dubious background – dubious, that is, to the Duke of Gloucester, the king's uncle, and the earls of Warwick and Arundel. Calling themselves the 'Lords Appellant', these three magnates, plus a number of other young nobles, including Gaunt's son Henry Bolingbroke (and possibly even Hotspur), 'appealed' to the king in order to silence those who had virtually taken their place in authority. The demand, finding no immediate political remedy, rapidly escalated and the resulting battle ended in disaster for the king's forces at Radcot Bridge, where the royalist party was defeated after a sharp skirmish over the River Thames.

The whole affair was an affront to Richard's kingship, and it is extremely unlikely that the king ever forgot Henry Bolingbroke's part in it. It was lucky for Bolingbroke, however, that his father enjoyed high office and this saved him from immediate rebuke, but the tragedy of Richard II was that he was 'cursed' with powerful uncles whose incessant intrigues against each other for the management of the kingdom were such a feature of his minority. As a result they paid no heed to the young king's formal training for kingship and this produced a situation that gave Richard ample room to formulate his own more 'creative' monarchy – a monarchy that was as personal as his own livery badge of the White Hart, worn by all his trusted retainers and later the bodyguard of loyal Cheshire archers, whose skill Hotspur would use to such devastating effect at the battle of Shrewsbury.

Fortunately for John of Gaunt, he was out of the country when the events of 1387 reached breaking point. With the aid of Thomas Percy and others of similar diplomatic quality, Gaunt had other things on his mind – he had decided to seek out his own personal kingdom elsewhere, namely the crown of Castile and Leon, which he claimed through his second wife Constance. As Gaunt had managed to escape Richard's blacklist of enemies, it was therefore his younger brother the Duke of Gloucester who first fell foul of the young king's acrimony, thereafter becoming Richard's mortal enemy and prime target for removal. In 1388 Gloucester wasted no time in making a clean sweep of Richard's more dubious friends and favourites by banishment, imprisonment, or beheading. Richard never forgave him, nor it seems his childhood friend, Henry Bolingbroke; it was a situation that would soon bring out the worst that King Richard had to offer, although he could never have anticipated what would materialise out of Bolingbroke's banishment ten years later. For the present his uncle, Gaunt, was out of the picture and the 'Merciless Parliament' was adjudicating the fate of Richard's favourite, Robert de Vere, Duke of Ireland – a sentence that once passed would have special significance for Hotspur, given that in the spring of 1388 he was summoned to London to receive yet another chivalric accolade.

Sir Henry Percy is mentioned as a Knight of the Garter in a wardrobe account recording the issue of red robes for his attendance at St George's Feast. Twenty-one knights and thirteen ladies attended the ceremony at Windsor Castle in 1388 and Hotspur's seat on this auspicious occasion was, rather ominously, none other than the one previously occupied by the recently banished former Duke of Ireland – the thirteenth.[33] However, as Hotspur sat feasting with the highest in the land, with his lady at his side, and with the most noble Order of the Garter encircling his thigh, he could never have anticipated that his next chivalric exploit would ensure that his name would be preserved forever in both ballad tradition and chronicled history. Everything considered, all the romance of chivalry that constituted the Garter celebrations would soon pale into insignificance and be transformed into a fight to the death by the light of a full moon. The ensuing battle would give Hotspur legendary status in his own lifetime and guarantee that the most famous of all Anglo-Scottish border encounters – the battle of Otterburn – would go down in Scottish history as the most heart-rending of all Scotland's sanguinary conflicts.

FOUR

Otterburn: 19 August 1388

⁶'Lord James, Earl of Douglas, made a promise . . . that he would be present in person with the army of the Earl of Fife on the West March. But, I know not by what council, he withdrew and collected his friends and followers . . . and found that he had 7,000 valiant warriors, with whose assistance . . . he seemed easily able to subdue the northern coasts of England. So making an expedition towards the south, he led his army, burning and pillaging towards Newcastle.'³⁴ John Fordun's chronicle, the *Scotichroniconi*, continues with the main details of how the Scots invaded northern England in the summer of 1388. The eastern offensive, under Sir James Douglas, crossed the border into Northumberland on St Oswald's Day (5 August), while the Earl of Fife, with a much larger main force, headed for Carlisle and the west march; both men hoped to take advantage of an England still in the political turmoil caused by the Lords Appellant. However, it was a far less strategic or planned course of events that brought about Hotspur's fateful encounter with Douglas at Otterburn on 19 August, and herein lies the fascination of this unique battle, it being more the product of classic chivalric pride than an outcome fashioned by the application of sound military judgement.

The evidence supplied in the *Scotichroniconi* is contemporary with all the events described, and so provides one of the most interesting 'Scottish' accounts of Otterburn in existence. As with all medieval chronicles that record battles, however, the *Scotichroniconi* contains only a certain amount of tactical information, and this – inevitably, but naturally in the case of Otterburn – is somewhat biased against the English side. Alternatively, Froissart's *Chronicles*, the longest and most famous foreign account of the battle, is pro-French, therefore also pro-Scottish before 1400, the result being that it is also not without its difficulties regarding the English version of events. Notable for his plethora of heroic speeches and chivalrous deeds,

51

Jean Froissart was also obsessed with embroidering the facts and even fabricating the story to heighten the drama, so much so that the truth becomes, like the act of medieval battle itself, distorted by the fog of war. For example, on numerous occasions Froissart gets carried away with the romance of the events he is describing, declaring at one point that Otterburn was 'of all the battles and encounterings that I have made mention of herebefore in all this history, great or small, this battle was one of the sorest and best foughten without cowardice or faint hearts'.[35] Given that Froissart had previously written about such notable English victories as Crécy and Poitiers, it is surprising that he included the battle of Otterburn in his history at all unless, of course, the battle was unusual in some way or that he had met with men who gloried in telling him about it at first hand. And here, arguably, is the real value of Froissart, who states quite emphatically that he had acquired his evidence from two English squires who fought and were captured there. These men he calls John Chateauneuf and John of Cantiron, who, along with two other unnamed Scottish soldiers, give Froissart's account of Otterburn a slight edge over other chroniclers who fail to mention their sources.

Heroic speeches and chivalrous conduct aside, Froissart's lengthy account of Otterburn generally agrees with the *Scotichroniconi* regarding the main facts, while five other secondary sources have their merits in providing interesting, if rather conflicting, information on Hotspur's first pitched battle. These are Walsingham's *History of the English*, John Hardyng's *Chronicle*, Andrew de Wyntoun's *Orygynale Cronykil*, Ranulph Higden's *Polichronica*, and Henry Knighton's *Chronicle*. That Otterburn was primarily a chivalric contest between Hotspur and Douglas is born out by the fact that a number of famous ballads were also written soon after the event, namely the two versions of 'The Battle of Otterburn' (English and Scottish) and, most notably, but hardly the most useful with regard to contemporary dating, the airy hunting ballad aptly christened 'Chevy Chase', or more correctly 'The Hontynge off the Cheviat'.

Extreme battles fought for little more than personal idealism come no better than Otterburn, and it is primarily as a result of this romance that the cut and thrust of the fighting is hard to pinpoint with any degree of accuracy. However, armed with a handful of chronicles, an appreciation of a relatively unchanged landscape and the vital knowledge of how medieval battles were fought, we can resurrect Otterburn if we bear in mind the impetuous character of Hotspur. There is no doubt that most medieval battles have their own unique grey areas; the important thing is to strip down the evidence and apply a degree of logic to what we know is corroborated by chronicled evidence. Events that immediately preceded Otterburn must also be analysed and applied to what occurred once battle commenced. What caused the battle to be fought was far from typical, and although we may conclude that strategically Otterburn solved nothing with regard to Anglo-Scottish relations, the root cause of the fight is best sought in the precepts of chivalry, not in the workings of military theory. Being more a contest between two arrogant knights who refused to give in to reason, Otterburn holds its fascination better than most as the quintessential medieval night battle, so great has been its hold on the popular imagination.

What actually occurred on a gloomy August evening in 1388 was carnage on a scale possibly not foreseen by either side initially. However, the great tragedy of Otterburn was that it was fought at all, and that ultimately it was 'won by a dead man'.[36] Under these special circumstances it is perhaps beyond anyone's capacity to resurrect the event completely, especially if one considers that a medieval night battle is perhaps not the most enlightening place to begin formulating any sound tactical reconstruction. Yet, despite this fact, the enduring legacy of Otterburn is that it has been related over the years through a number of heart-rending tales of classic chivalry that have embellished its dark mantle like an impenetrable shield. That such slaughter was played out in what should have been a perfectly tranquil scene is certain, but the fact that so many writers have gloried in telling subsequent generations about the great tragedy is harder to fathom. The ballads of Otterburn remain nostalgic and graceful renditions of a horrific border encounter, but they contain only a few lines of useful historical evidence. However, concealed within the chronicles there are clues to how the battle was fought, and also a useful reminder of Hotspur's real character in an embittered story of vainglory, mistake, pride and, above all, carnage.

Scottish preparations for invasion had been going on since the beginning of the year and it is said that some 50,000 Scots were mustered at Aberdeen in July 1388 under the royal banner of Robert II's second son, Robert

Stewart, Earl of Fife. Chief among the Scottish leaders under the earl were the 'Black Douglases', namely Sir James Douglas, 2nd Earl of Douglas, and his cousin and later successor Sir Archibald Douglas, Lord of Galloway. Soon after a feint dispersal of their forces – a ruse no doubt intended to confuse the English wardens of both east and west marches – the Scots reassembled their forces somewhere north of the Cheviots at Yetholm or Southdean near Jedburgh. Here, at a council of war, reputedly in a church described by Froissart as Eglise de Zedon or Sion,[37] it was decided that the border would be crossed in two places: the great bulk of the Scots army under Sir Archibald Douglas was given the task of ravaging Cumberland and attacking Carlisle, while the rest, commanded by Sir James Douglas along with the earls of Dunbar and Moray, were ordered to lead a diversionary attack on the English east march – Percy territory. For the sallow-faced and black-haired Sir James it was an opportunity to strike a blow at his traditional enemies, and his rapid march into Northumberland caught the English garrisons temporarily off guard.

The unprepared posture of the Earl of Northumberland and his son Hotspur can perhaps be attributed to two factors, the first of which was purely down to how a medieval Scottish army was equipped and travelled. Jean Froissart, who visited Scotland in 1365, gives this account of the Scottish 'mode of warfare':

These Scottish men are right hardy and sore travailing in harness and in wars. For when they will enter into England, within a day and a night they will drive their whole host twenty-four miles, for they are all a horse-back, unless it be the followers and the laggards of the host, who follow afoot. The knights and squires are well horsed, and the common people and others on little hackneys and geldings: and they carry with them no carts nor chariots because of the diversities of the mountains that they must pass through in the county of Northumberland. They take with them no provision of bread nor wine, for their usage and soberness is such that in time of war they will pass in the journey a great long time with flesh half cooked, without bread, and drink of the river water without wine, and they neither care for pots nor pans, for they seethe beasts in their own skins. . . . Wherefore it is no great marvel that they make greater journeys than other people do. And in this manner were the

Scots entered into the country and wasted and burnt all about as they
went, and took a great number of beasts.[38]

Such was the speed at which the Earl of Douglas invaded England in
1388 that soon his forces had reached the gates of Durham and, it is said,
had also entered parts of North Yorkshire, causing a great deal of concern
to the people of York. Although this deep, penetrating raid cannot be
confirmed with any great certainty, it is recorded that a contingent of
troops was sent northward under the command of the seneschal of York,
Sir Ralph Lumley, establishing the fact that Scottish raiding was at least
feared in those parts of Yorkshire that had suffered from it previously.
However, despite this highly publicised ravaging of northern England, there
may be some truth in Froissart's remark that the Scots failed to adopt their
usual practice of laying waste everything in their path immediately. In fact
when Douglas crossed the border into Percy territory, the adoption of
covert action, as opposed to all-out terrorism, was the main reason why
Hotspur and the English garrisons were taken by surprise, '. . . for they [the
Scots] rode a great pace under covert without doing of any pillage by the
way or assaulting of any castle, tower or house, but so came into the lord
Percy's lands and passed the river of Tyne without any let a three leagues
above Newcastle not far from Brancepeth, and at last they entered the
bishopric of Durham, where they found good country. Then they began to
make war, to slay people and to burn villages and to do many sore
displeasures.'[39]

Striking at both marches simultaneously was confusing enough for
English commanders, but the stealth tactics adopted by Douglas, followed
by a policy of all-out devastation, was a crippling blow to the existing
northern defensive system that required time to counteract. That Douglas
had it in his mind to strike deep into the east march at the behest of the
Earl of Fife's diversionary strategy is certain, but we cannot neglect the fact
that he must have also intended to draw his enemies, the Percys, out into
the open with an even bolder strategy of his own making. As for his first
objective, to confuse the English into thinking that the east march was the
Scots' only target, Douglas succeeded admirably. However, his second
objective was far less certain, or indeed planned, other than to say that he
must have relished the thought that soon his devastation and raiding could

not be ignored by his border counterpart, the warden of the east march, and his chief rival, the fiery 'Haatspore'.

It is perhaps useful at this point to take a brief look at the Scottish army that accompanied Sir James Douglas into Northumberland during the summer of 1388. Froissart's famous snapshot of how quickly this kind of self-sufficient force could penetrate into England speaks for itself. However, the first thing that becomes obvious about Douglas's invading army, or more specifically about how it was mustered during the second half of the fourteenth century, was how similar this recruitment system was to that of the English.

Although William Wallace introduced a form of Scottish conscription soon after the battle of Stirling Bridge in 1297, this method of gathering troops did not continue after his death, and a return to 'Scottish Service' survived until at least the late fourteenth century. Almost a carbon copy of the English 'Statute of Winchester' employed by Edward I in 1285, 'Scottish Service', like English 'Commissions of Array', mustered a levy of all able-bodied men aged between sixteen and sixty for military duty. Similarly, in the second half of the fourteenth century, money contracts called bands, or bonds of retinue, had become widespread north of the border. As the Scottish counterpart to contracts of indenture in England, these contracts between man and master were extremely parochial and involved a hierarchy system of Scottish lords who could not only pay their kinsmen and retainers to fight for them, but could also demand that their service go unpaid in time of war by the workings of feudal law. Hence great armies could be gathered at a moment's notice, every man knowing his place in the system, and every soldier expecting to do his duty in return for either payment, land, or protection from his local enemies.

Very similar to the English in only its recruiting methods, the most distinct advantage of a Scottish army was that it could move with remarkable speed, virtually all the army being either mounted or lightly armed infantry. More like a gigantic raiding party than a conventional medieval army of conquest accompanied by wagons and unwieldy baggage trains, Scottish soldiers were armed according to their status, each town and village being checked yearly by commissioners for equipment, horses and ability to serve. Laymen possessing goods worth £10 were expected to have at least one aketon (a quilted linen jacket), one helmet, gauntlets, sword and spear, extending to a somewhat more expensive coat of plates or a mail corselet if such luxuries could be afforded. So-called 'small folk' (tenant farmers with goods only amounting to the value of one cow) were required to have a long spear or a serviceable short bow, but no other cumbersome equipment was demanded, for a very simple reason – if the common soldier had no horse he was expected to keep up with those in the army who had.

Although many Scottish knights and men-at-arms were equipped much the same as their English counterparts, it is apparent that most Scottish troops were poorly provided with armour. According to Froissart, in 1385 the Scottish army was provided with 1,200 sets of armour by their French allies, 'to the great delight of the recipients, who were otherwise ill-equipped'.[40] Similarly, the Scots' *ribaudaille* or ribauld lacked any comprehensive plate armour. Representing the great bulk of Scottish armies, most of these 'naked' levies had only their shields, long spears and axes for protection, hence their vulnerability to the English longbow, which, on numerous occasions prior to the battle of Otterburn, had devastated their ranks with its rapid 'firepower'.

According to Charles Oman, quoting the major Scottish disasters at Dupplin Moor, Halidon Hill, Neville's Cross and later Homildon Hill, the moral of all such battles against the English was the same:

Invaluable against cavalry, the Scottish pikemen were helpless when opposed to the judicious combination of lance and bow. It was in vain that enlightened men in the northern realm, like King James I, tried to encourage archery: for want of old tradition and hereditary aptitude, Scotland never bred a race of archers such as flourished south of the Tweed. When she got the better of England in war, it was always through careful adherence to 'Good King Robert's Testament', by the avoidance of general engagements, the harrying of the land before the advancing foe, and the confining of offensive action to ambushes and night surprises.[41]

Thus did the Earl of Douglas adhere to the Scottish 'mode of warfare' when he attacked Northumberland in August 1388. By riding swiftly into the very heart of Percy territory 'under covert without doing of any pillage by the way',[42] he gave his enemies no warning of his precise whereabouts until it was too late. When the Scots started to burn and raid the area around Durham, the English garrisons were only just beginning to come to terms with the invasion. In one unconventional act of military audacity, Douglas had not only struck a formidable blow at his opponents, but he had also managed to redirect his army back to Brancepeth and the River Tyne intact. From there he determined to attack the Percys on their home ground, as it is clear from what occurred next that the Scottish earl was not prepared to quit Northumberland without a 'proper' fight with his border counterpart.

Hotspur was at Alnwick Castle when he heard the disturbing news of the Scottish raiding. With the vulnerability of Newcastle being the Percys' next major problem, the Earl of Northumberland swiftly dispatched Hotspur and his younger brother, Sir Ralph Percy, south to join forces with other English captains who had been summoned in order to check Douglas's advance. Although the Scottish raiding was doubtless a shock to the elder Percy, Froissart puts the great earl in a rather relaxed frame of mind, declaring to his two sons that he would 'tarry at Alnwick, which is a passage that [the Scots] must pass by'.[43] Thinking that Douglas might retreat into Scotland via the coast road, it seems that the earl had decided to trap the Scots somewhere between Newcastle and Alnwick. However, Percy badly misinterpreted Douglas's intended line of march back across the border. It was probably the best strategy that he could think of at the time, but as at Shrewsbury, fifteen years later, it would be his son who would bear the brunt of his mistake not to attack his enemies in person.

As for Douglas, facing the fiery Hotspur in single combat was too good an opportunity to miss. As wardens of a territory they had sworn so recently to protect, there was no way that the Percys could avoid him. The panic-stricken people and merchants of Newcastle welcomed their young champion into the fold, eagerly anticipating that the very presence of Hotspur might force the Scots to retreat to their own country. They failed to take into account Douglas's determination and chivalric pride. According to Froissart, on about 15 August, as the whole Scottish army passed under the walls of Newcastle, Douglas issued a stern challenge to his adversary in person.

When the Scots arrived outside medieval Newcastle it was surrounded by a ditch and a 20-foot-high wall built in the reign of Edward I. In the fourteenth century the chief export of the town was north-country wool, supplemented by coals from pits situated on either side of the River Tyne. Second only to York in northern importance, Newcastle was, according to a foreign traveller in 1436, the last 'civilised' point of contact with the rest of Europe. That it was populated by a sophisticated merchant class is supported by the historian H.L. Trevor Roper who, following Lord Dacre's musings, confirmed that the merchants of Newcastle 'constituted a single element of civilisation . . . separating them from their elder brothers who bit their fingernails in draughty castellated farmhouses and murdered each other over the bitting of a greyhound or even less important matters of dispute'.[44]

Militarily, Newcastle's role was to provide English armies with a forward headquarters and supply depot against northern invasion and raiding; however, the town was not considered a front-line fortress in the war against Scotland. Therefore, all things considered, a victorious Scottish raiding force, blowing its famous horns and parading its trophies of war around its walls must have been a matter of deep concern to all within, especially when the Scots encamped north of the town and started to launch several surprise attacks against Newcastle's gates.

Repelling these assaults on the English side of the 'barriers' were men like the captain of Berwick, Sir Matthew Redmane; Sir Thomas Umfraville, a kinsman of the Percys; Sir Robert Ogle; Sir Thomas Grey; Sir John Felton, and other well-known northern knights including Hotspur himself who, chief among the English leaders, immediately accepted Douglas's challenge of single combat in a moment of typical impetuosity. Froissart eloquently describes the heroic nature of this chivalrous encounter between the two knights, which was no doubt watched from Newcastle's high walls by citizens and soldiers alike:

> . . . there was fighting hand to hand: among other there fought hand to hand the earl Douglas and Sir Henry Percy, and by force of arms the earl Douglas won the pennon of Sir Henry Percy, wherewith he was sore displeased and so were all the Englishmen. And the earl Douglas said to Sir Henry Percy: 'Sir, I shall bear this token of your prowess into Scotland and shall set it on high on my castle of Dalkeith, that it may be seen far off.' 'Sir,' quoth Sir Henry, 'ye may be sure ye shall not pass the bounds

of this country till ye be met withal in such wise that ye shall make none avaunt thereof.' 'Well, sir,' quoth the earl Douglas, 'come this night to my lodging and seek for your pennon: I shall set it before my lodging and see if ye will come to take it away.'[45]

Contrary to what we know of Hotspur's reckless nature, Douglas's mocking challenge was not taken up immediately. Dissuaded from taking back his pennon, no doubt by other English captains fearing that an ambush, or some other form of trickery, might put both their leader and Newcastle in jeopardy, Hotspur was persuaded that caution was the best part of valour. According to Froissart the English decision to postpone the inevitable clash of arms was also because no one knew for certain whether Douglas commanded the only Scottish army in the vicinity. Douglas had admittedly won an important moral victory over Hotspur by achieving his precious pennon, but it was highly unlikely that any Scots army, lacking the resources necessary to conduct a siege, would risk staying in the open for long. Sure enough, the next day, no doubt hurling much abuse at the English army, English captains were proved right: the Scots army was seen to strike their camp and march north-west towards Ponteland, a town which they pillaged, burning its castle to the ground.

Meanwhile, news had arrived at Newcastle that a relief force under the Bishop of Durham was advancing to help the English. However, it is clear from Hotspur's dismissive reaction to clerical support that he had already made up his mind not to heed any further warnings of caution, nor to wait for any reinforcements. Instead, fired up no doubt by Douglas's slight to his honour, and most certainly incensed by the frustrated attempt to recover his priceless pennon from under his enemy's nose, Hotspur now made a move that was to prove both impulsive and reckless to the point of madness. What probably changed the mind of English captains to follow his lead in what can only be called a purely selfish mission to redeem lost pride was the simple fact that soon the whereabouts, position and strength of Douglas's army could be established with certainty.

Following the palls of acrid smoke rising from a string of burnt-out farmsteads and peel towers, English scourers were soon able to gather enough intelligence to confirm that Douglas was lacking any support from his kinsman the Earl of Fife, and that he was heading north-west for the border with a depleted army of some 2,500 men. According to Froissart, these same English scouts had also been able to locate the Scottish camp at Otterburn, some thirty-two miles away, no doubt relating to Hotspur that they had seen the ominous sight of his priceless pennon fluttering menacingly outside Douglas's tent.

Studying Froissart may be our only clue to Hotspur's more chivalrous adventures prior to the battle of Otterburn, but the story of the lost pennon may well be a fabrication of the truth, since neither the *Scotichroniconi* nor Thomas Walsingham's *Historia Anglicana* give any credence to missing pennons or lost honour, only perhaps to an intense rivalry – a rivalry that we know had existed between the houses of Percy and Douglas for generations. According to Walsingham:

> . . . with a great display of arrogance they [the Scots] approached Newcastle upon Tyne, and camped at Otterburn. Henry Percy junior was then in Newcastle with his brother Ralph, both were knights, both eager for military glory, both hostile to the Scots, but Henry the more so, because of his great valour. Henry [Percy] himself was enraged that the Scots were rampaging about unchecked, and so, because they had challenged him to fight, he promised that he would join battle with them in three days, although his forces were far below theirs in number.[46]

The *Scotichroniconi*, on the other hand, is more to the point, and because its writer gave a rather uncharacteristic report of Scottish incompetence prior to the battle, there is reason to believe that there is some truth in the theory that Otterburn was a chance encounter rather than a set-piece action. Indeed, according to this important source, it seems that the Scots were the victims of a surprise attack by Hotspur:

> While the Earl of Douglas was trying to get back to his own country, the said Henry Percy sought to find the army of the Earl of Fife; but as it was large, he turned away to attack the army of the Earl of Douglas, then in pitched camp at Otterburn in Redesdale. The Earl of Douglas did not suspect any evil from his foes, so with the earls of March and Moray, his two brothers, and many other knights and nobles, he and they were dressed, unarmed, in gowns and long robes, ready for the feasting on the

day of St Oswald. As they reclined at table a certain Scot came into them, sitting on a saddled horse, calling frantically to all to fly to arms, '. . . because our enemies are speeding upon us!' At his voice all jumped up from their supper, and flew to put their armour on . . .[47]

No mention of pennons here. However, we should not dismiss this romantic story of lost honour out of hand, as it seems that the very pennon stolen from the tip of Hotspur's lance in the confused melee before the gates of Newcastle may once have existed, at least in the mind of one cleric. According to Bishop Thomas Percy of Dromore, writing in the late eighteenth century, he actually saw the relic, although he goes on to describe its appearance as bearing the badge of Douglas rather than Percy. According to an old manuscript preserved at Syon House, Middlesex, Bishop Percy stated that he was told that the Earl of Douglas gave Hotspur's pennon to his squire, Douglas of Cavers, before he died at Otterburn and that it continued in the latter's family – who were hereditary sheriffs of Teviotdale – thereafter. Tradition further states that Hotspur pursued Douglas of Cavers from the battlefield and that it was because of this impetuous chase that Percy was eventually captured. During a visit to Cavers in September 1774 the bishop was shown the pennon which tradition says passed from Douglas's dying hand in order that it might be carried to safety. However, this artefact has no doubt been confused with another battle standard that is extant, namely the tattered, but surprisingly well-preserved Douglas standard, said to have fallen and then been raised again at the battle of Otterburn, just before Sir James died of his wounds on that fateful day.[48]

Romantic musings about lost relics and chivalry, as with all great battles, are natural failings made by all those who seek to perpetuate an important event in time. So much so, that anecdotes such as the Percy pennon, and others of equal disadvantage, tend to infuse the battle of Otterburn with so much conflicting evidence and unconfirmed rhetoric that the real story of the fight is totally obscured from view. To be armed with all the extant information and evidence supplied by the chronicles is one thing, but to heed the more fanciful meanderings of antiquarians is quite another. A much better course of action is to seek out the chronicled evidence and apply to this reasoning the mechanics of weapons, modes of warfare, and the history of a relatively unchanged moorland landscape. Supplied with this more tangible evidence, it is possible to re-create what may have occurred at Otterburn on that moonlit evening in 1388 without resorting to myth. The conclusions drawn are slightly different from the existing model and probably represent a new perspective on Hotspur's first pitched battle in the barren outlands of his ancestors.

HILL, RIVER, PASS AND MARSH

Before 1952 there was only one detailed and independent account of the battle of Otterburn in print. Written in 1857, Robert White's book[49] was the standard work until almost a century later Col A.H. Burne included a more lucid rendering in his *More Battlefields of England*. That Burne had much trouble understanding some of the finer points of Froissart's account is admitted by him on at least two occasions, although in the same breath he accepts the fact that Froissart was probably the only writer who was able to speak to eyewitnesses who had fought at Otterburn in 1388. Burne's version, indeed all his work on battles and battlefields, is incomparable; however, some of his conclusions are flawed in a number of ways, more specifically when one considers that his famous works were written when he was waging another more personal battle of his own with fellow historian and battlefield writer, Sir James Ramsay.

In Ramsay's *Genesis of Lancaster* another account of Otterburn exists which breaks the mould by placing the battlefield one and a half miles to the east of the generally accepted site. Burne predictably disagrees with Ramsay's account and employs his famous IMP[50] to maximum effect while at the same time attacking White's standard work by saying that the writer was 'a civilian, without practical knowledge of war and, like Sir James Ramsay, he sometimes enunciates military absurdities'.[51] Unfortunately, as with all challenges taken up personally, numerous mistakes are inherently made in order to prove an alternative scenario, and Col Burne's work is no exception to this rule. Perhaps a more worthwhile tactic is instead to apply the chronicled evidence, for when personal opinion and criticism are taken away, all that remains to consult are the reports of those who were closest to the event and who saw battles like Otterburn as relatively recent history.

Today, a multi-tiered stone plinth and obelisk, inappropriately named Percy's Cross, marks the battlefield for posterity. The monument stands in a rectangular tree-lined grove on the right-hand side of the A696 road from Newcastle to Scotland in the picturesque valley of the River Rede. In 1388 this main road was one of three medieval roads in and out of the east march of England and it is therefore extremely likely that the Earl of Douglas and his army used this same route when they crossed into England prior to their successful pillaging campaign, and returned by it when they encamped at Otterburn on or about 17 August. However, what immediately becomes apparent when visiting the site is the fact that the battlefield is located on sloping ground, with the main road running almost parallel to the river and the combat zone being situated on the right-hand side of the road if approaching Redesdale from the south. Indeed, the rolling moorland landscape, sloping gently away from east to west, constitutes one side of a shallow valley variously called on early Ordnance Survey maps Battle Croft or Battle Riggs. This same slope descends from a maximum height of about 232 metres to the banks of the fast flowing River Rede which runs through the valley some 1,000 metres away at a general height of about 147 metres above sea level. Thus the battle of Otterburn was fought in an extremely limited area, the river preventing any appreciable movement by both armies to the west.

Otterburn Castle (or the peel that once stood there in 1388) was purposely constructed at the eastern end of this shallow valley as a lookout post and safe haven against Scottish attack. Located on the saddle of a hill overlooking the road and the Otter Burn – a small rivulet that follows the contours of another more pronounced valley into the River Rede below – the castle once commanded the area, and, of course, was bound to attract a certain amount of Scottish attention. Indeed, Froissart states that the Otterburn peel came under immediate siege on 17 and 18 August 1388 and was apparently not subdued by Douglas and his retreating army because 'it stood in the marsh'.[52] Accordingly, the Scots 'assaulted [the peel] until they were weary, and did nothing',[53] which proves that something other than military might prevented them from taking their objective. Let us remember that only the previous day Douglas and his men had taken the castle at Ponteland and had not only burnt it to the ground, but had also captured its keeper, Sir Edmund Alphel. Can we therefore establish why the Scots had such problems this time against a simple border peel? In short, did some natural obstacle, such as Froissart's marsh, exist at the entrance to the valley in 1388? And if so, did this feature protect Otterburn Castle against Douglas's many spirited attacks?

The lie of the land may provide a clue here, although Froissart's repeated use of the word *marish* in conjunction with the Scottish camp is a little ambiguous, although not impossible to explain. What is impossible, of course, is to tell exactly what the weather was like in August 1388. Other than accepting Froissart's glib comment that at the time of the battle 'it was the month of August and the weather was fair and temperate',[54] little is known about the conditions before or after this date. However, it is recognised that rivers in moorland valleys have marshes bordering their banks in all seasons, unless they are exposed to extremely arid conditions. Therefore, it is possible that some form of marshland did exist at either side of the River Rede in 1388, more likely at a lower level, namely at the confluence of the Otter Burn and the River Rede, directly below the position of the Otterburn peel. This marsh may have prevented the Scots from approaching and capturing their objective, although Froissart's evidence alone is by no means conclusive.

What is certain, though, is the position of the 'pass' between the Otterburn peel and the river, and the significant problem that this natural obstacle made for Hotspur's army when it finally arrived at Otterburn on 19 August. Indeed, this pass, and the subsequent effect it had on the English, later dictated how the actual battle was fought. However, we must first briefly sketch Hotspur's movements from Newcastle to Otterburn and conclude, as near as possible, what time of day the English arrived on the battlefield. After receiving news from his scourers that Douglas was isolated from the main Scottish army with about 2,500 men under his command, Hotspur persuaded his followers that here was an opportunity not to be missed. According to Froissart, the Bishop of Durham was fast approaching Newcastle with reinforcements, 'but Sir Henry Percy would not abide his coming, for he had with him six hundred spears, knights and squires, and eight thousand footmen. . . . Thus they departed from Newcastle after dinner and set forth in good order and took the same way as the Scots had gone and rode to Otterburn.'[55]

Froissart gets confused with distances here, and as a result places the Scottish camp only a few miles (leagues) from Newcastle, whereas in reality Otterburn is a good thirty-two miles distant – a forced march, at least, for any conventional medieval army to complete in a day, let alone in an afternoon. If these timings are accepted, then it must be argued that Froissart was not only mistaken about distances, but also about footmen. To arrive at the pass overlooked by the Otterburn peel by dusk (roughly seven o'clock in August), it is clear that Hotspur must have commanded a mounted force. Indeed, he must have led a large raiding party of knights, men-at-arms and hobilars (mounted footmen) into Redesdale.

A.H. Burne briefly discusses this problem of distances and troop types in his work on the battle: if a pace of five miles per hour could be maintained by the English army (no great feat if Hotspur's men were all mounted), then it is perfectly feasible that his army could complete the thirty-two miles to Otterburn before dusk – although the suspicion is that it was much later than seven o'clock when the English arrived there given that the *Scotichroniconi* suggests that Douglas's knights had already taken their armour off and were preparing for supper.

This idea of an English mounted army can be developed further, especially when we call into question the unusual way the battle of Otterburn was fought. However, to proceed further we must know the position of the Scottish camp, and this poses the greatest problem of all regarding the tactics employed by both armies. Froissart was convinced that there were two separate camps, one, or both, bordering his elusive marsh, but most modern writers, Burne included, are inclined to believe that there was only one camp beside the River Rede. Froissart writes that 'they made many lodgings of boughs and great herbs, and fortified their camp sagely with the marsh that was thereby, and their carriages were set at the entry into the marshes and [they] had all their beasts within the marsh . . . therewith suddenly the Englishmen came upon them and entered into the lodgings, weening it had been the masters' lodgings, and therein were but varlets and servants'.[56]

Next, Froissart tells us that the Scottish lords sent a company of footmen to support their varlets and servants at the entrance to the camp, 'and in the mean time [the lords] armed and apparelled themselves, every man under his banner and under his captain's pennon',[57] a clear indication that Douglas, March, Moray and their retainers were situated somewhere other than in the camp by the marsh. Froissart does not give the exact location of this second camp, but it is clear that its position was somewhat advantageous to the Scots, who had without doubt been taken by surprise by their enemies. As also indicated in the *Scotichroniconi*, this attack on the servants' camp was wholly unexpected. However, it is also clear from the chronicles that in order to launch this surprise assault, Hotspur had to solve a terrain problem of his own. Indeed, it is apparent from both Froissart and the *Scotichroniconi* that the English were forced into splitting their army into two separate 'battles' or divisions, and this brings us back to the pass below the Otterburn peel.

Although it may be safe to assume that both sides prior to the battle of Otterburn had envisaged some form of plan to outwit their opponents, it remains the classic characteristic of all land battles that terrain always plays a key role in deciding how the most carefully laid plans come to fruition. Passing below the Otterburn peel in the gathering gloom, Hotspur's army may have heard the thankful cries of relief from the beleaguered English garrison above them, but at the entrance to the valley it is clear that something other than impetuosity forced Hotspur's hand to divide his force, hence weakening it. According to the *Scotichroniconi*: 'Henry Percy found that his men were crowded together, so he divided his army into two. He led one part himself, with Ralph Percy, his brother; the other part he entrusted to the lords Maurice [Matthew] Redmane and Robert Ogle, to destroy pavilions and tents . . .'[58]

The marsh, or indeed the pass between the river and the high ground, may have caused this manoeuvre to occur in the narrow width that was available to Hotspur's army. However, the sudden division of the English force could have been more deliberate than this, if there were in fact two Scottish camps, one containing the so-called varlets, beasts, baggage and plunder, and a second adjacent to this reserved for Douglas, his knights and their followers, that was chiefly responsible for supporting the former in the marsh.

Both concepts are utterly plausible given the circumstances, but what is certain, and in accordance with the information supplied by Froissart's eyewitnesses, is that some plan resulting in a well-timed ambush had been arranged by the Scots beforehand. In accordance with all the precepts of 'Good King Robert's Testament', this theory becomes all the more credible if one considers Charles Oman's theories of how the Scots waged war against the English in the fourteenth century. Although no military concept can be proved conclusively, there is every reason to believe that Douglas had been planning his attack on Hotspur for at least two days. It would be foolish to think otherwise; the only thing that Douglas failed to do was to forecast the arrival of his enemies in the valley. However, what Douglas did succeed in doing, like all good commanders, was to use the Redesdale terrain to his advantage despite being taken by surprise, and here both the *Scotichroniconi* and Froissart are in agreement that a mountain, or hill, played a decisive part in the ensuing battle.

After deciding to split his force into two (probably unequal) parts at the entrance to the valley, Hotspur directed his captains, Redmane and Ogle, against the Scottish camp situated beside the river. With this strong raiding party winging its way down Redesdale, Hotspur and his brother Ralph were now able to manoeuvre their forces more easily in the valley. But was the fiery Hotspur in some way unsure of the actual position of his rival's camp, or was he in fact hedging his bets? His main objective must have been to seek out Douglas (and ultimately win back his priceless pennon), but it seems that some confusion had arisen as the setting sun began to gently graze the western hills of Redesdale.

Cooking fires had been lit in the Scottish camps by this late hour; therefore it seems feasible that if Hotspur had seen these two separate constellations of light from afar then he may have purposely divided his forces in the hope of taking both positions at once. The *Scotichroniconi* clearly states that at first the Scots were taken by surprise by Redmane's men as they rode roughshod over the Scottish varlets' camp. Douglas, quickly responding to this first attack, tried to support his men as best he could; indeed, 'so quickly did [he] apply himself to the order of battle that he was prevented from putting on his armour properly; so that night he was fatally wounded in his face and neck, by unknown persons'.[59] However, despite this apparent confusion in the Scots camp, Hotspur chose not to attack his enemies simultaneously along with Redmane, and this mistake gained Douglas precious time to play a trick on the English. Immediately after sending some of his own footmen to help his hard-pressed forces below him, he drew his contingents together, 'and [they] without any noise departed from their lodgings and went about a little mountain, which was greatly to their advantage. For all the day they had been well advised of the place and said among themselves: "If the Englishmen come upon us suddenly, then we will do thus and thus, for it is a jeopardous thing in the night if men of war enter into our lodgings. If they do this we will draw to such a place, and thereby we shall win or lose."'[60]

Similarly, the continuation of the *Scotichroniconi* gives startling evidence of this ploy by Douglas, as well as how this ambitious manoeuvre resulted in a well-timed ambush on the English right flank: 'The arrival of the English increased the alarm amongst the Scots, who took flight, keenly pursued by Redmane and Ogle. But when the part led by Percy was waiting for the fugitive Scots, and was rejoicing at the prospect of their flight, the Earl of Douglas got his best men to mount their horses and advanced unseen through thickets and thorn brakes. They approached the field unseen by the English, and suddenly burst out near the English line, with twelve banners unfurled, and gleaming in the setting sun.'[61]

Marching along the sloping valley, no doubt heading for Douglas's camp – possibly located a little further along the valley and to the left of the varlets' quarters – it was now Hotspur's turn to think quickly under pressure. If reducing his total strength by half had been a necessary evil to either circumnavigate the pass or to bring both parts of his army to bear on Scottish camps simultaneously, then Hotspur had badly misjudged his opponents. In a stroke of Scottish ingenuity, Douglas had melted into the gathering gloom, leaving Hotspur and his men at the mercy of a Scottish attack right where it was least expected. Hotspur had become a sitting target, isolated from the rest of his army who were, by all accounts, oblivious to his predicament. Redmane and his cavalry were busy killing Scotsmen below, not to mention recovering English loot and burning the Scots camp to the ground. As far as Redmane's detachment was concerned the battle was won: there could be no doubt that Hotspur was well capable of taking care of Douglas on his own.

Given Hotspur's impetuosity in all things chivalrous, it is perhaps understandable that his main aim was to face Douglas in personal combat. Given the circumstances of his family feud with the Douglases, his captured pennon, and his highly combustible character, Hotspur's selfish need to prove himself in battle can perhaps be understood. But the ghastly mistake of dividing his forces in the face of the enemy cannot be forgiven so easily, and the tactic would cost him dear. But poised above the two Scottish camps at the head of his men, Hotspur could hardly have foreseen what would emerge from the tree line to his right, nor that the real battle of Otterburn was only just beginning.

HOTSPUR VERSUS DOUGLAS

The English chronicler John Hardyng, who later fought alongside Hotspur at Homildon Hill and Shrewsbury, wrote a short poetic account of Otterburn in which the blame for his master's defeat is levelled at the confusion of medieval warfare:

> The earle Douglas and the earle of March also,
> Northumberlande, by West the Newe Castell,
> Unto Morpath norwarde dyd mikyll wo
> At Otturborne, as chronicles doo tell,
> Henry Percy with small hoste on him fell,
> And slewe Douglas, and many put to flight,
> And gate the felde upon his enemyes right.
>
> He sent the lorde syr Thomas Umfreuyle,
> His brother Robert, and also, sir Thomas Grey,
> And sir Matthew Redmayne beyond the Scottes that while,
> To holde them in so they fled not awaye;
> Wherfore the Scottes releved agayne always,
> Through which Henry was take there anone,
> To Dunbar led, for whom was made great mone.
>
> The felde was his all if it he were take,
> The Umfreuyle, Grey, Ogle, and Redmayne
> Helde the felde hole, it might so for his sake
> And knewe nothing whetherwarde he was gayn.
> The earle of Marche with prevy men alane,
> Full prively to Dunbarre with hym rode,
> And kepte hym there, for he was greatly ferde.[62]

Apart from a number of lyrical anomalies contained in Hardyng's stanzas, it is almost certain that the writer, as a member of the Percy household, knew something about the battle of Otterburn at first hand. Being initially employed by Hotspur, then by Sir Robert Umfraville, the second son of the same Thomas 'Umfreuyle' that Hardyng mentions, he was therefore in an excellent position to gather evidence for his history. However, being prejudiced against literally anything Scottish, Hardyng's evidence of Otterburn must be tempered with a certain degree of caution. Yet, despite the biased opinions, what emerges is interesting, if only to confirm certain facts that are contained in other contemporary accounts of the battle.

The first of Hardyng's stanzas clearly follows the obvious preliminaries of the campaign, although it is debatable whether Hotspur marched a 'small' force into Redesdale in August 1388. However, Hardyng next states that Hotspur 'gate' the field upon his enemy's right – an interesting statement if one considers the eventual split in the English army and his later right-hand position in the valley. Next, Umfraville, Grey, Ogle and Redmane are sent 'beyond' the Scots to hold them in the field, while all the time the Scottish camp was being 'releved' by others from elsewhere. Hardyng then tells us of the English defeat and that Umfraville and his knights 'helde the felde hole', but due to some confusion they 'knewe nothyng' of Hotspur's whereabouts or, indeed, that he was captured until it was too late. If we take into account the evidence of the *Scotichroniconi* this confusion is perhaps not so surprising given that, firstly, it was almost dark when the battle commenced, and, secondly, that as far as Umfraville and his men were concerned, the Scots were fleeing from the field and the battle was won.

Isolated on the slopes of Battle Riggs, and heading for what he thought was Douglas's camp, Hotspur barely had time to think before the Scots' attack came hurtling down the hill. The shock to the English right must have been devastating, even if we accept that Hotspur's force was superior in numbers to that of Douglas's. As the full moon began to cast its sombre shadow over the open heathland the cries of battle soon began to snuff out all the romance of the approaching evening in a cacophony of clashing weapons and yelling men. Hotspur and his men were on their own. Blood had already been spilled in the valley below, but now the main event would focus upon the madness of close-quarter medieval combat and the prize of an elusive piece of coloured cloth. The *Scotichroniconi* relates:

Knights and squires were of good courage on both parties to fight valiantly: cowards there had no place, but hardiness reigned with goodly feats of arms, for knights and squires were so joined together at hand strokes, that archers had no place of neither party. There the Scots shewed great hardiness and fought merrily with great desire of honour: the Englishmen were three to one: howbeit, I say not but Englishmen did nobly acquit themselves, for ever the Englishmen had rather been slain or taken in the place than to fly. Thus, as I have said, the banners of Douglas and Percy and their men were met each against the other, envious of who should win the honour of that journey.[63]

Froissart goes on to describe the battle of Otterburn in similar romantic terms, hardly a practical or useful method of reconstruction, but wholly in keeping with his age, and the age of chivalry. Given that such close-quarter violence had to be justified in some way so that others might condone more of the same, it is perhaps understandable that such psychological states as battle trauma and confusion are never discussed in any chronicles dealing with medieval warfare. As a result, most accounts are prone to a gratuitous distortion of the truth, the frenzy of medieval combat and what actually transpired when both armies finally clashed never fully being agreed upon, even with the benefit of so-called eyewitness accounts. Yet, in the case of Otterburn, there are a certain number of crucial events that are repeatedly woven into the pages of the chronicles, and therefore some semblance of order can be established out of the disorder and slaughter of battle.

In order to trace the ebb and flow of the final stages of Otterburn it is necessary to establish a mode of fighting, agree on what weapons were used, ascertain the ground over which both sides fought, and of course determine the size and ability of the forces engaged. If we say that the majority of Hotspur's army was mounted when it first entered Redesdale, then it follows that this was also how it appeared when Douglas launched his unexpected attack on Hotspur's flank. Archers had no place in the battle, we are told by Froissart, therefore it seems certain – given the surprise in the Scottish camp – that Hotspur's men, like the force of Redmane and Ogle, still enjoyed a slight advantage over the Scots – that is, if Douglas's men were, like their camp guards, dismounted when they attacked. According to the *Scotichroniconi* this can be confirmed with some certainty: 'Shortly before sundown they [the Scots] dismounted and attacked the English. But the latter, three times as numerous as the Scots, counter-attacked manfully with their lances, and a fierce conflict arose.'[64]

This initial clash of arms was sustained by the English who, according to Froissart, 'fought so valiantly that they reculed the Scots back'.[65] The Scottish chronicler, Andrew Wyntoun, gives a rather lyrical description of how the English managed to redress both the situation and the disadvantage of being ambushed when the Scots emerged from the tree line:

> Thai knyt them noucht in swilk array,
> As thai before awysyd were.[66]

Froissart reiterates Wyntoun's point by adding that Hotspur managed to form up some of his men, 'ilz se arresterent', against this sudden assault. Then the extremely brutal hand-to-hand battle began in earnest: 'And at the first encounter many were overthrown of both parties; and because the Englishmen were so great in number and greatly desired to vanquish their enemies, they rested at their pace and greatly did put aback the Scots, so that they were near discomfited.'[67]

Overwhelming English numbers (by all accounts a ratio of three to one) suggest that the Scottish element of surprise lasted only briefly. But why did Douglas order his men to dismount at the outset of their attack when surely the Scots were quite capable of launching a mounted flank attack of their own just as effectively? The solution is hard to fathom, but part of the answer may be found in the way the Scots waged war.

An oral tradition, attributed to Robert Bruce, records the basic guidelines of Scottish warfare, namely that troops should form up for battle on foot in close-order divisions usually described by chroniclers as *schiltrons*. These shield walls, bristling with long spears, some 12 to 14 feet in length, looked similar in appearance to a Greek phalanx, and against unsupported cavalry a Scottish *schiltron* could be particularly lethal. The most favoured position for this formation appears to have been on a hill with a wood to the rear and a brook or marshy ground to the front. However, there was one fatal flaw to the *schiltron* and yet another in its usefulness when close-quarter combat began. First, English archery could wreak havoc among such closely packed formations, and second, when both sides resorted to hand-to-hand combat, the long Scottish spear was difficult to wield effectively against shorter melee weapons such as the short axe and the stabbing sword.

If Douglas's men were mounted when they left their camp, then it is highly likely that they dismounted before they attacked in order to use their long spears against Hotspur's cavalry. This would have put the English horses at a grave disadvantage. But once Hotspur's superior force was obliged to dismount to face the advancing *schiltron*, then the balance of arms would have been immediately redressed, hence the giving way of the Scottish line and the resort to bolder tactics by the Douglas household.

According to the evidence, it was at this point in the battle that the fighting got particularly savage, both sides obviously trying to gain some advantage over the other in the uncertain half-light of the full moon (the moon was full on 20 August). Pushed back by the English men-at-arms, it seems that Douglas's standard, the 'bludy hert', accidentally fell in the mayhem of tumbling bodies that heralded another break in the Scottish line. The loss of the Douglas banner was unthinkable and, immediately, two of the earl's knights, both named Patrick Hepburn, father and son, launched themselves forward into the melee to rescue it from the English. Although this blind act of courage did nothing to heal the bloody breach that had been made in their retreating front ranks, the standard was won back after a fierce fight. However, it was clear that something more drastic had to be done in order to bolster Scottish ranks, and to resist the superior numbers stacked against them, and it is here that two of the chroniclers of Otterburn are at odds with each other.

Froissart states that the Earl of Douglas, seeing his battle line buckle under pressure, decided to attack the English line single-handedly: 'he took his axe in both his hands, and entered so into the press that he made himself way in such wise, that none durst approach near him, and he was so well armed that he bare well off such strokes as he received. Thus he went forth like a hardy Hector, willing alone to conquer the field and to discomfit his enemies . . . some of his knights and squires followed him, but not all, for it was night, with no light but the shining of the moon'.[68]

No doubt some of Douglas's household men followed their master into battle in order to protect him, but it is clear from the chronicles that there was a great deal of confusion over who made the first move to stabilise the

Scottish line. According to the *Scotichroniconi*, 'While this struggle began, a very experienced, strong, and brave Scot, John Swinton rushed forward into the English line and did fearful execution there. Because of this the Scots were able to penetrate the English line with their spears, so that the English were forced to give ground to this strong force.'[69]

John Swinton served a number of Douglas lords between 1378 and 1402. He was a very experienced soldier, not only maintained by Scottish lords but English ones too, including John of Gaunt, Duke of Lancaster. A veteran of several English campaigns in France, Swinton returned to Scotland in 1378 and became part of the inner circle of the Douglas affinity, marrying into the Douglas household and becoming stepfather to Sir James – clearly an important asset to James's family, especially in military matters.[70] At Otterburn, Swinton's distinctive role as Douglas's retainer would have been to protect his master, along with others who primarily fought as a battle group using their lords' heraldic standard as a rallying point. Swinton managed to survive his celebrated attack on the English line to fight another day, but Douglas, who was probably the main instigator of the assault, was suddenly cut off from his fighting group by the gathering tide of English men-at-arms. Trying to cut a bloody path through to his rival Hotspur, it appears that the sallow-faced Scot passed beyond the point of no return, not to mention his own front line. Immediately his famous black hair and gaunt complexion were seen to be swallowed up in a thicket of English weapons. Froissart gives an unconfirmed, but entirely plausible account of how Douglas was cut down in the savage melee that enveloped him:

. . . but at last he [Douglas] was encountered by three spears all at once, the one strake him on the shoulder, the other on the breast and the stroke glinted down his belly, and the third strake him in the thigh, and sore hurt with all three strokes, so that he was borne perforce to the earth and after that he could not be again relieved. . . . Thus the Earl Douglas was felled to the earth, he was striken into the head with an axe, and another stroke through the thigh. The Englishmen passed forth and took no heed of him, they thought none otherwise but that they had slain a man of arms.[71]

On the other side of the field Douglas's fate would have been unknown even to the closest of his followers. Given the general confusion of medieval battle, and the fact that Otterburn was fought in a kind of confused half-light, it seems incredible that the battle was pursued with such vigour into the night. Other than to their immediate front, it is extremely likely that both sides were now fighting in a number of tightly packed 'knots' and it is reasonable to suppose that this is why the Scots won the fight on an individual basis. Indeed, several bewildered cries of 'Follow Douglas!' may have given the Scots a much-needed boost of morale, heralding yet another counter-attack by the earls of March and Moray, who very soon succeeded in pushing back the English ranks and capturing Hotspur's brother, Ralph Percy, in the process.

Given Ralph Percy's situation, it is perhaps safe to assume that Hotspur himself was on this side of the field, his brother being 'entered in so far among his enemies that he was closed in and hurt'.[72] As English ranks suddenly pivoted back down Battle Riggs towards the River Rede, Hotspur's brother was soon, like Douglas, swallowed up in the crush of falling bodies. Craving mercy and declaring to his captors that his hose and greaves were full of blood, the younger Percy was immediately taken prisoner by Sir John Maxwell, who entrusted him to one of his men in order that his wounds might be bound up behind the lines. Across the flashing sea of weapons the fiery Hotspur, seeing the unthinkable happen before his eyes, probably could only watch as his brother was led away to the rear. Indeed, hacking about him like a madman, Hotspur may have already exposed himself to capture as he tried in vain to rescue his wounded brother from the turning tide of battle.

It must be emphasised here that as the battle of Otterburn progressed and the hours of night advanced so any semblance of order and formation must have deteriorated on both sides. Medieval battle was an extremely confusing and disorientating experience by day – hence the need for rallying cries and respites from fighting – without the added problem of bad visibility to contend with. Thus the field at Otterburn would have become strewn with a series of fights, with the superior English numbers adding hardly any significant advantage to an already confusing situation. However, it is here, in the disorder of history, that the battle enters its legendary phase and boasts probably the finest death scene in Scottish history. Froissart's highly stylised prose briefly lightens the slaughterhouse experience of medieval warfare in a scene that later moved many a Scotsman to tears.

Now let us speak of the young James Earl of Douglas, who did marvels in arms before he was beaten down. When he was overthrown the press was great about him, so that he could not be relieved, for with an axe he had his death's wound. His men followed him as near as they could, and there came to him Sir James Lindsay his cousin and Sir John and Sir Walter Sinclair and other knights and squires. . . . Then Sir John Sinclair demanded of the earl how he did. 'Right evil, cousin,' quoth the earl, 'but thanks be to God there hath been but few of mine ancestors that hath died in their beds. . . . But cousin, I require you think to revenge me, for I reckon myself but dead, for my heart fainteth oftentimes. My cousin Walter and you, prey you raise up my banner which lieth on the ground. My squire Davie Collemine is slain, but sirs shew neither to friend nor foe in what case ye see me in, for if mine enemies knew it, they would rejoice and our friends be discomforted.' The two brethren of Sinclair and Sir James Lindsay did as the earl had desired them and raised up again [Sir James's] banner and cried 'Douglas!' Such as were behind and heard that cry drew together and set on their enemies valiantly and reculed back the Englishmen and many were overthrown, and so drave the Englishmen back beyond the place wereas the earl lay, who was by that time dead.[73]

Sir James Douglas was only thirty years old when he was killed at Otterburn, according to his probable date of birth in about 1358. He is said to have fallen approximately 200 metres north-east of where a battle stone was later erected as a permanent memorial to his blind and dogged act of courage. No vestige of this original monument exists today, but set upright in the very same stone socket is the present obelisk, called Percy's Cross, a name which is particularly ironic given that Otterburn was to be a victory for the Scots and not the English. However, with extreme fatigue now setting in on both armies, it must be said that by midnight the English were some distance from both these battlefield markers.

In fact, according to the chronicles, Hotspur's line must have been non-existent as a battle formation. Given that it is recorded in all the various accounts of Otterburn that the Scots were well rested before the fight began and the English had force-marched their way into Redesdale, it is certain that they were very badly mauled too. It will be remembered that Hotspur's army had marched thirty-two miles that afternoon, and had fought a battle at the end of it. It therefore takes very little imagination to visualise what occurred when a renewed Scottish attack, preceded by the ghostly image of Douglas's standard, swept the last vestiges of hope from English hearts. Froissart graphically recounts that 'in the last skirmish . . . the Scots passed through the [English] battles',[74] which is probably a good description of what the ensuing rout from the field looked like as several detached fragments of Hotspur's army began to turn their backs on the enemy and run for their lives – each man being sought out, brought down and hacked to death in the monotone hell of moonlight.

Hotspur, caught up in this chaotic free-for-all, apparently fought off a number of separate attackers, chief among these being Sir Hugh Montgomery, his subsequent captor. Still no doubt unaware that Douglas had been killed on the slope above him, Hotspur is said to have matched the stamina of his enemies to the end, until at last he was overwhelmed, wounded and taken prisoner. The author of the *Kirkstall Chronicles* also reveals the tragic fate of one of Hotspur's household men in this final phase of the battle. As the English army routed, 'the valiant follower and war-like standard bearer of Lord Henry Percy, called John Waltham, killed many Scots in the battle, and received many wounds himself from the hands of the Scots, [until] finally, after being fatally wounded, he died at last'.[75]

According to English sources, including the above chronicle, Hotspur was captured by George Dunbar, Earl of March and later taken to his castle in Scotland, which if anything is perhaps a rather 'English' way of providing Hotspur with a more worthy opponent and subsequent captor, although Dunbar's castle may have been Percy's later place of confinement. It is also alleged by English writers that Hotspur was personally responsible for slaying Douglas, which seems highly unlikely given the confusion of the battle and the fact that Froissart would have revelled in describing such a chivalrous and glorious encounter between the two knights as a fitting climax to his history. According to Andrew Wyntoun's chronicle, 'no man knew in what manner Douglas died'.[76] Add to this a degree of uncertainty as to whether Hotspur was later exchanged for Sir Hugh Montgomery – who had somehow been captured by the English after the battle – and the full extent of medieval propaganda and biased opinion is apparent, given the fact that Otterburn was such a decisive victory for the Scots. However, aside from all the speculation and propaganda, there is ample evidence to support the assertion that Hugh Montgomery was indeed Hotspur's captor, as the former was later able to build his castle at Polnoon in Renfrewshire from the proceeds of Hotspur's ransom.

As for the rout from the field, Froissart tells us that English fugitives were pursued for at least five miles, presumably in the direction of Newcastle and towards the Bishop of Durham's advancing army of some 7,000 men. But what had happened to Sir Matthew Redmane and the others who had chased the Scots out of camp at the beginning of the battle? Did the Captain of Berwick fail his leader at the eleventh hour due to the fog of war, or was it perhaps something less straightforward?

Froissart informs us that when Redmane returned to the battlefield after chasing the Scots 'varlets' out of their camp, he found that Hotspur had already been defeated. Seeing his comrades, 'yielded them on every side',[77] Redmane barely managed to escape the field with his life. In fact, Sir James Lindsay managed to capture him before accidentally blundering into the Bishop of Durham's army en route to Otterburn and becoming a prisoner himself in the confusion that existed after the fight.

Redmane, as it transpired, was saved by an incredible stroke of luck, but he was not the only bloodstained fugitive to alert the Bishop of Durham to the disaster at Otterburn. News of the English defeat, the capture of Hotspur, and the uncertainty of what might suddenly appear out of the north could not be concealed from the rank and file of the bishop's army indefinitely, and soon the fainthearted began to desert in droves. After re-forming an even larger army at Newcastle, the bishop decided to advance once more up the Otterburn road. He reached the battlefield without incident, but this time he was beaten back by a clever Scottish ruse and a show of unforgivable hesitancy by English commanders. The Scots only had to blow a few times on their famous hunting horns to shake the English into disarray. Melting away across the previous day's cull of nearly 2,000 bloated corpses, the battle of Otterburn was well and truly over.

The famous night battle was a resounding victory for Scottish 'fay'. According to Froissart the English dead numbered 1,840; 1,000 more of Hotspur's army were wounded on Battle Riggs, and the Scots managed to secure 1,040 prisoners despite the lateness of the hour and the difficulty of rounding up so many men in the dark. It is said that Douglas's army sustained only 100 casualties, with some 200 more taken in the initial rout from the field, and although confirmation of the English dead may be corroborated by the chance discovery in 1877 of approximately 1,200 skeletons buried under the parish church of Elsdon, which was built in about 1400, the number of Scottish casualties may be a gross exaggeration by Froissart considering the fierceness of the battle.

The day after the abortive attack by the Bishop of Durham's army, the Scots struck their camp at Otterburn and returned home, taking with them the body of their beloved leader to be buried at the abbey of Melrose. Here the battered and bloody corpse of James Douglas was 'laid in a tomb of stone [with] his banner hanging over him', a perpetual reminder that chivalry and courage beyond the call of duty were still alive and well in the heart of Scotland. Likewise, after hearing tidings of Otterburn, the Earl of Fife ordered his western army home, Archibald Douglas no doubt hearing of his cousin's death in battle and being first among many who wished to avenge his death. Duly appointed the new Earl of Douglas in place of his courageous brother who had died a death worthy of his illustrious clan, it was now up to Archibald 'the Grim' to conduct the next bout of aggression against Hotspur's England while its famous warden was temporarily out of action.

As for Hotspur, he had been extremely fortunate to escape the maelstrom of medieval combat to fight another day. Taking advantage of the laws that granted mercy to those who could pay handsomely for their release, Percy and his badly wounded younger brother were hurried into Scotland as prisoners of war. Shackled to their captors by the velvet bonds of chivalry, they could only hope and pray that their esteemed father or the English crown could obtain their ransoms. If not, then they were doomed to perpetual exile. An English chronicler later wrote:

> Thys fraye bygan at Otterborne
> Bytwene the nyghte and the day:
> Ther the Dowglas lost his lyfe,
> And the Percy was lede awaye.[78]

FIVE

France: 1391

The English defeat at Otterburn, together with the high drama of Hotspur's capture, sent shock waves throughout England. However, despite the military and personal alarm caused by the battle, contemporary English chroniclers delighted in acclaiming Hotspur as their champion, chiefly due to the fact that the Scots had decided to withdraw their forces back across the border.

Hotspur's injuries at Otterburn had been minimal, but his brother Ralph, according to Froissart, had been seriously wounded in the lower part of his body, possibly in a leg or thigh considering that his greaves had filled up with blood. Consequently, it is recorded that the younger of the two Percys was allowed to return home soon after being captured, due to his deteriorating health – the codes of chivalry once again showing that among equals mercy was keenly expressed to those who had attained knightly positions. Hotspur, too, would soon come to know how important influential prisoners could be, especially when they had to be protected from those who chose to disregard the workings of chivalry. Indeed, far from levelling criticism against those who had detained him, there is every reason to believe that Hotspur chose to respect his enemies, both sides clearly understanding that any knight worthy of his spurs would accept defeat in much the same way as he might glory in victory. Not to recognise this principle, or honour the lucrative business of ransoming prisoners of war, would be in breach of the traditional laws that limited death among the nobility. Regulated by the codes of chivalry, ransom was thus a very important part of post-military activity, any deviation from the norm being taken very seriously indeed by those who might suffer from its abuse.

Therefore, unlike the liberation of some who came after him, Hotspur's freedom was assured, and in the summer of 1389 he was speedily ransomed for the princely sum of £3,000, a portion of this figure being willingly funded by the crown and suitably recorded in the Issue Rolls of Richard II: 'To Henry de Percy, son and heir of the Earl of Northumberland, for money paid to him by assignment made this day in part payment of 1000*l.*, which the Lord the King, with the advice of his counsel, commanded to be paid to the said Henry of his gift in aid of his ransom having been lately taken in the Scots war: 500*l.*'[79]

With Hotspur's ransom paid in full, his galling defeat at Otterburn was soon forgotten. In fact, once back in England it was agreed by Richard's council that the custody of Carlisle, together with that of the west march, should be committed to him for five years at the rate of £6,000 per annum. Command of the east march was added later, although it is recorded that in 1391 the Earl of Northumberland held this position, both Percys, father and son, now becoming autonomous as chief wardens of the marches in place of their rivals, the Nevilles, who had yet to find an experienced leader.

With the reinstatement of Hotspur as overall march warden, the government of Richard II had once more allowed the Percys to acquire sole command of the border. However, this time it was not the needs of war, but the desire to win their favour that caused Richard's government to act so magnanimously towards them. The royal council was well aware that Percy autonomy in the north could not be allowed to become unmanageable, but as yet there was no means to counterbalance their rule. With the death of John Neville in 1388, it was simply not possible to follow John of Gaunt's policy of pitting Neville against Percy in order to achieve a balance of power. As for John Neville's son Ralph, as yet lacking any real experience in border affairs, he could only wait for a more favourable time to upstage his rivals. Created 1st Earl of Westmorland in 1397, Ralph Neville would very soon find himself in the precarious position of supporting usurpation as a means to ensure the survival of his house. That the Percys played the most dominant role in this 'kingmaking' process is certain but, as previously explained, it was to be the ever-present threat of the Nevilles that caused the Percys to act so decisively in an effort to protect their territorial and political interests in northern England.

When Hotspur was given command of the east march in October 1389, Richard II was ruling independently. At the age of twenty-one the king made public his intention to shake off his long minority, and he immediately took steps to place the government into his own hands.

Thomas Walsingham poignantly recorded how the king did this in his *Historia Anglicana*, when after asking his council how old he was Richard astonished his peers by exclaiming, 'Well! Know that I have for long been ruled by tutors, and it was not possible for me to act at all, or almost not at all, without them. Now henceforth I will remove those from my council, and, as heir of lawful age, I will appoint whom I will to my council, and conduct my own affairs. And I order that in the first place the chancellor should resign to me his seal.'[80]

Soon after this the Duke of Gloucester and the earls of Warwick and Arundel were removed from office, and others, 'who were [more] pleasing to [the king's] eye',[81] added in their place. It was no mistake that all three former 'appellants' had been plucked from Richard's blacklist. However, far from causing a major stir in English government, the next four or five years were the most cordial of Richard's reign, which proves that this change of direction had the desired effect, especially against those nobles who up until then had enjoyed a relatively free rein in his administration.

The possibility of peace with France and the ratification of a brief truce with Scotland also allowed a fair measure of financial recovery to take place in England, during which time Hotspur was constantly on the move, both at home and abroad, being retained for life in the king's service at £100 per year, a figure that was in addition to his wages as a warden of the east march.

During 1390 Hotspur was based at Calais, where he conducted several daring raids towards Boulogne. Later in the same year he was helping to raise the siege of Brest with his uncle Thomas Percy, but Hotspur's craving for action was short-lived: in 1391, when a more permanent truce with France was negotiated, he was once more returned to England, where he no doubt anticipated another long period of inactivity. How wrong he was. Soon after arriving back home, he received news of what later was to be hailed as one of the most famous tournaments of the century. The contest was to be held at St Inglevert, ten miles south-west of Calais, where three French knights had issued a challenge to meet all-comers on the field of honour. Apart from showing his talents in the tourney, here was an ideal opportunity for Hotspur to strike a blow for England without infringing international affairs of state, and he immediately joined Henry Bolingbroke's retinue of knights who were embarking for France, his former Lancastrian companion-in-arms having taken his father's advice to vanish tactfully from the English court while his erstwhile 'friends' were being dealt with by the vengeful King Richard.

Headed by their most famous captain, Jean de Boucicaut, later Marshal of France, the epic encounter at St Inglevert was very soon the talk of Europe. The venue for the tournament was in itself significant: the place of combat bordering the English 'pale' near the port of Calais was a blatant provocation by the French against one of the richest and most influential havens of English trade abroad. However, the French challenge was also audacious enough to interest knights not only from England, but also from countries all over Europe. Thus Hotspur soon found himself rubbing shoulders with knights from Bohemia and Germany who, similarly bored with inactivity in their own countries, had converged on St Inglevert in order to pit their skill against Boucicaut and his men. Although they were unable to fight their enemies in the traditional fashion, the French challenge was extreme in that they sought to hold the field against all-comers for the incredible period of thirty days.

The first English challengers arrived in France at the beginning of March 1390. These were the Earl of Huntingdon, the Earl Marshal, the Lords Beaumont and Clifford, Sir Peter Courtenay and Thomas Mowbray. Hotspur arrived in Bolingbroke's retinue towards the middle of the month along with nine other knights, including John Beaufort, Henry's step-brother, and Thomas, the son of John of Gaunt's most famous mistress, Katherine Swynford. According to the *Religieux de Saint-Denys*, 'These foreigners [the English] were recognised as the bravest of all the challengers',[82] simply because they engaged in a more dangerous fight than the other knights. If this is to be believed, then it is certain that Hotspur and his companions were putting their lives on the line. Given a choice of combat by either striking a white 'shield of peace' or a black 'shield of war' displayed before their pavilions, more often than not the English competitors chose the latter option as their preferred mode of battle. This latter choice of tipped lances obviously compounded each man's chance of being wounded or even killed in the thrilling but highly dangerous contest of skill that followed the more ceremonial aspects of tournament life. However, even when blunted or 'coronel'-shaped lance heads were used, fatalities were not uncommon. Because these weapons were designed not to pierce armour plate but to spread the force of impact over a large area (either to unhorse the knight or to break the lance in two), the personal risk of being hit at full 'tilt' and injured was tremendous. Even with specially designed tournament armour, which was much more reinforced and heavier than war armour, a knight was constantly vulnerable to being catapulted out of his saddle and crashing violently to the ground.

Helmets, or the great 'frog-mouthed' helms worn by competitors proved heavy and cumbersome, not to mention limiting vision, and although they provided adequate protection for the tourney, it was not unknown for a knight, hurtling at top speed, to insert his lance into the slit of his opponent's helm if his challenger did not raise his head the split second before impact. Similarly, shields and armour plate were invariably shattered, knocked off, or pierced by sharpened lances. At St Inglevert, for instance, the Earl of Huntingdon's shield was pierced by Boucicaut's lance which, after splintering his shield, slid over his right arm, missing his head by only a matter of inches. Thomas Mowbray was also lucky to escape serious injury when he was 'unhelmed' by an opponent. Add to this the danger of the 'free-for-all' that was such a feature of the tourney, and all the chivalric niceties of heraldic display and pageantry could very easily be transformed into a bloody gladiatorial spectacle of broken bones and ripped flesh.

Medieval manuscripts provide many colourful 'cartoon' depictions of baroque pavilions flowing with banners; medieval ladies accompanied by gaudily attired courtesans; knights tilting on unruffled warhorses – all set serenely against a backcloth of white spires and rolling hills. However, the reality of the tournament was far more extreme and dangerous for those who participated in it. Although the fifteenth-century illuminator of Froissart's *Chronicles* depicts two such knights running the course of a tilt barrier at St Inglevert, the fact is that fourteenth-century jousts were run without them, hence the additional hazard of a fatal head-on collision with an opponent's warhorse. The medieval tournament was a highly dangerous sport, and although nobles saw in it a chance to train in the absence of war (a cross between mock battle and the affirmation of their warlike status), it must be said that the justification for their participation in such martial events extends far beyond the competitive aspect of winning or losing and rests more on the basic premise of self-aggrandisement, which of course is what medieval chivalry was all about in the absence of real war.

It was therefore no accident that Hotspur and Henry Bolingbroke decided to compete at St Inglevert in March and April 1390. As renowned jousters in their own right, both were out to reaffirm their martial status in the only way possible during a truce – a reminder to their king and their contemporaries that they were still 'contenders' in the ever-changing world of honour and favouritism. In Henry Bolingbroke's case, he had been associated with those 'appellants' that Richard had so recently removed from office. Hotspur's ambitions at St Inglevert were probably based on a much more chivalrous idea, to be the best, like Chaucer's knight:

> And when the role was called, and every name was read,
> Their numbers checked to ensure no deceit,
> Then the gates were shut, and up goes the cry:
> 'Now do your duty, show your mettle, knights!'
> The heralds leave off spurring up and down;
> Now the loud trumpets, and the clarion
> Ring out; and on the east side and the west
> In go the spears, couched firm for the attack,
> In go the spurs, sharp in the horse's side.
> We'll soon see who can joust, and who can ride!
> There on thick shields the shafts shiver and split.
> One of them through the breast-bone feels the thrust.
> Twenty feet in the air the spears leap up;
> Out come the swords, like silver is their flash;
> They hew at helms, and hack them all to bits;
> And out in harsh red floods the blood now spurts.[83]

As previously explained, it was John of Gaunt's firm intention to keep his son, Bolingbroke, out of Richard's way as much as possible during the recent upheaval in his government. Therefore, it comes as no surprise that soon after St Inglevert, Gaunt was more than willing to fund another of his son's martial passions, an expedition to Prussia where he might spend some time campaigning with the Teutonic knights. Hotspur, on the other hand, was sent by Bolingbroke's father from Calais to Bordeaux as its new acting governor, an appointment that can hardly have been to Hotspur's liking considering that previously he too had intended to fight in Prussia but had failed to do so. Because it fell well short of what he saw as an 'active' military appointment, enforcing a lasting peace with France must have seemed like a prison sentence to him in its boredom, especially when at the very beginning of his office the citizens of Bordeaux refused to admit him because he came in the name of the much-hated John of Gaunt.

However, in keeping with Hotspur's restless need to remain active, there is evidence that sometime before 15 July 1393 he took the opportunity to travel to Cyprus on a good-will mission for King Richard. As England's special envoy to King James, Hotspur was received by Jacobus Dei Gratia Jerusalem et Cypri Rex (the King of Cyprus), who after Percy's return sent a letter to King Richard thanking him for having sent him such a gracious ambassador. Now twenty-nine years old, Hotspur was fast becoming a prime contender for more administrative roles. Indeed, he held the important office of governor of Bordeaux for approximately three years, from 1393 to 1395, although in 1393 he was recalled to Calais, then to England, where he was again nominated as warden of the east march and governor of Berwick in 1394. As a commissioner for punishing infractions of the Scottish truce during the same year, Hotspur managed to relieve the boredom of peacetime life by presiding over a number of private combats by royal licence. But by June 1394 he was back in France again as Richard's lieutenant when the French truce, now extended for a further four years, again prohibited any further military ambitions Hotspur may have harboured.

While in the north of England, Hotspur had probably spent a considerable amount of time with his family, especially with his wife, Elizabeth Mortimer, who had recently given birth to a son. Given the much-used ancestral name of Henry Percy, Hotspur's heir was later destined to succeed to the earldom of Northumberland and by incredible ill-luck play an active and, as it turned out, fatal role in the opening battle of the Wars of the Roses. However, born on 3 February 1394, this new addition to the Percy household ensured not only the survival of Hotspur's line, but also, being part Mortimer, the continuation of a much more controversial claim to greatness: Hotspur's child was descended of royal blood, a fact that could not be overlooked by anyone with regard to the workings of medieval succession. The Mortimer earls of March were yet to figure significantly in Hotspur's hectic life, but by the end of the century many men, especially those who opposed the rule of Richard II, would find that the Mortimer claim was an irritation they could well do without. Chief among these belligerent factions was the house of Lancaster which, having also staked its claim to the throne, tried everything to obstruct the Mortimer succession, even though the claims of March had been acknowledged and fully ratified by King Richard in parliament. Even Henry Bolingbroke's usurpation of 1399 failed to repress the battle for succession, and the threat to Henry's claim continued unabated for at least another decade, creating an extremely unstable environment, from which were spawned the Percy rebellions of 1403 and 1408.

The turbulent events of 1399, and the usurpation of the crown by Henry Bolingbroke, Earl of Derby are well documented. However, what scholars and historians call into question time and time again is the role played by the Percys in the revolution, and whether all three adult members of the family were innocently duped by Henry Bolingbroke, or did they know that their cousin intended to usurp the English throne from the outset? Their complicity in Richard's capture, abdication, and subsequent death allied the Percys more firmly to Lancaster than ever before, but the rebellion of 1403 changed the political climate against them enormously, and medieval chroniclers such as John Hardyng have distorted and perpetuated a number of falsehoods regarding their participation.

Hotspur in particular suffers from this popular bias more than his father or uncle, so much so that only his rebellious character surfaces from the firmament of history. Historical characters are notoriously hard to fathom, and given the circumstances that led to Henry Bolingbroke's usurpation in 1399, coupled with what is known of the intentions of the Percy family prior to this, we may wonder at Hotspur's part in the whole affair. On the other hand, it is perhaps worth remembering how important it was for noble families to survive such major upheavals in medieval succession, and as a result begin to understand what they might do to protect their families if threatened. The rumblings of unrest that led to Bolingbroke's usurpation can be traced back to Richard's need to punish those responsible for killing and exiling his friends in 1388. However, this need for revenge was exacerbated in 1397 when the king arrested his former enemies, the three leading 'appellants', Gloucester, Warwick and Arundel.

As previously discussed, Richard's decision to launch this pre-emptive strike against those who had conspired against him met with little public outcry, but the grisly task of Gloucester's 'disappearance' fell into the unstable lap of Thomas Mowbray, Duke of Norfolk who, acting as Richard's chief assassin, was forced into arranging Gloucester's death at Calais where the duke had been formally imprisoned. More executions followed Gloucester's demise, the Earl of Arundel's fate being more public when he was accused of treason and beheaded after a short trial by John of Gaunt on 21 September. The Earl of Warwick was next to be dealt with. Three days after Arundel's head had been severed on Tower Hill, the earl, faced with a similar fate, broke down and confessed his treason, only to be rewarded for his honesty by banishment for life to the Isle of Man. It only remained for the king to apportion the spoils of victory to his friends, and the king was generous to those who had supported his merciless enterprise, including Thomas Percy, who became the Earl of Worcester, and Ralph Neville, who was elected Earl of Westmorland – the latter promotion posing a direct threat to Percy supremacy in the north.

Henry Bolingbroke and Thomas Mowbray, despite their complicity in the events of 1388, managed to escape capital punishment and were pardoned on the grounds that they had, at that time, endeavoured to place a check upon the more violent inclinations of their fellow rebels. However, both men, especially Bolingbroke, must have wondered how long it would be before the king began to punished them for their rebellious conduct at Radcot Bridge. In Bolingbroke's case it was probably only the influential presence of his father that kept him alive for so long. As for Mowbray, he had already dipped his hands in royal blood and was evidently so disillusioned with his king's behaviour that he soon decided to conspire against him.

This was Richard's hour of triumph, and not only had the king managed the situation well, but he had also convincingly reasserted his authority by avoiding a wholesale bloodbath so reminiscent of the actions of those 'appellants' who had opposed him in 1387. In spite of everything, he had succeeded in removing the root cause of rebellion in only a few days of determined action. But already, as with most key political changes in government, the seeds of revolution had already been sown. By leaving Bolingbroke and Mowbray unpunished, Richard's apparent clemency soon led to factional intrigue, as well as another serious problem that the king cannot possibly have foreseen at the time.

Sometime between October 1397 and January 1398, a plot was hatched directed principally against the house of Lancaster. At this time King Richard was still childless, and this worrying situation was not helped by the fact that the king was then married to his second wife, Isabella of France, a child of only seven years old. Consequently, like all childless monarchs before him, Richard's succession was called into question. By tradition, the English throne was descended by primogenitary inheritance, and it followed that, in the absence of a legitimate heir, a successor had to be named. In this instance the Earl of March was appointed to this position, even though his claim to the throne came through the female line. Similarly, it is recorded in the *Continuatio Eulogii* and in John Hardyng's *Chronicle* that John of Gaunt had also petitioned parliament that his son Henry Bolingbroke should also be recognised as Richard's heir in right of 'tail male' (that is, in the male line). Not surprisingly, this caused a serious rift between Gaunt and March, the king on numerous occasions having to intervene to avoid bloodshed. Add to this the fact that Gaunt's landed estates were the greatest in all England, worth about £12,000 a year, and there must have been many nobles, including the king, who coveted a share in them. This uncertainty, bad feeling and overmighty greed to destroy the Lancastrian inheritance caused further discord in December 1397 when Bolingbroke, then Duke of Hereford, was met by Mowbray, Duke of Norfolk on the road between London and Brentford:

. . . The Duke of Norfolk overtook him [Bolingbroke] in great haste and spoke with him on diverse matters, among which he said, 'We are about to be undone.' And the Duke of Hereford asked, 'Why?' And he [Mowbray] replied that it was for the deed at Radcot Bridge. And the Duke of Hereford said, 'How should this be, for he [the king] pardoned us, and made a declaration for us in parliament, saying that we have been good and loyal towards him.' And the Duke of Norfolk replied, 'Notwithstanding this, it will be done with us as it has been done with others before, for he wishes to annul this record.' . . . The Duke of Norfolk said further that it was a wondrous world and false, 'For I know well that if it had not been for some persons, my lord your father of Lancaster and you would have been seized and slain when you came to Windsor after the parliament.' And he said that the Dukes of Aumale and

Exeter, the Earl of Worcester and he were pledged that they would never agree to undo any lord without just and reasonable cause.[84]

Although we only have Bolingbroke's word for what transpired at this meeting, Mowbray then went on to name other nobles, including the king, who were conspiring to overthrow Lancaster and lure the Earl of March to their side. Drawn to the attention of the king by John of Gaunt, these revelations, in the form of a petition, caused a suspicious Richard to order that Bolingbroke and Mowbray be brought before him at Oswestry. Once confronted with Bolingbroke's testimony, Mowbray flatly denied that he had ever spoken about such things and he threw down his gauntlet at Bolingbroke's feet in protest. Thereafter, it was agreed that the law of chivalry should determine matters, seeing that no proof of either noble's story could be established; in other words both men were ordered to fight it out by trial of battle:

> . . . therefore a duel was arranged and a day of battle given to them, namely the feast of St Lambert, bishop and martyr, in September, and on the appointed day great throngs of people converged on the place [Coventry] from all parts of England. When the two dukes in dispute had appeared in the lists, however, and were ready to do battle, the king, who remained, girded with his sword, in his royally furbished pavilion, ordered them to hold fast and under no circumstances to join battle, and he took the dispute into his own hands. Then he ordered his will to be proclaimed; namely that Henry Duke of Hereford, on account of his former disobedience towards the king, should be banished from the realm for ten years, and that Thomas, Duke of Norfolk should be banished from England forever.[85]

If Richard had been seen to bury the hatchet against his former enemies of Radcot Bridge, he certainly had not forgotten where he had buried it, and by the end of October 1398 both men had left the country to begin their respective exiles. Mowbray died of the plague in Venice a year later, but Bolingbroke managed to make new friends in France due to a rapid deterioration of Anglo-French relations.

Meanwhile, in the north of England Hotspur had once more taken up his position as warden of the east march, a commission that was issued on 12

June 1396 for ten years. Indeed, while Bolingbroke and Mowbray were setting sail for an uncertain future, Hotspur was once again fulfilling a more administrative role, signing – along with George Dunbar, his old enemy at Otterburn – a convention for a truce, Dunbar at that time having custody of the Scottish border as Earl of March. Dunbar figured significantly in Hotspur's life, so it is worth remembering that he was still maintaining a number of connections with England, his Anglo-Scottish links stretching far back beyond the border wars and being in complete contrast to those of the Black Douglases who campaigned against the English at every opportunity. Indeed, Hotspur's association with Dunbar was extremely significant in that both he and the earl shared a certain amount of common ground against the Douglas clan. It was a partnership that was to turn extremely sour when Hotspur rebelled against Henry IV in July 1403.

For the present, Hotspur had succeeded in wiping the Otterburn bloodstain from his doublet, but he could hardly have failed to notice that there was a strange uneasiness sweeping the kingdom. The cause of the suspicion was primarily of Ricardian origin, and in line with the king's latest coup against the 'lords appellant', Thomas Percy, Earl of Worcester was the first 'insider' to alert his family to its danger. Thomas had recently been favoured with a number of royal appointments, including the captaincy of Calais in January 1398; however, despite being favoured by King Richard, he continued to act as an attorney to his cousin, Henry Bolingbroke, during his banishment. Expertly equipped to conceal a certain amount of double-dealing, Worcester, forever the diplomat, was to play a key role in the events of 1399, although his first task was to warn his brother and nephew of a move against them by the unscrupulous king.

To understand the rift between Richard II and the two Percys, father and son, it is also essential to document the king's so-called tyranny, which became progressively worse when John of Gaunt died suddenly on 3 February 1399. As dutiful as ever, the king attended the old duke's funeral at St Paul's, but soon after this he found out that his uncle's death gave him a unique opportunity to carry out his most notable display of ill-will towards his exiled Lancastrian cousin. He immediately and unreservedly banished Henry Bolingbroke from England for life. To all the nobility, including the Percys, this new reversal of the king's earlier edict must have come as a considerable shock. Thomas Walsingham recorded how the despotic king further punished Lancaster by revoking the letters patent, which accorded Bolingbroke's attorney, Thomas Percy, powers to grant any inheritances or successions that fell to him: 'By revoking these letters the king showed manifestly how much he hated the duke, and that the reason why he had originally banished him was not, as he had dishonestly pretended, because of the quarrels or disturbances which might have broken out between his servants and retainers and those of the Duke of Norfolk, but in the hope that, when the chance came, he would be able to extend his banishment for life, and thus get his hands upon the duke's very considerable possessions and appropriate them for himself.'[86]

The Earl of Northumberland, and others of equal status, must have felt extremely vulnerable when this news finally broke. Indeed, apart from the king's own advisers, the Percys must have been the very first to receive information about Richard's ambitious intentions to destroy Lancaster through Thomas Percy, who was so closely associated with the appropriation of Bolingbroke's estates. Wondering who might be Richard's next victim, everyone's nervousness increased when the king's oppressions were levelled against the kingdom as a whole.

In 1398, the Earl of Northumberland had been appointed by the Shrewsbury parliament to execute the will of the king – namely to enforce the king's demands on his subjects – and it was to be this next round of Ricardian oppressions – including the signing of blank charters and the swearing-in of sheriffs to obey the king's commands directly, as well as the payment of insupportable sums of money by nobles not in royal favour – that made the Percys even more suspicious of Richard's intentions. In fact, the private feelings of the Earl of Northumberland may have compelled the fiery Hotspur to speak out against his sovereign. Maliciously accused of saying something clandestine under Richard's tyrannical rule was fatal, but even more so if that person was a well-respected celebrity like Hotspur. With a brood of Ricardian spies lurking everywhere under duress, it was only a matter of time before the king got word of Percy's 'treasonable language', and he and his father were soon summoned to answer for their 'crimes', prior to Richard's latest military expedition to Ireland.

Jean Creton, a French chronicler, and a self-confessed eyewitness to the events of 1399, is the only authority for the statement that it was Hotspur, rather than his father, who spoke out against the king, which if anything gives a clear indication that Creton thought that the younger Percy was certainly not happy with Richard's latest despotism. However, the king keenly targeted both Percys at once when the Earl of Northumberland refused to obey the king's command to appear with his retinues to embark for Ireland. Richard's reaction to the Percy rebuff was characteristic of his rule – he immediately banished both Percys from the kingdom.

Northumberland and Hotspur quickly made plans to take refuge in Scotland, but they were dissuaded at the last minute by Thomas Percy who, always the careful player, probably was well aware that the tide would soon turn against Richard. Percy, then admiral of the fleet, had 200 ships waiting for the king at Milford Haven, and therefore Richard postponed the execution of all his recent sentences until his return. It is perhaps no coincidence that as soon as the king reached Waterford in Ireland, the Earl of Northumberland opened communications with his cousin, Henry Bolingbroke, in France in an effort to ensure the survival of his family. This sequence of events, and the subsequent 'kingmaking' of 1399, can be strongly attributed to the elder Percys, and Thomas Percy in particular, who as Earl of Worcester was undoubtedly not only the inside influence of the Percy family at this time, but also a close confidant of the exiled Henry of Lancaster as his acting attorney.

The Earl of Worcester contributed 35 men-at-arms and 100 archers in aid of Richard's expedition to Ireland; therefore, upon contemporary authority, it is certain that far from deserting his king at this time, he seems to have outwardly carried out his martial duties with his usual efficiency and enthusiasm. Indeed, there was no reason for Thomas to do otherwise, or be seen as anything less than one of Richard's loyal supporters. He had been present, along with many English nobles, the Earl of Northumberland included, who had sworn an oath to uphold the judgments of the parliament that had revoked Henry Bolingbroke's rights of inheritance. However, now with members of his own family threatened with forfeiture, and possibly death, Thomas must have secretly harboured some thoughts of how his family could ever be reconciled with a king who had recently appropriated someone else's estates for himself. For the moment Thomas Percy could only wait for an opportune moment to act, and we can only guess at what he intended to do once he returned with Richard from Ireland.

As for Hotspur, his world had suddenly turned upside down. His treason was assured once his king set foot back on English soil and no doubt he was determined to act against his king if compelled to do so. He may have contemplated what actions could be taken against Richard, but no doubt his father betrayed what ambitious plans were stirring in France, although how much Hotspur knew of them is open to question. Rebellion was a certainty, but as for 'kingmaking' there were only two real choices – Lancaster or March. The house of Plantagenet had shown its true colours in the model despotic king bent on relieving his wealthiest subjects of their riches. The nobility could not tolerate the situation, and hence Richard II had to be removed.

In 1395, Roger Mortimer, Earl of March had been recognised as the king's heir, but while serving as Richard's lieutenant in Ireland, he had been killed in an ambush, leaving the Irish question unresolved. Richard's second expedition of 1399 therefore determined not only to punish the Irish for Mortimer's death, but also to put down a revolt that was to be forever a thorn in England's side. The resulting campaign came to nothing, but little did Richard know that neither he nor the Mortimer family would ever be allowed to rule in England again. Henry Bolingbroke, now Duke of Lancaster, had used his time in France well to make friends and plan his own revenge against Richard's rule. The invasion and revolution that he instigated would change the course of English history forever, and provide a convenient loophole through which the Percys might once again place themselves at the forefront of English affairs.

SIX

Doncaster: 1399

Unlike his father, the Earl of Northumberland, and his uncle, the Earl of Worcester, Hotspur's involvement in the revolution of 1399 is shrouded in mystery. The simple fact is that contemporary chroniclers scarcely mentioned his name in connection with any of the momentous events that led to Henry Bolingbroke's usurpation of the English throne, other than to say that he, like his father and uncle, was party to it. True to the overbearing father and son relationship alluded to earlier, it follows that Hotspur was the innocent victim of his father's will, and that being so inferior, he inadvertently became part of an ill-defined chorus line of onlookers who all made a distinct impression on events but who were innocently carried along by the sheer weight of the leading players. However, this is certainly not in keeping with the impetuous and outspoken Hotspur that chroniclers delighted in revealing to their readers. Indeed, according to Jean Creton, Hotspur had recently defied all accepted principles of spontaneity by not only criticising his king, but also getting himself and his father charged with treason. Therefore, can we believe that Hotspur's fiery nature was so consumed by his father's presence on this occasion?

Without doubt there is a strange truth concealed in Hotspur's apparent elusiveness, a truth that until now has never been fully explored by historians. The resulting tide of family betrayal and royal perjury remains a contentious issue, but undeniably the results of Bolingbroke's usurpation had a direct effect on Hotspur's view of kingship thereafter. It was no accident that the Percy family were first elevated by their new king, then smashed beyond all recognition; in fact, by 1408 all their adult members had been executed or killed in battle as rebels. As for Hotspur, the events of 1399 were to place a great weight of disillusionment in his mind and it was undoubtedly these same feelings of discontent, and ultimately guilt, that contributed greatly to his last irrevocable split with Lancaster prior to the battle of Shrewsbury in 1403.

Hotspur's feelings of personal guilt are, of course, hard to prove, but his actions subsequent to Henry's usurpation give a clear indication that he was clearly not pleased with the result of his labours. Understanding his mysterious role in the revolution of 1399 is also hindered by the way that some contemporary chroniclers tended to spin a rather complex web of misinformation about what actually occurred during the crucial months of July and August; therefore the actions of the leading protagonists have become obscured by a fog of biased opinion. To deal with such dogma the historian must see past the deceitfulness, the broken oaths and the downright trickery written into some of the chronicles, and instead focus upon the motivations, needs and ambitions of those involved. Powerful elements of propaganda later tried to exonerate the Percys from their complicity in Bolingbroke's usurpation, also Richard's death (or murder) at Pontefract Castle, sometime before 14 February 1400. Some of this evidence is corroborated by more than one source. Some is irrevocably questionable. In accepting modern research, the actual events of 1399 are not disputed here, but by redefining Hotspur's role in the revolution the instability of all such medieval usurpations is clearly exposed in the mind of one who later rebelled.

Chief among the propagandists who tried to exonerate the Percys from their part in Richard's demise was the extremely subjective northern chronicler John Hardyng. As he had been a staunch retainer of the Percys since childhood, his account of what occurred when his former masters met with the newly arrived Henry Bolingbroke at Doncaster on 16 July 1399 is an excellent, if highly suspect, version of Lancastrian perjury. However, following closely on the heels of Hardyng is an account written by the Dieulacres chronicler, who reinforces the opinion that Hotspur's complicity in the rebellion was certain, but secondary to that of his father and uncle, who were, along with Bolingbroke, the prime movers of the revolution. It is clear, according to official sources, that Bolingbroke intended after sailing from France with only a few hundred loyal supporters to steal Richard's crown and snuff out the memory of the man who wore it. Hotspur, like his father and uncle, was guilty of the same crime, although the younger Percy seems to have been unwittingly duped, not only by Henry Bolingbroke but also by the leading members of his own family.

When Richard left for Ireland in 1399, his brother Edmund, Duke of York had been left in charge of the kingdom. As regent, York's powers were wide-ranging and on 4 and 12 July he dutifully sent out orders for the garrisoning of castles up and down the country in fear of an expected invasion, although at this stage no one was quite sure who was mounting the offensive or where the suspected landing was likely to take place. Bolingbroke, on the other hand, had managed (intentionally or otherwise) to confuse everyone about his movements, and this left the Duke of York at a grave disadvantage. Uncertainty gave way to indecision during the summer months, and this allowed Henry ample time to disembark his men, plan his moves, and gather his strength, the Percys being his chief recruiting agents in the north of England.

Most sources generally agree that Bolingbroke's small flotilla of ships scraped ashore on the shingle beaches of the east coast of Yorkshire somewhere between Bridlington and Ravenspur (modern Spurn Head) on 4 July 1399. From here Henry moved inland to Pickering Castle before turning west to Knaresborough, installing his own garrisons in each town. Proceeding south, he and his motley crew of adventurers, including a number of battle-hardened veterans such as John Norbury and Sir Thomas Erpingham, proceeded to Pontefract where they clattered across the drawbridge of the castle on or about 14 July. Moving on to Doncaster a day or two later, Bolingbroke awaited the arrival not only of the Percys, but also of Ralph Neville, Earl of Westmorland, who had also chosen to back the Lancastrian mission – a fact that was bound to intensify feelings of rivalry with the Percys and promote a multitude of hasty reactions from the Earl of Northumberland which he might not otherwise have entertained.

Meanwhile, the Duke of York had managed to extricate himself from London. After much dithering and realigning of his position, he dispatched urgent messages to Richard in Ireland, sending out equally pressing summonses to the shires in order to muster an army in defence of the realm. Once supplied with a nucleus of military support, York advanced first to Aylesbury, then Oxford, where his force increased to about 3,000 men. However, York's previous indecisiveness had wasted precious time, and it soon became obvious that in order to keep his army intact he must link up with his king as soon as possible when he returned from Ireland. Only by achieving this could he hope to confront Bolingbroke's superior northern contingents on equal terms, although it must be said that at this time, York's sympathies, and those of his followers, seem to have been divided – each one of his royal captains recognised the legitimacy of Bolingbroke's claim to recover what was his by rightful inheritance.

While York's fickle army marched west in the hope of making contact with King Richard, Bolingbroke, not short of support himself, was making his pitch to the ageing Earl of Northumberland in words unequivocal with regard to his ultimate objective of usurping the throne. A grant dated 2 August 1399, under the seal of the Duchy of Lancaster, gives credence to the possibility that Henry Percy senior knew all along what his Lancastrian cousin was planning:

> Henry by the grace of God, King of England and of France and Lord of Ireland. To the Treasurer and Chamberlains of our Exchequer greeting. Since our very dear and faithful cousin Henry Percy, Earl of Northumberland, by force of our commission made unto him under our seal of the Duchy of Lancaster has had the custody of our castle and town of Carlisle and of the West march towards Scotland from the second day of August last past until the 23rd day of this present month of October, we wish of our especial grace and order you that to our same cousin you should cause to be paid from our treasure from the duration of the said time, in the way that he takes at present by virtue of the indentures made between us and him for the custody abovesaid. Given under our privy seal at Westminster the 31st day of October, the first year of our reign.[87]

According to this important document, Bolingbroke (then king in October 1399) admitted, at least on paper, that he had usurped regal powers soon after his landing in England. The complicity of the Earl of Northumberland in accepting Henry's grant of the west march at this same time not only condoned his cousin's audacious assumption of royal prerogatives, but also assured his collusion in the events that were to follow. In short, the Earl of Northumberland was once again showing his true colours in an effort to protect his family interests against the Nevilles under the pretence of a new regime. It is highly likely that the office of warden of the west march was a condition of Northumberland's support of

Bolingbroke, and considering that both men had suffered from Richard's tyranny previously, it is not unreasonable to suggest that Percy willingly condoned his cousin's aim to take the crown, if not from the outset, then according to the grant of wardenship, at least a fortnight before Richard was captured in Wales.

However, did Hotspur know of Bolingbroke's covert plan to depose Richard? This matter is more difficult to ascertain, which brings us back to the events at Doncaster when Bolingbroke allegedly swore an oath before all his supporters that he had returned to England only to recover what was rightfully his, namely the duchy of Lancaster. After joining forces with Bolingbroke, Hotspur and his father bore witness to what was to become the foundation stone of later Percy propaganda, a ceremony that was to add considerable weight to what most contemporary chroniclers thought was Bolingbroke's only reason for returning to England. The biased chronicler John Hardyng was certain that both Percys were ignorant of their cousin's ultimate aim to usurp the throne, because Bolingbroke 'wase crounde ayenst his oath made in the White Ffreres at Doncastre to the seid erle of Northumberlonde and other lordes, ayenst the wille and counsel of the seide erle and of his sonne, and of sir Thomas Percy earl of Worcestri, for which cause they died after, as I knew well, for that tyme I wase in the feelde at Shrewsbury with sir Henry Percy, of the age of xxv yere, armed, and afore brought up in his house of xii yere age'.[88]

On the face of it Hardyng's words ring true. However, as previously explained, John Hardyng was unbelievably biased towards the Percys, and he wrote his famous apology some years after the famous rebellions of 1403 and 1408, which casts considerable doubt on his testimony. To add weight to this, it is also alleged that Hardyng actually forged important documents and, like most medieval chroniclers, reworked his history to suit both Lancastrian and Yorkist regimes thereafter, begging the question – can he be trusted at all on this important matter? Yet, as a comparison, the Dieulacres chronicle has no apparent link with the Percy family, but its support of Bolingbroke's oath is equally damning, therefore equally convincing. On the eve of the battle of Shrewsbury, Hotspur declared that he opposed Bolingbroke's crowning, 'because Duke Henry swore to the other two Henrys [Northumberland and Hotspur] on the relics of Bridlington that he would never seek the Crown, and then said that, if anyone more worthy of the Crown was found, he would willingly withdraw; he declared that the duchy of Lancaster would suffice for him'.[89]

If the above evidence is correct, then not only did the Earl of Northumberland connive with Bolingbroke to depose Richard, but so too did Hotspur. However, careful examination of the above passage reveals another possibility that cannot be ignored, and this concerns the Mortimer claim to the throne, a claim with which Hotspur had very close associations. His marriage to Elizabeth Mortimer, and therefore his affinity to Roger Mortimer's seven-year-old heir Edmund, Earl of March, could hardly have slipped Hotspur's mind. After all, Mortimer's right to the throne had been previously condoned by parliament by right of medieval succession and this was still in force as far as most people were concerned. The fact that Bolingbroke had announced at Doncaster that he only intended to recover the duchy of Lancaster made perfect sense to a man like Hotspur, given that the Mortimer succession was more worthy of the crown.

In fact, it must have struck a chord in the minds of many people who were tired of Richard's tyrannical rule and wished for a radical change of direction. As for Hotspur's subsequent involvement with Bolingbroke, his cousin's fair words were probably enough to make him compliant with the entire concept of usurpation, providing that Bolingbroke would willingly withdraw in favour of a more worthy claimant if one could be found. With Richard deposed and Mortimer crowned King of England, the Percys, as his nearest blood relatives, would no doubt be favoured above all others in England. Therefore, seen in this light, the later usurpation of Bolingbroke, and the bad blood that accompanied the Percy rebellion of 1403, give us every reason to believe that Hotspur was not only duped by his usurping cousin, but also that he was misled by his own father right from the start.

For his integrity in believing the widely held notion that Bolingbroke was championing his own inheritance, rather than seeking the crown, Hotspur may be forgiven; many men, including the chronicler Thomas Walsingham, thought the same and recorded as much in their histories. However, for his complicity in helping his father depose an anointed king, Hotspur must surely be condemned as it is certain that he and his fellow rebels had every intention of overthrowing Richard II and installing another in his place. In both these aims, all three Percys were most certainly in agreement, even if Hotspur's own vision of the future king did not run parallel to that of his co-conspirators.

The weight of Hotspur's military support for Bolingbroke at Doncaster is also a key point to remember, not only in connection with the rebellion of 1399, but also with regard to Hotspur's developing magnetism as a military leader. Second only to his father, who received £1,333 in wages for his troops, Hotspur was paid £666 by Henry's receiver when he came to the throne, for men provided. Like many other Lancastrian supporters, Hotspur remained under arms until after Bolingbroke's first parliament at Westminster in October/November 1399, proof that he certainly approved of Richard's removal, if not with who had been chosen to succeed him. The total paid out to Henry's army was approximately £4,900, which gives us some idea of how vital the combined Percy contingents were to the success of the revolution. In fact the total wages paid out to Hotspur and his father were almost half the cost of Bolingbroke's entire outlay.

Although numbers of men are not specified in this instance, Bolingbroke's northern army was certainly large by the standards of the day, the lowest estimate being approximately 30,000, a figure which included the larger contingents of William, Lord Willoughby, Robert Waterton esquire, Sir Walter Blount, William Lord Roos, Sir Thomas Wendesley and, rather ominously for the Percys, Ralph Neville, Earl of Westmorland, who was paid £146 for his support. The long list of men who attended Henry at Doncaster bears out the observation of the Dieulacres chronicler that 'numerous noble and warlike men from the north and from Lancaster, Derby and Stafford gathered with him'.[90] However, it must be said that Bolingbroke's army, and therefore his credibility as a contender for the throne, would not have been so effective had it not been for the strength of the two Percy contingents. The experience of their men as battle-hardened border warriors was a significant psychological advantage over Henry's enemies.

Meanwhile, Richard II had heard of Bolingbroke's landing around 10 July at the latest, but it was not until 18 or 27 July that he, along with Thomas Percy, landed at Milford Haven on the Welsh coast. Admittedly, the king had previously dispatched the Earl of Salisbury to secure Conway Castle and attempt to recruit an army in Wales and Cheshire, but the king's delay in Ireland had already cost him dear. A further setback in England forced the newly arrived Richard to suddenly change his plans, due to an appalling lack of support, and this developing situation also caused

Thomas Percy, Earl of Worcester, then steward of Richard's household, to formally break his rod of office and opt to join forces with his brother and nephew in England.

However, the major impediment that resulted in the dispersal of the king's forces in Wales was of the Duke of York's making. Soon after quitting Oxford, York did the unthinkable under the circumstances and decided to split his army. Marching with the mainward, such as it was, via Stow-on-the-Wold and Gloucester to Berkeley Castle, he presented Bolingbroke with an ideal opportunity to strike. Forcing York to submit, due in part to his much-depleted and vacillating army, Bolingbroke's army marched on Bristol – the last bastion of Ricardian support. Here, news of the summary execution of some of Richard's chief supporters forced the king to abandon his original plan in favour of reaching Cheshire and the pool of support that he knew could be mustered there in his name. Slipping away from his own followers in Wales, with only a few intimate supporters in his entourage, he secretly made his way to the north, leaving Thomas Percy out in the cold. This abandonment by the king is said to have forced Percy's hand to join Bolingbroke, although the Whalley chronicler says that the reason for Richard's flight was far more suspicious, namely that the king had been warned that he was about to be captured (by Thomas Percy?).

According to the French chronicler Jean Creton, who was actually with the Earl of Salisbury at Conway, Richard 'rode hard' for North Wales, expecting to find a great army already gathered there in his name. However, those troops originally mustered by Salisbury in Wales and Cheshire had already deserted when they discovered that the king was not at Conway in person. Fearing for his life, and with Bolingbroke marching on Chester, Richard had little room for manoeuvre. He could either flee into exile or stay where he was and hope to mediate with his disaffected cousin. Despite the derogatory image of Richard II that has come down to us, the king showed no lack of courage by choosing the latter option.

Chester submitted to Bolingbroke's forces on 8 or 9 August, although it was clear that the troubles within the town and the surrounding district were far from over and needed a much firmer hand. According to the chronicler, Adam of Usk, who was with Bolingbroke's army towards the end of July, certain Cheshire diehards refused to accept Bolingbroke's authority and thus the order was given for the Lancastrian army to pillage the surrounding countryside: 'And I, the writer of this chronicle, spent a not uncheerful night in the tent of my lord of Powis. Many in neighbouring places, drinking of the poisoned cups given to them by the people of Chester, perished. There also from divers water-cisterns, which men probed with spears, and from other hiding places, vessels and much other goods were drawn forth and taken for plunder, I being present with the finders.'[91]

When Richard's envoys finally arrived in Chester amid this increasingly hostile situation, Bolingbroke immediately detained them and made plans to dispatch his own emissary to the king. This involved sending the 57-year-old Earl of Northumberland – with whom Bolingbroke had obviously pre-planned the whole affair – to Conway. Before he left, Northumberland was briefed on what action to take against Richard; however, the details of the king's capture were probably left entirely open-ended due to the uncertainty of what might greet Northumberland when he arrived in North Wales. Hotspur, playing no further part in the plot to capture the king, probably remained in Chester at this time as only one chronicler suggests that he accompanied his father to Conway. The reasoning behind Hotspur's stay at Chester is based firstly on the fact that the town was still a hotbed of royalist support; secondly, that it had to be brought under military control by a competent leader, and indeed held for Lancaster while Bolingbroke was elsewhere; and thirdly, that the evidence of Hotspur's appearance in command of the Lancastrian army at Flint Castle soon *after* Richard's capture is evidence that his was a separate force from that of his father.

Hotspur's part in the subjugation of Chester is supported by the claim that he succeeded in gaining the respect and loyalty of the people 'in kind' – a loyalty that would serve him well in the Shrewsbury campaign of 1403. Also that he was chiefly responsible for winning the town over to the rule of Henry IV when he came to power, and that in the first year of Henry's reign he was made justiciary of the town and given the constableship of its castle. Finally, according to the *Annales Ricardi Secoundi*, it was none other than Hotspur who was responsible for beating off the half-hearted attacks of the Cheshiremen who, it is said, 'continued to launch furtive attacks on the duke, assaulting his baggage-train and plundering the local residents, until through the valour of the younger Henry Percy, their presumption was punished and their boldness repaid in kind'.[92]

Hotspur's responsibility and link with Cheshire were therefore established in August 1399. However, his departure, along with that of his father and uncle from the town, is recorded by the Monk of Evesham, so some shadow of doubt must be cast over Hotspur's continual involvement in Wales even though his name is not associated with any of the events surrounding Richard's capture. What is more of a possibility is that Hotspur may have accompanied his father to Conway, then rode back to Chester to deliver a message to Bolingbroke that Richard was safe in his father's custody. Obviously the absence of Hotspur's name in connection with Richard's capture is not conclusive proof of his non-attendance, but there is no proof of his presence either, although we may be sure that Hotspur knew what his father intended.

It is said that the Earl of Northumberland and the previously deposed Archbishop of Canterbury, Thomas Arundel, arrived at Conway with no more than seven attendants, while a much larger force, commanded by Thomas Erpingham, Bolingbroke's most loyal captain, was left in concealment 'between two mountains' a few miles down the coast, somewhere between Conway and Rhuddlan Castles. Northumberland and Bishop Arundel, acting as Henry's chief emissaries, both promised Richard – indeed they swore upon the newly consecrated host – that he would be permitted to retain his royal power, provided that Henry's inheritance was restored to him. This Richard agreed to do, and three days later he was escorted from Conway towards Flint:

The earl [of Northumberland] then left [Conway] with his seven attendants, as he arrived, and rode to the mountain where he had left his men in ambush; who all made very merry, for he said to them, 'We shall very soon have what we are looking for.' King Richard, who was ignorant of all the villainy and treason which the said earl had concocted, mounted on his horse with all his company, who were only twelve in all, and rode as far as the mountain. And as he and his companions were going down the mountain, they perceived the people of the Earl of Northumberland who were in the valley, and who all armed; and he said to the Earl of Salisbury, 'Do you not see below banners and streamers?' The Earl of Salisbury replied, 'Certainly, sire, I do; and my heart forebodes ill.' 'Certainly,' said the Bishop of Carlisle, 'I strongly suspect that man has betrayed you.'[93]

When the forces of Thomas Erpingham ambushed the royal party there was no escape for the trusting Richard. The Lancastrian coup was complete, although once again Northumberland swore to the king that he had his security at heart and that he would immediately convey him safely to his cousin who was waiting for him at Flint Castle. At this point Hotspur was possibly dispatched to Chester to inform Bolingbroke that all had been accomplished. Percy may have been given charge of the town while his cousin rode to Flint in order to seal Richard's fate, given that Adam of Usk states that Bolingbroke took with him 20,000 men, 'the rest of his host being left behind to guard his quarters and the county and castle and city of Chester'.[94]

The rest of Richard's tragic story is well documented and it seems was fully agreed by all three Percys who, along with Bolingbroke, first conducted the king to Chester, then to London, vehemently pursued by bands of Cheshiremen who could not believe their sovereign's fate. Once confined in the Tower 'for his own safety', Richard resigned his crown, but the matter of placing Bolingbroke on the throne was a more difficult matter to resolve, although, as it turned out, not impossible to manufacture. For Hotspur, Richard's deposition was still a clear-cut case of honouring the right of succession. However, when the Mortimer claim was ignored this must have soured his relationship with Bolingbroke considerably. Indeed, his characteristic halting and explosive speech must have been difficult to contain under the circumstances. According to John Hardyng:

> . . . they decided on a free election; but on account of the youth of Mortimer – who was at that time by rightful descent earl of March, and nearest heir of England to King Richard, as was clear at the time – and on account of Duke Henry's might, they chose him king, as nobody can deny. At that time the Earl of Northumberland had, on the advice of Duke Henry, sent his troops home, as had his son Henry, who whished to act truly: for they did not think that the duke would in any way go against his oath which he had taken. He and his followers, however, as was clear at the time, kept their troops with them until he was crowned. The earls of Northumberland and Worcester, Sir Henry Percy and the earl of Westmorland all advised [Henry] not to do anything contrary to his oath: and although he listened to their request in the evening, on the

following day he took private counsel and decided that he would undoubtedly be crowned king.[95]

Thus the Lancastrian dynasty was founded and its seed of discontent planted for future generations to fight over in the Wars of the Roses. Echoing across the next century like a clarion call to arms in the minds of all those who sought legitimate leadership, Bolingbroke's usurpation was to be the central theme of Yorkist propaganda thereafter. With regard to the future heirs of Lancaster, Richard's subsequent death in Pontefract Castle poured an incurable sense of guilt on those kings who succeeded him. Some, like Henry V, sought to purify Richard's memory, yet others, such as Henry VI, stood idly by and let others shape the course of history. As for the Percys, John Hardyng's claim that they were unhappy with Bolingbroke's 'perjury' is a matter that only continues to cloud their involvement. Thomas Percy was, according to the *Chronique de la Traison*, among the first in parliament to cry out 'Long live Henry of Lancaster, King of England', and considering that all three Percys took part in Henry's coronation, the Earl of Northumberland carrying Lancaster's sword 'curtana' before the procession, and Hotspur being made a Knight of the Bath on the eve of the pageant, Hardyng's claims of perjury remain unfounded.

However, there is another matter to take into account with regard to Hotspur's more open dissatisfaction with Henry IV. Indeed, the Dieulacres chronicler suggests that Hotspur actually 'absented himself from the festivities on the day of the coronation, which had undoubtedly been carried out against his wishes'.[96] Although at first sight doubtful, considering that Hotspur and his wife had previously received gowns for the occasion, this statement cannot be set aside, particularly if we consider that the hint of Hotspur's discontent had originated from Cheshire – a focus of Ricardian support.

The Dieulacres chronicle was compiled at Dieulacres Abbey in Staffordshire and was written in two distinct parts by two different authors. The first author, covering the years 1381 to 1400, is strongly sympathetic to Richard II, while the second writer is an advocate of Henry IV. It has been suggested by J. Taylor that the first section of the chronicle was originally written in Chester (in other words it constitutes a town chronicle), which would explain its strong Ricardian sympathies, and that this work was later copied out by a second author who was a monk at Dieulacres Abbey. Therefore, singling out Hotspur as the 'discontented Percy' is a very interesting premise, particularly if the first chronicler was actually a native of Chester as Taylor suggests.

Following this line of enquiry further, this evidence makes the possibility of Hotspur's rebuff of the new king a likely 'sentiment' in those parts of England still loyal to Richard II. If not, how did Hotspur manage to control the staunch Ricardians of Chester and repay 'their boldness in kind' if he did not sympathise with their argument to some degree? The fact that he later managed to win the people of Chester over to his side, when so many of them, including Cheshire's famous archers, had previously supported Richard, is also incontrovertible proof of Hotspur's feelings of betrayal. The importance of his involvement with Chester as its justiciary for life confirms that he was well respected, not only for employing a firm hand when it was needed, but also for administering a degree of tolerance in matters much closer to his heart. No doubt Hotspur's fame and chivalrous reputation preceded him in this respect. Indeed, his impetuous, rebellious nature probably added considerable weight to his acceptance by this important Ricardian recruiting ground, an area which three years later would be instrumental in supporting his own rebellion against the man he had so unwittingly helped to the throne.

As for Bolingbroke's broken oath, this was to echo down the centuries, promoted chiefly by all those biased chroniclers, like John Hardyng, who wished to absolve the Percys from their part in the usurpation. How else could their later rebellion of 1403 be sanitised, other than by clearing their name prior to this? Hotspur's mistrust of Henry IV probably derives primarily from the failure of Bolingbroke to observe the right of the Mortimer claim to the throne, not from the oath-breaking at Doncaster. Other reasons for Hotspur's dissatisfaction were yet to materialise, although for the moment, despite his anger, he was not slow in strengthening his position by reaping the rewards of Richard's downfall. One of King Henry's first acts (21 October 1399) was to confirm Hotspur as warden of the east march and governor of Berwick and Roxburgh. Carlisle and the west march were already allocated to his father by the dubious act of 2 August under Lancaster's seal. However, Hotspur soon received £3,000 a year in time of peace or truce and £12,000 a year in time of war for his services to the crown, figures that were exactly double the wages of his father, who commanded in the west. Percy strength in Northumberland was also increased by a grant to Hotspur of the castle and lordship of Bamburgh for life, while his father received the ultimate accolade of Constable of England for his services to the crown. Regaining control of the border over the Nevilles was obviously of paramount importance to the Percy family; however, Ralph Neville's appointment to the office of Marshal of England and the lordship of Richmond for life as his reward for supporting Henry can only have placed a question mark on the Percys' northern domination.

If the Percys had openly opposed Henry IV in 1399, as Hardyng suggests, then their power would hardly have been increased on this scale. Their financial, political and strategic gains were much greater than those of Henry's other supporters, giving rise to the famous boast that the Percys alone were responsible for placing Henry on the throne. They certainly had engaged in 'kingmaking' for their own ends, and as a result both father and son strengthened their already lofty positions in the north, Hotspur also increasing his power in other parts of the kingdom, including Wales, by the year-end.

Thomas Percy, Earl of Worcester, also benefited from his support of Lancaster and received rewards for his defection to Henry, although some historians believe that he was compensated to a lesser extent than his brother and nephew. Together with all the grants Thomas had amassed under Edward III and Richard II, he received 500 marks a year for life, and as steward of Henry's household, Admiral of England, Treasurer and Keeper of the Privy Seal, his devotion to the new regime was assured for the present. In fact, Thomas was one of the peers who assented in parliament to the imprisonment of Richard II, an unlikely action if he felt in any way unrewarded for his part in the kingmaking process.

The death, or murder, of Richard II in Pontefract Castle was the direct result of Henry Bolingbroke's ambition, and the Percys, by virtue of their support in the revolution of 1399, were therefore accessories to this 'crime'. However, the revolt in Richard's name known as the Epiphany Rising cleared a path for Henry IV, although once king it was obvious that his problems were far from over. Both physically and mentally the burdens of medieval kingship were great, some sources suggesting that constant opposition, rebellion and sickness, coupled with the spectre of Richard's death at Pontefract, troubled Henry for the rest of his life, his conscience gnawing at him ceaselessly with regard to the latter if the chronicles are to be believed.

As for Hotspur, he had seen at first hand what northern military might was capable of achieving in a relatively short space of time. Returning home into the north soon after Henry's first parliament, he must have been astonished at how easy it had been to displace one king for another. Helping topple Richard from his tyrannical throne was one thing, but how well would the perjured Henry sit in his place? A precedent set by the previous deposition of Edward II had foretold that Henry's act of usurpation was nothing new; the sanctity of medieval kingship had already been threatened by the reality of creative kingmaking. However, for Hotspur at least, the wrong king had been crowned at Westminster on 13 October 1399, and the muddy roads of medieval Yorkshire must have seemed like a sad reflection of his own far from certain future as he left London behind him.

As he dug his well-worn spurs into the flanks of his horse and sped further into the north, his impulsiveness to act may have cooled in the bleakness of his native land. Despite his popularity and renown, there is no doubt that Hotspur still craved to fulfil the chivalric ideal; however, that ideal had been marred considerably by the deceit and double-dealing that had lately poisoned his family to prey on the instability of kingship.

SEVEN

Wales: 1401

After the displacement of Richard II and the return of his young queen to her father in France, Henry IV could hardly have expected amity with Charles VI. The mistrust between the two kingdoms gathered momentum when it was rumoured that a French invasion was planned and that letters had already been exchanged between France and Scotland declaring Henry a traitor.

It will be remembered that on 26 October 1398, Hotspur, as warden of the east march, had signed – along with his old enemy of Otterburn, George Dunbar – a convention for a truce with Scotland. However, now that a renewal of hostilities both with France and with Scotland was a distinct possibility, Hotspur was put on full border alert in order to combat any incursion that might arise when the old northern truce expired. Hotspur's appointments to office soon after Richard's deposition indicate that Henry IV had every confidence in his northern warden's ability, and as governor of Berwick, Roxburgh and Bamburgh Castle, Hotspur once more found that he was in an ideal position to play a leading role in the anticipated next bout of cross-border activity. With the west march superintended by his father, the Earl of Northumberland, Percy dominance in the north could hardly have been more stable than at the turn of the century. So it must have come as a considerable shock to both father and son that at a great council meeting at Westminster on 9 February 1400, Henry declared his intention to undertake an expedition against the Scots in person, heralding a pre-emptive invasion that may have derided Percy ability to deal with the border unaided.

As previously stated, tapping the minds of historical characters is a very difficult, if not impossible, task given the circumstances of time and lack of historical evidence. However, what we do know is that the Earl of Northumberland had taken offence against this form of border intrusion before. Hotspur, on the other hand, was unlike his father in many ways, so more honourable intentions may have spurred him on to follow his king with the very best chivalric intentions in mind. Since Hotspur readily accepted the chance of even the slightest warlike activity, it is highly unlikely that he was at all cautious regarding any attempt by Henry to belittle his family's northern achievement. In fact, given his recent inactivity against the Scots, Hotspur must have welcomed the expiry of the existing truce and the king's decision to emulate his ancestors by demanding that Robert III pay him homage in the time-honoured fashion.

Even though Hotspur may still have had some misgivings about how Henry had achieved his throne over his relations the Mortimers, there is no conclusive proof that he was outwardly showing any disloyalty towards his king at this time. He and his father had previously accompanied both Richard II and John of Gaunt when they invaded Scotland, and there was probably every reason to believe that some honour might be achieved out of the coming venture, whereby Percy territorial influence might be further extended across the border.

However, previous English invasions into Scotland had been generally disappointing and this fact must have coloured Percy thinking considerably with regard to how Henry might break the stalemate. Specifically, would Henry's invasion achieve anything other than another fragile truce? Could the English actually bring the Scots to battle, given their enemies' reputation for guerrilla warfare? The questions posed by other abortive English invasions into Scotland were endless. On the other hand, Hotspur knew that Henry IV was no pushover as a soldier. He had proved his worth in combat on many occasions, both at home and abroad, and his martial skills were equal to, if not better than, those of any man in England. Moreover, Henry had something else to prove: unlike his predecessor Richard II, Henry's claim to the throne, and hence his authority over his subjects, was built on very insecure foundations. He had much to lose by invading Scotland, but perhaps everything to gain if some small victory could be achieved in the first year of his reign. By August 1400 all preparations were complete and Hotspur was ready to forget his cousin's indiscretion against his in-laws and follow his comrade of St Inglevert into battle against the Scots.

Earlier that year – in fact only a week after the king had discussed his invasion plans in parliament – a strange letter had arrived from Scotland, which in some ways may have encouraged Henry to act more decisively than ever before. The letter came from a refugee and outlaw who begged for safe conduct into England. The fugitive was none other than George Dunbar, Earl of March who, in revenge for private wrongs against his family, had recently seceded from the Scottish court. At first, Dunbar was careful to avoid contact with his old enemies the Percys, asking Henry if it were possible that the Earl of Westmorland or his kinsman, Lord Neville of Furnival, might give him safe conduct into England. However, soon after being given shelter in the north, the forceful Scot was looking to the Percys for support against a common enemy. Immediately after receiving news that his castle had been handed over to the eldest son of the Earl of Douglas, Dunbar took the opportunity, aided by Hotspur, to retaliate against his former kinsman. Together with his erstwhile opponent of Otterburn, both men were soon racing into the north with a large raiding party, long before Henry's royal army had been fully mustered for invasion. Marauding through the Lothians as far as Hailes, it seemed for a while that the wheel of fortune had turned full circle against the Black Douglases. But Hotspur and Dunbar's impetuosity was short-lived and they soon overreached themselves in enemy territory. After being forced to turn back through lack of victuals, they were finally beaten off by Douglas in a sharp skirmish at Cockburnspath, nineteen miles north of Berwick-upon-Tweed.

The impulsive raid by the two former enemies achieved very little, other than perhaps helping to forge an unlikely alliance between their two houses. Sharing common ground in their private feud against the Douglases, their partnership was bound to rekindle a measure of cross-border activity and also ignite more general feelings of Scottish resentment against Dunbar, who was now seen by his countrymen as a traitor. For the moment, Dunbar's treachery served England and the Percys well, but the stage was set for a resurgence of border warfare with a native Scot in England's employ, the true significance of which would only materialise three years later on the field of Shrewsbury, when Dunbar's dubious loyalty had such drastic results for the ever-trusting Hotspur.

Meanwhile, the king's Scottish invasion was gathering momentum and in late June 1400 Henry was at York with an army of 13,000 men, 11,000 of these being archers. It was an English army built in the traditional French invasion style and focusing on the power of the longbow, 500 of the archers being mustered from Cheshire and formerly in King Richard's employ. By 7 August 1400 the army had reached Newcastle, where King Henry issued a proclamation to all Scottish nobles demanding that they induce their king, Robert III, to pay homage to him at Edinburgh on the 23rd of that month. Henry was doubtless testing the loyalty of the Scottish nobles over recent cross-border activity, a key factor of allegiance that he had so recently employed when he made his own successful bid for the throne. Ten days later, after receiving no reply to his demands, Henry advanced further north and on 14 August, with banners displayed, he entered Scotland with Hotspur and Dunbar in support. However, like so many other invasions before it, Henry's 'adventure' backfired in a matter of days due to a combination of logistical problems, continuous guerrilla warfare, and reluctance by the Scots to conform to Henry's demands. After reaching a well-held Edinburgh, Henry's army was soon forced to retrace its steps into England with only a fragile promise from the Scots that they would give some consideration to Henry's claim of 'overlordship'. A tenuous six-week truce was the only outcome of the costly enterprise, and this naturally placed command of the northern border once more under Percy supervision. In fact, according to John Hardyng, the biased Percy chronicler, the border was left practically undefended by the king:

> The ii. Yere of his reygne then he [Henry IV] went,
> In harvest tyme so into Scotlande,
> And Edenburgh with the countre brente,
> I whiche tyme the Scottes brent our lande,
> All Bamburgh shyre in Northumberlande;
> For both wardeyns with the king were gone,
> No wardeyn there, but husbandes by their owne.[97]

The Scots' response to Henry's audacity was inevitable, and had it not been for the resilience of the northern border garrisons and the defeat at Fullhope Law of a large Scottish force by Sir Richard Umfraville, one of Hotspur's kinsmen, the consequences of Henry's invasion might have been much worse. The king was never to invade Scotland again. Indeed, he was destined to be the last English king to cross the border at the head of an army of invasion.

The abortive summer expedition of 1400 was, however, not Henry's only military predicament. In September 1400, as his weary and downhearted army began to march south, news of another crisis was suddenly delivered up into his already problematic reign. The first spark of what later ignited a full-blown rebellion would not only affect Hotspur and his relationship with the king, but in later years would also cause a severe drain on Henry's war chest and hence contribute greatly towards bad feeling, distrust and finally the open rift with the Percy family. Henry's dilemma first centred on a local issue over land rights, which later escalated into a well-organised insurrection led by probably one of the most remarkable personalities in Welsh history – Owain Glyndwr.

At this point it is worth fleshing out some of the characters who would play leading roles in the tragedy of Hotspur's final years. The king's eldest son Prince Henry, then Prince of Wales, had previously accompanied his father into Scotland during the August 1400 campaign and was fast becoming a major focus of attention. Now thirteen years old, he had previously attended King Richard in Ireland, returning to England in either August or September 1399 in the company of Humphrey, Duke of Gloucester, who died during the journey. Despite his father's usurpation of the throne, it is said that the prince had a genuine fondness for Richard II, although this assumption is hard to corroborate with any certainty other than to say that when Henry Bolinbroke became king he set about purifying Richard's memory by erecting a number of chantries to pray for his soul, and carefully reburying his remains in Westminster Abbey. What is known with greater accuracy, however, is that shortly after his father's abortive invasion of Scotland, Prince Henry came directly under Hotspur's expert military guidance and here there may have been some genuine affinity between pupil and mentor.

The physical appearance of medieval personalities is a notoriously difficult area to paint with any degree of accuracy. Jean Fusoris, a Frenchman who visited the English court in 1415, described Henry V's appearance as more suited to the Church than to the battlefield. According to him, Henry did not resemble a warrior at all, unlike his brother the Duke of Clarence who, according to Fusoris, really did look like a soldier. Evidently, Prince Henry was also an athletic figure, a runner and jumper, but certainly not the traditional Englishman by any means. Compared to his father, Henry IV – who was by all accounts of stockier build, although not as tall as his predecessor Richard – the prince was lean, of average height, and above all handsome, with a straight nose and thick brown hair. His earlier days of Shakespearian pranks and riotous behaviour can be discounted here, and his ability to lead men accepted, probably due in part to Hotspur's skilful guidance in the Welsh marches. Almost certainly as dashingly elegant and exhibitionist as his mentor – for whom we have no positive physical description – here the similarity between the two men must end as there is no firm evidence to suggest that any impetuous streak ran through Prince Henry's studious mind; quite the opposite in fact, his later years show that Henry V was a more self-possessed figure than Hotspur, who was by 1400 – contrary to Shakespearian myth – at least twenty-three years his senior.

Henry IV, on the other hand, was a contemporary of Hotspur, albeit two years his junior. Born in April 1366, Henry was thirty-four in 1400 and was almost certainly suffering from the disease that would kill him thirteen years later. Although probably not apparent at the time of Glyndwr's rebellion, the illness, variously described by the chroniclers as a cross between leprosy and syphilis, was already weakening the king's health considerably. Later in his reign this incapacity contributed greatly to his many problems as king in that it not only disfigured his face, but also caused him to become an aged invalid at the early age of forty-six. However, King Henry's physical appearance at the turn of the century was probably much like fifteenth-century miniatures of him; that is, of a broad thick-set man with a rather heavy face, forked beard and curling moustaches reminiscent of the highly stylised figure wearing the distinctive, and slightly ridiculous, tall black hat in Jean Creton's *Metrical History of Richard II*. Thomas Elmham described Henry IV as 'calm and fearless, he excelled as a knight, earl and duke; a king distinguished alike for his bodily vigour, mind and stature'.[98] There is no disputing Henry's martial skill and ability for quick, decisive action in his early years, and even though his Scottish invasion may have ended in failure, we do know that Henry was an extremely fast thinker. In fact, had it not been for his swift judgement in 1403 against Hotspur, Henry would have probably lost both his crown and his life to rebellion.

Helping to allocate crowns had recently become a Percy speciality, and this passion for kingmaking was to continue for a number of years, although in the first few of Henry's reign the Earl of Northumberland and his brother Thomas, Earl of Worcester seemed to have been content with their lot. With regard to the great earl who had weathered the storm of usurpation with such uncompromising ease, the bearded figure outside Beverley Minster in Yorkshire, and the contemporary illustration of him in Jean Creton's *Metrical History* convey an image of a rather regal, wise old gent, given more to stately affairs than to the shrewd and self-motivated survivor that he was. Northumberland could be as deceitful and as scheming as any nobleman of his age, and by 1400 he was fifty-eight – ancient by medieval standards. As a leader of men he can be seen carrying a poleaxe in Creton's miniature depicting Richard's capture in Wales. In it Northumberland wears full leg armour and is sporting an English standard (mail collar) around his neck. His greying hair and long pointed beard accentuate a rather thin nose set into a gaunt, slightly drawn face. Clearly stylised, but wholly in keeping with similar unique portraits of Richard II and Henry Bolingbroke, Creton's caricature of Northumberland closely resembles the statue of him set into the edifice of Beverley Minster, although some believe the figure to be that of Hotspur and not his father.

Clearly, the most military adept and politically experienced member of the Percy family at this time was Northumberland's younger brother, Thomas, Earl of Worcester. However, it appears that the personality, and indeed the motivations, of this 'lesser' Percy are also the most difficult to pin down with any degree of accuracy. In 1400 Thomas was fifty-six, two years younger than his brother and although many neutral sources describe him as the perfect diplomat, honest to the core and meticulous with regard to everything he did, there is a side to the Earl of Worcester that is deeply unfathomable. After his part in the desertion and deposition of Richard II, Thomas is found once more serving in France – first conducting peace negotiations at Leulingham, then, in his capacity as Admiral, commanding a fleet to Aquitaine to quell a bout of threatened disaffection there.

In the spring of 1400 Thomas Percy was appointed to treat for the restitution of Richard's child queen Isabella to her father in France, where by all accounts he was well respected for his complete honesty and graciousness. King Henry's trust in his chief mediator and former attorney, soon to become lieutenant of South Wales, seems to have been unshakable. But if this were wholly true, we may wonder why Thomas decided to join forces with his family in rebellion against Henry in 1403. Indeed, the common accounts represent the Earl of Worcester as a prime mover in the events leading up to the battle of Shrewsbury in July of that year. Other authorities speak of Thomas's great uneasiness at the memory of his share in Richard's downfall, while Shakespeare portrays Worcester as the cool intriguer. Perhaps, like all other great movers of history, Percy's ultimate objectives are far too complex to fathom today, other than to say that by July 1403 Thomas was caught between two extremes: constancy to his king, or loyalty to his family. As a confirmed bachelor he was unable to found a house of his own, and therefore his fortunes were very much tied to his brother and nephew, although he certainly had a shrewd strategic side to his character, fooling even his king at one point when he joined forces with the rebels right under his son's nose.

The character of Owain Glyndwr, on the other hand, is even today painted much larger than life, being well immersed in Welsh ballad tradition and folklore. More a giant shadow of medieval Welsh nationalism than a tangible man among many, Owain's name evoked awe and admiration both in England and Wales during his lifetime. In 1400 his home and lands at Sycharth in the lordship of Cynllaith Owain, on the other side of the Berwyn Mountains from Glyndyfrdwy bordered those of Lord Grey of Ruthin, an English marcher lord and a great personal friend of Henry IV. However, by 1400 Owain (of the Glen of Water) had become a great landowner himself – in fact, one of the wealthiest landowners in Wales – and it was only a matter of time before the marchlands of his ancestors became a hotbed of Anglo-Welsh rivalry.

Owain was descended from ancient Welsh princes and had previously studied law at Westminster; becoming a soldier, he had accompanied English armies into Scotland. Using his skill in English law, Glyndwr had already petitioned parliament in 1399 regarding the ownership of certain estates that his neighbour, Lord Grey, had previously laid claim to. Despite that, probably owing to Grey's influence with the king, nothing had come of Owain's formal pleas, so in autumn 1400 Glyndwr decided to take the law into his own hands. On 16 September he proclaimed himself Prince of Wales and took up arms against the English. On 18 September he collected his retainers, numbering some 270 men, and attacked the market town of Ruthin, setting fire to it and carrying away a great deal of plunder.

Spofforth Castle, Yorkshire. *(G. Wheeler)*

Alnwick Castle, by Canaletto. *(G. Wheeler)*

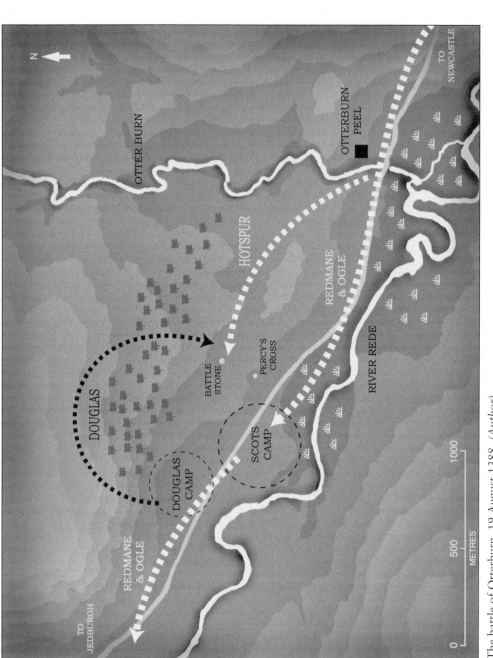

The battle of Otterburn, 19 August 1388. (*Author*)

The Percy Cross, marking the site of the battle of Otterburn. *(Author)*

The 'Cavers' Douglas standard thought to have been carried by Sir James Douglas at Otterburn. It is now believed that this standard, though similar to the original, dates to the late sixteenth century. *(National Museums of Scotland)*

The battle of Otterburn, where Hotspur was defeated by Sir James Douglas. *(Bibliotheque Nationale)*

The capture of Richard II by the Earl of Northumberland. *(British Library)*

Richard Neville, Earl of Westmorland,
Staindrop church, County Durham.
(G. Wheeler)

The jousts at St Inglevert as depicted in the
*Chronicles of Froissart. (Bibliotheque
Nationale)*

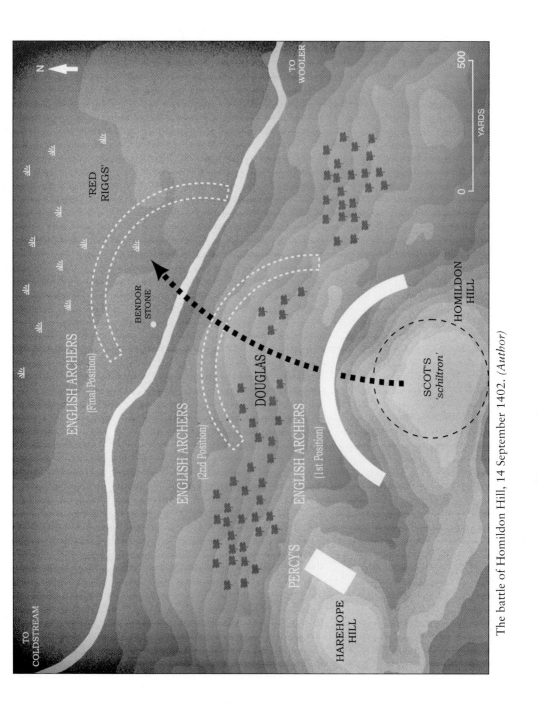

The battle of Homildon Hill, 14 September 1402. (*Author*)

The slopes of Homildon Hill, looking south from the 'Bendor Stone' in Red Riggs. *(Author)*

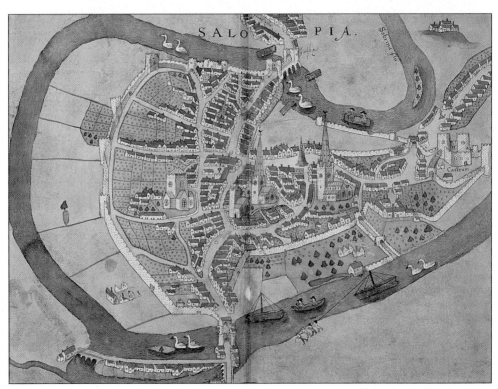

The 'Burghley' map of Shrewsbury, showing the castle (far right) and the English and Welsh bridges over the river Severn. *(British Library)*

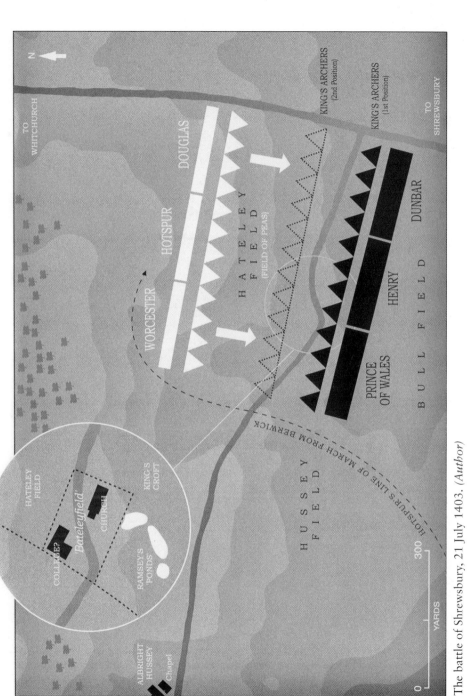

The battle of Shrewsbury, 21 July 1403. (*Author*)

Battlefield church and the area known as 'Bateleyfield'. *(Author)*

The death of Hotspur at Shrewsbury. From an engraving by the Victorian artist E. Caton Woodville. *(G. Wheeler)*

Hotspur's death at the battle of Shrewsbury, from the *Beauchamp Pageant*. *(British Library)*

However, Glyndwr did not stop at Lord Grey's principal domain, and he went on to attack the English garrisons at Denbigh, Rhuddlan, Flint, Hawarden and Holt. Ravaging their way southwards, his army then marched on Oswestry and Welshpool, only to be stopped on the banks of the River Severn by a hastily raised force under Sir Hugh Burnell, who scattered the rebels after a short fight.

Thus, the first bout of Glyndwr's rebellion was over and he and his followers soon disappeared into the Welsh hills. But Owain's military demonstration against English rule sparked off other similar risings in Wales, insurrections that caused the king to immediately regroup forces that had recently campaigned in Scotland, turn west and set about punishing the audacity of his once-loyal Welsh supporter. Along with the irate Lord Grey, still smarting from the recent burning of his township, the king marched by way of Chester into North Wales. Moving through Bangor and Caernarvon, his coastal reconnaissance met with little resistance and even penetrated into Montgomeryshire unopposed.

Thus the routine of the king's Welsh wars was established and other than confiscating the estates of Owain and two of his followers, Henry was soon forced into retracing his steps to London through lack of finance. Had he at this point made any effort to enquire into the grievances of Glyndwr and the Welsh people, it is possible that further rebellion might have been averted. Instead, the views of his parliament were repressive and narrow-minded, especially when alarming reports soon confirmed that Welsh students were abandoning English universities to fight for Owain and that Welsh labourers were leaving the countryside to bolster his army. Later English laws placed severe restrictions on the Welsh people, and so intense was the alarm of the English at this time that according to the chronicler, Adam of Usk: 'I heard debated very many harsh things to be put in force against the Welsh, to wit: that they should not marry with the English, nor get them wealth nor dwell in England, and many other grievous things.'[99]

It was also rumoured that parliament had decreed that the Welsh language should be suppressed; an act, according to Adam of Usk, that would have been insisted upon had not God 'mercifully ordained the recall of this decree at the prayer and cry of the oppressed'.[100] Consequently, there was no doubt in English minds that the Welsh problem had to be dealt with very urgently. Popular opinion pronounced that Wales was fast becoming a breeding ground for revolt, even though ideas for full-blown rebellion were still only simmering beneath the surface. English marcher lords, including the vindictive Lord Grey and Edmund Mortimer, Earl of March – the latter no friend of Henry IV – were keen to show their mettle in the coming fight. Like their northern counterparts against the Scots, such men had everything to lose if their hard-won estates were overrun by the Welsh; therefore they placed themselves willingly at the forefront of English resistance, even though in the beginning Henry may have still hoped for a more conciliatory approach to the crisis.

Henry needed men like Grey and Mortimer's support in the Welsh marches, but it is clear that he also wanted someone else who could both fight fearlessly when called upon to do so and also negotiate with impartiality, an action that neither Grey nor Mortimer could do with impunity. The question was, who had gained similar experience of border warfare elsewhere and who could provide the vital prerequisite of neutrality that Henry sought? Who better to carry out English policies in such a hostile environment than the renowned Hotspur?

The Welsh poet, Gruffudd Llwyd, who was perhaps attached to Owain's household, describes Glyndwr as 'resplendent in gold and scarlet trappings of the finest kind . . . fighting in tournaments, shattering men's bodies and overthrowing a hundred knights'; therefore, it is certain that Hotspur would have met his Welsh opponent at some point during the round of tournaments that annually graced the meadows of many English towns during the medieval period. Hotspur may even have fought alongside Glyndwr at either Berwick in 1384, or more likely in Scotland in the following year, where both men served in the army of Richard II. It is also extremely probable that their paths crossed at the Scrope–Grosvenor trial in 1386. Either way, it is plain that each man knew of the other, even though Glyndwr was about ten years older than Hotspur.

Hotspur was well aware that his new appointment in Wales would be no bed of roses. Given that his opponent would follow the same hit-and-run tactics as the Scots in a similar terrain of mountains, forests and valleys, the prospect of capturing such an elusive figure as Glyndwr, or indeed quelling his revolt, was a great challenge – a challenge that not only brought along with it a host of other responsibilities, but also a measure of difficult logistical problems that needed a good deal of financial backing from Henry's government. Once he was given his commission, Hotspur's new command included the justiciary of Chester, North Wales and Flintshire, and the constableship of the castles of Chester, Flint, Conway and Caernarvon. Hotspur was also given a grant of the Isle of Anglesey for life, making such a wide theatre of operations clearly a great undertaking. However, wide-ranging commands were nothing new to a man who, 'while others were given to sleep, he was wont to watch over the enemy'.[101] Swapping border for border, Hotspur was soon astride his favourite horse and eagerly spurring for Chester in anticipation of accomplishing yet more praiseworthy feats of arms.

As indicated, under his expert guidance at this time was the youthful Prince of Wales, sent by his father to learn the arts of war from his most fearless fighter. It was a short tutelage for the future Henry V, but one that clearly had a great effect on him. Experience of how border war was conducted would serve the prince well in the coming years of Welsh rebellion, but first-hand knowledge of the impetuous Hotspur would be equally beneficial in a far more imminent conflict that would prove disastrous for his mentor outside a famous Shropshire town in 1403.

Meanwhile, in the spring of 1401, the Tudor brothers, Gwilym and Rhys, operating independently from their cousin Glyndwr, had managed to capture Conway Castle while its complacent English garrison was at church. As it was too strong to be taken by direct assault, Hotspur determined to lay siege to it, and for the next four weeks he and the Prince of Wales, along with a force of 120 men-at-arms and 300 archers, set about seizing it. Assaults were frequently attempted, but Conway was finally recovered through conciliatory rather than military action, the Tudor brothers' lives being spared on the condition that nine of their accomplices were betrayed to the English and beheaded in their place. A letter from King Henry to the Prince of Wales later thanked his son and Hotspur for 'their great pain and diligence'[102] in maintaining the siege, which reputedly cost Hotspur some £200 of his own money. However, short of this vote of confidence, it is doubtful whether Henry's council ever intended to repay Hotspur for his efforts immediately, and although this was to prove the first in a long sequence of bad debts that Hotspur ran up while campaigning in Wales, there is reason to believe that in the following year (19 April 1402) Hotspur received the outstanding £200, 'in assignments', for charges incurred while besieging Conway for a period of four weeks at his own expense.

A famous succession of letters from Hotspur to the king's council dates from this period and this has given rise to an argument that he was badly treated by Henry prior to his famous rebellion in 1403. On 10 April 1400 Hotspur wrote from Denbigh that he had received the king's recent ordinances and that he would do all in his power to further English affairs in Wales. However, on 2 May he wrote another letter from Caernarvon reminding the king's council that his soldiers at Berwick and the east march were suffering great poverty from lack of payment. He prayed the council to 'remember how I have repeatedly applied for payment of the king's soldiers at Berwick and in the East Marches of England who are in such distress as they can no longer bear or endure for want of money and I therefore implore you to order that they may be paid as was agreed upon between the treasurer and myself at our last meeting, if better means cannot be adopted, otherwise I shall have to go to you in person to claim payment, to the neglect of other duties'.[103]

A further letter from Hotspur was sent from Denbigh on 17 May, indicating that this time his Welsh troops were suffering through lack of payment, although every effort was still being made to continue the war against the rebels. Indeed, in early June, Hotspur, marching south from his base at Denbigh, routed a Welsh force in Snowdonia near Cader Idris, while another English contingent under the command of John Charlton, Lord of Powys narrowly missed capturing Glyndwr himself, seizing part of his armour, along with some of his servants. It is also said that Hotspur actually met with Glyndwr at this time in the hope of bringing him back to the king's allegiance, all of which proves that at least some major funding was in place if the fight was to be continued in Wales. According to an anonymous chronicle printed by Giles, Glyndwr wished to seek a royal pardon, along with a three-month armistice, 'but certain of the [king's] council said that it neither was nor could be honourable and benefiting the king's majesty to remit to such a malefactor his offence'.[104] Others in the council went further and advocated Glyndwr's murder, to which Hotspur replied, 'that it was not in keeping with his rank to use the oath of fealty as a means of deception'.[105] It is probably no accident that Hotspur's last communication from Wales was sent shortly after this.

His famous letter of 4 June, again from his headquarters at Denbigh, is blunt and to the point. He writes, '. . . that if good and speedy remedy do not come . . . and if I depart from this country before some order is taken, which becomes a matter of necessity to me for I cannot bear the costs I am at, then the complete success of the rebels is assured'.[106] Hotspur continued his letter by reminding the council that after having made repeated applications for payment of his troops, and having from time to time been put off with evasive answers, he had written personally to the king warning him that if any town, castle or march under his rule should be overrun for want of subsistence for his troops, they who would not make payment in accordance with royal commands must bear the blame. He stated that he was quite at a loss to understand how the council could plead their inability to meet the charges that he and his father had applied for, which only amounted to £5,000, while the council had no difficulty in providing £37,000 for military defences elsewhere. Finally, Hotspur concluded his letter by apologising for his forthright style, no doubt in the hope that the council would heed his need for immediate action. Suffice to say, the action never came, and Hotspur was forced into leaving Wales in the hands of the young prince. Indeed, by the end of June Hotspur, as hyperactive as ever, was back in the north killing Scotsmen.

This desperate situation left the young Prince of Wales trying to organise, at his own expense, the continued fight against Glyndwr. With Hotspur out of the picture, it was no accident that he too was soon complaining to his father about the scarcity of ready money – a fact which if nothing else proves that Hotspur's letters of that summer were true accounts, and that actual cash was still not forthcoming from the king's council. As an apology for this lack of funding, the council said that the king was planning to lead another invasion into Wales in person, but in the interim Sir Hugh de Despenser would be sent to shore up the breach left by Hotspur. Thus, in the late summer of 1401 the situation in Wales had been temporarily stabilised, even though Glyndwr had managed to recover the counties of Caernarvon (although not Caernarvon Castle) and Merioneth in another bout of determined guerrilla activity.

When Henry did finally invade Wales in October 1401, the struggle was taken one stage further by the English. According to Adam of Usk, a Welshman himself, there was no respite for his fellow countrymen against the aggressor: 'The English, invading those parts with a strong power, and utterly laying them waste, and ravaging them with fire, famine, and sword, left them a desert, not even sparing children or churches; nor the monastery of Strata Florida, wherein the king himself was being lodged and the church of which and its choir, even up to the high altar, they used as a stable and pillaged even the patens; and they carried away into England more than a thousand children of both sexes to be their servants.'[107] The apparent treatment of the Welsh at this time is notoriously biased and unconfirmed, but what can be said is that, apart from executing one or two prominent followers of Glyndwr and despoiling the above-named Cistercian abbey, the king's foray into Wales had done almost nothing to reduce Welsh resistance.

Hotspur, meanwhile, was still somewhat soured by the rough treatment that he had received from the king's council in the principality and it seems that his financial problems were still far from over. In a letter dated 3 July 1401 from Swynshede in Lincolnshire, Hotspur described his frustration at yet again failing to secure payment of his revenues from assignments made on the customs of London, Hull and Boston. In his letter he expresses in the strongest terms his surprise that the lords of Henry's council made so little effort to safeguard the financial needs of the northern defences. Hotspur again warned Henry's council that serious trouble might result in the marches if his soldiers were left unpaid; however, some shadow of doubt must be cast over whether the outstanding expenses were as bad as Hotspur made out.

According to J.M.W. Bean in his study of the relationship between the Percys and Henry IV, there is every reason to believe that, above all, Hotspur was struggling to come to terms with Henry's unwillingness to provide adequate funding. Bean argues that 'there is clear evidence that the Percies had some grounds of complaint against Henry IV in that they found it impossible to secure prompt payment of all the revenues due to them for their duties on the Marches'.[108] However, Bean also suggests that after examining Percy accounts, he felt that nothing sinister was attached to the incidence of 'bad tallies' against them, 'since they [the bad tallies] were a natural hazard encountered in service with the Crown'.[109]

Financial burdens aside, by the end of 1401 the situation on the Scottish border was as volatile and delicately balanced as ever. Although cross-border raiding was still prevalent, all-out war had been avoided by Anglo-

Scottish mediation, and while Hotspur was otherwise employed in Wales, inroads had been made by the Earl of Northumberland to agree a formal truce with Scotland. According to a signet letter dated 10 April, King Henry had received letters from the Duke of Rothesay who wished to meet with the Earl of Northumberland at Melrose Abbey to discuss terms for a lasting peace. However, due to a more militant policy pursued by Archibald Douglas, these more formal efforts at mediation were doomed to failure for as long as he and his family held the major share of border power. Indeed, it was clear that Douglas aggrandisement depended on there being no respite for the area.

Archibald Douglas, who became 4th Earl of Douglas after his father's death in 1400, had led the force that had recently opposed and driven back Dunbar and Hotspur's men at Cockburnspath. But Archibald, later called 'Tyneman' (the loser), figures most significantly in Scottish history as the man who lost almost every battle he took part in, from Homildon Hill in 1402 to Verneuil in 1424. Yet apart from this more obvious military failing there was another side to Douglas's character that proved increasingly annoying to his enemies, and this was his ability to survive by straying from convention. There is no doubting Douglas's courage as a soldier, his prowess in battle, and personal ability to muster large Scottish armies against the English, but he was also a cunning opponent whose ability to fight on any side is seen by following his varied military career. Indeed, by the end of 1403 Douglas had received, and had recovered from, several horrendous war wounds to both his face and his body, showing that in combat he was no coward. His political stance alongside the more militant members of the Scottish nobility against their English oppressors is also proven by his willingness to oppose the status quo, all the more so now that his Scottish rival, George Dunbar, had recently gone over to the English side to aid in his overthrow.

An even darker side of Archibald's character can be seen in his capacity to plot the downfall of others. During the spring of 1402, Douglas's name was associated with the Duke of Albany, whose covert aim appears to have been to usurp the Scottish crown by disposing of its rightful heir. When the Duke of Rothesay suddenly died in mysterious circumstances, the complicity of Douglas and Albany in the crime can only be wondered at considering that shortly after Rothesay's death the King of Scots' only surviving son was also killed by Douglas's own brother. However, aside from plotting inwardly for power, Douglas 'the Tyneman' seems to have been the most fearsome and mercenary of them all; it was a talent that Hotspur came to recognise when he recruited Douglas to fight alongside him at Shrewsbury in 1403.

During the early months of 1402 there were several Scottish raids into England, all of which were prompted by Archibald Douglas in his bid to further consolidate his position as a major war leader. Sir John Haliburton of Dirleton returned from the first of these forays loaded with booty; however, Sir Patrick Hepburn of Hailes, who had previously distinguished himself at Otterburn in 1388 and was a very close friend of Douglas, fell foul of Hotspur and George Dunbar's forces at Nesbit Moor, a few miles north of Wooler. The ensuing battle, 'apud Nesbit-More in Marchia' and the subsequent loss of life incurred there would prompt the Scots to launch their most devastating bout of cross-border raiding yet. In fact, the fateful culmination of this raiding would end in yet another Percy versus Douglas border encounter that would go down in history as one of the most decisive longbow battles ever. Both conflicts would certainly have long-term implications for the Percy family and not only lead to Hotspur's final, irrevocable split with Lancaster, but also signal his last impetuous ride into the pages of medieval legend.

EIGHT

Homildon Hill: 14 September 1402

The battle of Nesbit Moor signified not only a change of fortune for Hotspur and the men of the English border garrisons, but also dealt a severe blow to Scottish pride – a fact that was bound to result in a major border reprisal by the Scots before the end of the 1402 campaigning season. Today, little evidence survives of what actually occurred at Nesbit Moor on 22 June, but by all accounts a small English force, commanded by Hotspur and Dunbar, attacked a Scots raiding party under the command of Sir Patrick Hepburn as it tried to gain the relative safety of the River Tweed. In the sharp but extremely bloody fight that ensued, the Scots were decisively beaten, and many Scottish knights, including Hepburn himself, were either killed or taken prisoner. According to a signet letter of Henry IV's council, the Earl of Northumberland, who was then warden of the west march, dutifully informed the king of the resounding English victory. The resulting correspondence from Henry IV to his council illustrates just how dangerous the situation in the marches had become:

30 June 1402. Market Harborough. To the Council. The earl of the March of Scotland [the Earl of Northumberland] has informed the king that he and his son with the garrison of Berwick-upon-Tweed to the number of 200 have defeated 400 Scots. John Haliburton, Robert Lewedre, John Cokbourne and Thomas Haliburton, Scottish knights, were captured, and Sir Patrick Hepburn and other Scots killed and taken to the number of 240. There is also news from the letters of the Earl of Northumberland, and reports from the bearer of these that 12,000 Scots have been near Carlisle, but have done little damage. The earl says that the Scots are proposing to enter the kingdom with so great a power that it appears that they wish to give battle. The council is required hastily to examine arrangements with Northumberland and his son, and to ensure that no harm comes to the marches through their negligence.[111]

Careful reading of the above letter seems to attribute the English victory at Nesbit Moor to the forces of the Earl of Northumberland and Hotspur, even though other sources agree that George Dunbar was also present at the engagement. Considering that the border defences had already been breached by Sir Patrick Hepburn and his men – Dunbar's enemies – it is also a possibility that all three of these men were present at the battle. However, it is highly likely that the Earl of Northumberland was absent and was still languishing in the west march, since it was he who had gained first-hand knowledge of the large Scottish army threatening Carlisle and had sent word of this to Henry IV by special messenger. As for George Dunbar, he was almost certainly with Hotspur on this occasion bearing in mind that he still had a score to settle with both Archibald Douglas and Sir Patrick Hepburn over land rights. Moreover, Dunbar knew that lately Douglas had won over to his side many of his own former vassals, including Hepburn, who naturally saw Dunbar's absence in Scotland as an opportunity to confirm a measure of independence with the Scottish crown. With such a chance to redress the balance a distinct possibility, it is extremely unlikely that Dunbar would have missed such an ideal opportunity to punish those who had recently taken it upon themselves to overrun his ancestral lands.

Hotspur, on the other hand, was more directly affected by Hepburn's punitive raid. As acting warden of the east march he was responsible for its safety, and in this respect he was probably more than willing to oblige Dunbar in his own hunt for justice so that order might be preserved. After all, who better to advise Hotspur on the best way to confront the Scots than a native lowlander? Given how difficult it had been to confront the Scots and bring them to battle on many previous occasions, Dunbar's assistance would have been invaluable. Indeed, it is highly likely that Dunbar had a lot to do with how victory was achieved over his former countrymen at Nesbit Moor. The death of Sir Patrick Hepburn on the field of battle, and the capture of Dunbar's other ex-tenants and councillors, must have been sweet revenge for the humiliation he had suffered the previous year.

Dunbar's more obvious usefulness in English ranks was also to be repeated in many other border fights; however, apart from his role as a military adviser the wayward Scot seems to have been somewhat of an embarrassment to many English commanders, even possibly to the Earl of Northumberland, who may have seen him as a direct threat to his own . territorial ambitions in Scotland. Hotspur had worked well with his Scottish ally previously, so doubtless he recognised that a clear advantage could be gained by having Dunbar's assistance in military matters. Dunbar's ability to anticipate his former allies' strategy; his skill in knowing how and where the Scots might strike next; his capacity to predict what roads they might use in order to launch their raids into England; and, more importantly, his knowledge of how to confront their bristling *schiltrons* in open battle, were therefore great assets to established English strategy. Hotspur was the perfect light cavalryman, impetuous and courageous to the extreme, but Dunbar was a cool tactician of the first order, and in English ranks against his own people he was to prove a formidable opponent, not only at Nesbit Moor, but also a few miles further south on the slopes of Homildon Hill against a more formidable opponent of old.

Indeed, with the Scots punished for their recent incursion into England and Sir Patrick Hepburn lying dead in the heather, Archibald Douglas could not have been expected to remain idle for long. Infuriated by the recent glut of border inactivity, he was soon seeking revenge upon the men responsible for slaying his friend. Upon hearing news of the bloodbath at Nesbit, the large Scottish army that had been threatening Carlisle immediately transferred itself from the west to the east march and very soon set about raiding deep into Northumberland. It was clear that this large Scottish invasion had been anticipated for some weeks, therefore the Percys had had ample time to muster their forces in order to fulfil their duty as march wardens. The question was, where could Douglas's marauding army be stopped with a clear English advantage?

Hotspur probably knew that the Scots army – variously estimated at between 10,000 and 12,000 men – had crossed the River Tweed in early September 1402, and after raiding as far as the River Tyne, it was anticipated that it would be on its way home by the middle of the month. Attending Douglas were his own tenants from Galloway, men from the west and middle marches, Clydesdale and Lothian. Under his banner of the 'bludy hert' rode George Dunbar's brother, Patrick of Biel, two of Dunbar's principal Berwickshire vassals, Adam Gordon and Alexander Hume, and George Earl of Angus with his kinsmen from Liddesdale. Douglas had also called in a favour from the Duke of Albany, his former partner in crime and now Scottish regent, and he had responded favourably by supplying Douglas with a retinue of knights led by his heir Murdoch Stewart, Earl of Fife. Also present in the Scottish army were the earls of Moray and Orkney, the lords of Montgomery, Erskine and Grame, along with veterans of Otterburn, including John Swinton, the renowned crusader John Edmonton, and William Stewart. A contingent of thirty French knights were also present in Douglas's ranks, all eager to strike a blow at the English while peace treaties were being argued over in Paris.

The historian, Bower, described Douglas's large host as 'his army'; that is to say it comprised men who had supported the war against the English (and George Dunbar) since 1400. According to M. Brown in his excellent study *The Black Douglases*: 'Although, as justicar and sole march warden, Douglas represented the merging of public and private power in the south, the host he raised in 1402 was built, primarily, on obligations of leadership, not on the duties of national service.'[112]

The considerable amount of men who flocked to Douglas's standard in 1402 is a testament to his emergence as a military leader, as well as a clear indication of how far some Scottish nobles would go to punish traitors, in this case George Dunbar, Earl of March. The usual campaign of pillage and destruction had its attractions for many 'small folk' in the Scottish army and, undoubtedly, striking a blow at the English for purely selfish reasons was certainly a major consideration for many of those nobles who did not come directly under Douglas's ever-broadening sphere of influence. However, it must be said that overall, the Scottish army of 1402 was a more unified force than ever before, although its size, probably no exaggeration at some 10,000 men, was always going to become unwieldy and vulnerable to a better-organised English army in the open field.

According to the chronicler Andrew Wyntoun, the Scottish army had penetrated as far as Newcastle, plundering towns, burning crops and killing Englishmen on a wide front, and although its exact route into Northumberland is not known, it is safe to assume that the main body of Douglas's army probably crossed the River Tweed at Coldstream. After extensive raiding in England, the likelihood is that Douglas attempted to follow this same road back into Scotland via Wooler and the valley of the River Till, although due to conflicting evidence this cannot be established beyond doubt. John Hardyng, who was, by his own admission, with Hotspur at the battle of Homildon Hill, claims that Douglas's army:

> Had brent the lande by South, Northward tho,
> To Homildon, where on Holy Rode daye,
> The earle [of Northumberland] them met in good and stronge araye.[113]

George Dunbar's skill in anticipating the movements of Scottish forces would now be employed to good effect. Moving ahead of the Scottish army, which was almost certainly hampered with a vast amount of plunder, Dunbar advised the Percys where best Douglas might be apprehended. The place chosen for the concentration of English forces was Milfield-on-Till, six miles north-west of Wooler, only a few miles from the bloodstained moor of Nesbit, where the bones of the dead probably still peppered the ground. However, the Percys' strategic position at Milfield was not seen as a defensive position, nor was it considered to be the final battlefield where the two armies might meet. Quite simply the English position blocked the main road into Scotland and the crossing of the River Tweed at Coldstream. Confronted by such a formidable obstacle as an English army in the open, Dunbar anticipated that the Scots would react in the usual manner. Indeed, as soon as they received word that the English were in the vicinity they sought advantageous ground of their own choosing. Immediately after reaching Wooler they picked the ideal place to stand and fight: a commanding hill to the west of their line of march offered a distinct advantage to their time-honoured strategy. This was the modern-day Humbleton Hill on the periphery of the Cheviots almost 1,000 feet above sea level. Thomas Walsingham confirms the site of this significant border battle in his *Historia Anglicana* – that is, after railing with his usual egotism against Hotspur's opponents:

> At that time the Scots, made restless by their usual arrogance, entered England in hostile fashion; for they thought that all the northern lords had been kept in Wales by royal command; but the Earl of Northumberland the Lord Henry Percy, and Henry his son, and the Earl of Dunbar who had lately left the Scots and sworn fealty to the King of England, with an armed band and a force of archers, suddenly flung

themselves across the path of the Scots who, after burning and plundering, wanted to return to their own country, so that the Scots had no choice but to stop and choose a place of battle. They chose therefore a hill near the town of Wooler, called 'Halweden Hil', where they assembled with their men-at-arms and archers.[114]

Marching alongside Hotspur in two divisions was the cream of the northern border garrisons, a large contingent of English border archers and a picked force of knights, all of whom had some personal stake in the coming fight. According to a letter of Henry IV to his council dated 20 September 1402 – which incidentally included a schedule listing certain persons who were 'not to ransom any Scottish prisoners without instructions from the king'[115] – some of the knights who rode with Hotspur can be identified. These were the lord of Greystoke, Sir Henry Fitzhugh, Sir Ralph de Yver, the lieutenant of Roxburgh and the constable of Dunstanburgh. Also present in the Percy contingent were Sir Robert Umfraville, John Hardyng (who was at this time one of Hotspur's retainers), and a contingent of traders from Newcastle who were eager to heap revenge on the Scots for their recent plundering of the Tyne valley. The Earl of Westmorland, despite his rivalry with the Percys, had also sent a contingent of men and archers, probably to better stake a claim to any victory that the Percys might otherwise reap for themselves.

However, again, there must be some element of doubt whether the Earl of Northumberland was with the English army at this time, as in a letter to Henry's privy council the wording can be taken both ways: 'The earl of Northumberland has informed the king by letter and by his squire, Merbury, that a force of 10,000 Scots led by the earl Douglas has been defeated by Henry Percy, son of Northumberland, and the Scottish earl of March, at Homildon Hill [*Homeldon joxt Wallore*], Northumberland, on the feast of the Exaltation of the Holy Cross [14 September].'[116] According to the tone of the letter, the earl was not present at Homildon Hill, a fact that would have relinquished command of the English forces to Hotspur, with Dunbar acting as his chief adviser. As warden of the east march Hotspur's influence over his men, and on the field of battle, would no doubt have been assured in the absence of greater authority. However, this is unlikely to have been the case. John Hardyng, the soldier who later turned historian, relates that he was an eyewitness to the battle, and although he reports almost nothing about the fight itself, he does state quite unmistakably that the Earl of Northumberland was at the battle in person. Indeed, taking into account the last lines of Hardyng's stanza, 'To Homildon, where on Holy Rode daye, the earle them met in good and stronge araye', it is clear that Hotspur was acting in a more subordinate role to both his father and George Dunbar who, as it turned out, played an integral role in how English strategy was planned:

> His sonne also, Henry Percy, was there,
> George of Dunbar was in theyr company,
> And with the Scottes that daye fought full sore,
> Discomfyted them and had the victorye.[117]

Doubtless throwing much abuse at the English, and also George Dunbar – a traitor in their eyes – the Scots army was in no mood to be frightened from its chosen elevated position. Now crowning and massing its great bristling *schiltrons* on the slopes of Homildon Hill, it saw that its superior position offered a distinct advantage over its enemies marching below. If it could only weather the storm of arrows it knew would undoubtedly precede the English attack, it was conceivable to use the gradient of Homildon to launch a downhill charge to break the English line in the water meadows beyond. As Archibald Douglas peered at the English ranks ascending the successive tiers of the Cheviots he must have welcomed the opportunity to confront both his mortal enemies in battle at once.

As indicated, the Scots army is said to have numbered some 10,000 men; both Hardyng and the Earl of Northumberland's letter to Henry's council confirm this, but how large was the combined Percy contingent in comparison? Firstly, its complement of archers must have been numbered in thousands rather than in hundreds, considering that it carried the first phase of the battle so effectively. Naturally, the required amount of 'bows' deemed necessary to cause the Scots to quit their defensive position depended on how massed their target was. Considering the size of the Scots army and its closely packed formations, it may be safe to assume, lacking documentary evidence to the contrary, that the Percy forces were practically wholly composed of archers, as English armies had been during the French wars. Fully mustered, and according to what manpower was available in the northern garrisons at the time, Percy's army may have comprised approximately 5,000 archers, although the Monk of Evesham estimates the English at 19,000 men, 7,000 of these being archers and the rest men-at-arms.[118] A figure of 5,000 would have given the English adequate 'firepower' to inflict the maximum amount of damage on the Scots with minimum loss of effectiveness.

Previous experience with the longbow (although known only as a bow at the time) had proved to English commanders that archers had to be counted in thousands to be successful. A hundred or so archers were no use at all on the medieval battlefield, given that they had to deliver as many arrows as possible, as fast as possible, to a fairly narrow area (depending on the formation of the target). The resulting barrage had to be unbearable enough to cause disarray and this was precisely the outcome if the situation was favourable. Given that at Homildon Hill the English archers would be shot back at by the Scots, who also had bows – with admittedly less impact due to the imbalance of training, numbers and efficiency – it is safe to assume that the delivery of English arrows would have been as many as six or eight arrows per minute (approximately 5,000 arrows in the air at any one time). With the rate of reloading accepted by modern tests and comparisons, the result of one volley of arrows would be devastating enough, especially if directed at masses of practically unarmoured Scottish levies, to cause terrible casualties. However, English border archers would have almost certainly carried two sheaves of twenty-four arrows on them at any one time, as well as those available from their baggage train. It is quite remarkable that the resulting barrage, lasting no more than a few minutes at Homildon Hill, would have the capacity to deliver more than 30,000 arrows to a massed target in one minute, and depending on how many arrows were available after that, a pro rata figure until arrow supplies were exhausted.

It is not surprising that this clattering 'hail storm' of wood and steel shot in quick successive volleys had attracted George Dunbar's eye before. The English successes against the Scots at Dupplin Moor and Halidon Hill were practically recent history in 1402, and no accident in an age when the longbow continued to reign supreme as the principal English 'secret weapon'. The bow was especially destructive against unwieldy masses of men and horses, any formation being broken by English archery provided the circumstances were favourable. Certainly Homildon Hill was one of those more special occasions where, against mostly ill-equipped Scottish ribaulds, disarray and death would be dealt in a matter of minutes. The only question that remained in Dunbar's mind was what would happen if the arrow storm failed to move the Scots off the hill. It was fortunate that in Hotspur he had the perfect mechanism to deliver the coup de grâce – that is, if he could cool the hot-tempered northerner for just a few minutes longer.

As the marching continued along the Till valley the waiting game above caused the Scots in their frustration to begin blowing their famous hunting horns in an effort to unnerve the English. By all accounts Hotspur was getting increasingly agitated in his saddle. To be at the enemy in true medieval style, head on, with honour, against 'The Douglas' was his only wish. All the murky thoughts of moonlit Otterburn and his inglorious capture undoubtedly flooded back into his mind at this time. In truth he probably had already decided to charge the enemy without anyone's consent, but his illustrious father was riding beside him and although, according to the *Scotichroniconi*, Hotspur tried desperately to persuade Dunbar to initiate a mounted attack *uphill*, he knew that if he even so much as attempted to ride the Scots down single-handedly, there would be hell to pay in the Percy household.

As stated by the English chronicler, Thomas Walsingham, part of the English army then 'left the road in which they had opposed the Scots and climbed another hill facing the Scots'.[119] This smaller hill, also situated on the periphery of the Cheviots, has been identified as Harehope Hill, immediately adjacent to Homildon and to the north-west of it. With a ravine separating the two elevations and, according to Walsingham, a dale where the English archers deployed to take into account, this leaves only two options open with regard to the opening location of Percy's army. Either the English knights and their archers left the road and took up position on the slopes of Harehope Hill together, their archers being purposely formed in the ravine below to harass the Scots *schiltron* or only the English knights climbed Harehope Hill while their archers took up position below Homildon Hill to the north of it with their backs facing the road. Both options show that archers were detached from men-at-arms. However, the main question regarding the archers' opening position

135

undoubtedly rests on whether the ravine between the two hills can be considered a suitable place for the deployment of missile troops, not forgetting the obvious fact that their arrows had to reach the target.

In both scenarios, further questions need to be considered regarding where the archers would have been most effective. The ravine (or above the ravine) position would have provided a clear height advantage whereby the English archers could have been arrayed in successive lines on the slopes of Harehope Hill, thereby providing an excellent platform to shoot continuous volleys of arrows across the ravine towards the Scottish ranks massed before them. In the second version, the deployment of the English archers is of less importance, since there is ample room for manoeuvre and for the arrangement of a more traditional formation given the lie of the land. But in accepting this more favourable position, can we be certain that the archers would have accepted such isolation away from their men-at-arms, who Walsingham describes as safely positioned on the hill to their right. In both instances it is clear that other dynamics must be brought to bear in order to solve the problem.

Establishing range efficiencies is easily done. Modern replica war bows of yew of 100- to 150-pound draw-weight, using 4-ounce war arrows of approximately 30 inches long, can be shot 240 yards with great accuracy. This fact, though, does not take into account that most medieval archers had been drawing heavy war bows from an early age, so it is safe to assume that even greater distances and rates of 'fire' could be achieved by archers who probably saw the bow as a natural extension of their body. With these mechanics in mind (and ranges established at between 240 and 300 yards), it is clear that only one of the above positions can be accepted. The ravine between the forward slopes of Harehope and Humbleton hills is approximately half a mile across, clearly not a distance achievable by the medieval war bow. The ravine position is also not a logical battle position, given that this would have placed the English archers at a disadvantage considering the impetus of a downhill charge by the Scots. However, the second position to the north tends to favour both massed archery (the necessary embodiment of men to cause maximum destruction in the field) and the accepted mechanics of the bow. Moreover, this second site is in agreement with what the chroniclers say occurred next (the only evidence we have of the events described).

A STORM OF RAIN

If the English archers formed up before Homildon Hill in the 'dale' described by Thomas Walsingham, then the first thing they would have had to do was to move into range of the Scots army. Obviously it is impossible to tell what the weather conditions were like on 14 September 1402, but what is known is that the topography of Homildon Hill would have caused a slight detrimental effect to the range of the longbow, owing to a steep gradient. Swarming in a great sweeping mass halfway up the grassy slopes of the hill, the English would have first emptied out their arrow bags and leisurely set about planting their missiles point down in the ground. The Scots, on the other hand, must have been extremely wary of what was about to occur approximately 240 yards below them. Most of Douglas's men would have probably seen an English arrow 'storm' before, but none dared quit their position in the face of the enemy. Above all they knew that if they turned their backs on the enemy, then the Percys, their knights and their men-at-arms poised on Harehope Hill would most certainly ride them down. All they could do now was stand behind their shield wall and wait for the deadly, drawn-out hiss to fill the air.

Humbleton Hill is terraced in three tiers. The lowest tier, comprising the road, the battle stone (traditionally known as the Bendor Stone) and the low-lying land – later given the name Red Riggs – are features that figure predominantly in local legend, the latter name being attributed to the final act of killing in the water meadows of the Till valley. The second tier of Homildon is situated about 100 metres above the road and this is probably where the English archers took stock of the situation and finally stood to shoot their first volleys at the Scots. The final tier is the summit 200 metres above this at a height of almost exactly 305 metres above sea level. It is highly likely that there was a good distribution of trees on the lower and second tiers of the hill, although this is very hard to confirm today, but doubtless the English captain of archers found that the second tier of Humbleton would provide his men with the best possible view of the enemy *schiltrons* and therefore instructed his men accordingly to adopt the best position from which to enfilade the Scottish ranks. As for Hotspur, the Earl of Northumberland and George Dunbar – the last of whom had undoubtedly contrived the English strategy to best outwit his countrymen – they too, like their enemies, could only await the outcome of the arrow storm, harnesses and armour rattling, in anticipation of a favourable outcome.

The opening barrage of archery probably lasted only a few minutes at the most, but this provoked an immediate response from the Scots. Thomas Walsingham confirms that 'Without delay, our archers, drawn up in the dale, shot arrows at the Scottish schiltron, to provoke them to come down. In reply the Scottish archers directed all their fire at our archers; but they felt the weight of our arrows, which fell like a storm of rain, and so they fled.'[120]

Scattering over the reverse slopes of Homildon Hill, the ensuing panic to be free of the deadly hail would have immediately created huge ragged holes in Scottish ranks, especially where a proliferation of English archers meant that proportionally increased casualties would occur. Men injured by many arrows protruding from their heads, limbs and upper bodies would have been instantly incapacitated where they stood, while great heaps of dead and dying would have no doubt built up on the lower slopes of the hill as a result of the shock and sheer force of the heavy war arrows. For the 'small folk' in the Scots army the battle was over almost before it began, but Archibald Douglas and his blood allies had clearly not had enough of the slaughter: 'So [Douglas] seized a lance and rode down the hill with a troop of horse, trusting too much in his equipment and that of his men, who had been improving their armour for three years, and strove to rush on the archers. When our archers saw this, they retreated, but still firing, so vigorously, so resolutely, so effectively, that they pierced the armour, perforated the helmets, pitted the swords, split the lances, and pierced all the [Scots'] equipment with ease.'[121]

In the 'rush' to ride down the English bowmen the Earl of Douglas was hit by a great cluster of arrows that punctured his elaborate armour at least five times. John Swinton, called by some the instigator of the Douglas charge, was killed outright, not far from his speeding master, while the impetuous Scottish attack carried forward until it was brought to an abrupt halt in a tumbling mayhem of screaming horses and broken bodies. Their men-at-arms never penetrated the English line. Indeed, those who attempted it were most likely severely wounded and soon finished off or captured behind the lines. Veering away from the plummeting arcs of hissing arrows, most of Douglas's mounts would have instinctively tried to flee, but as the English retreated before them down the hill, loosing their great bows in frantic rage, there was no escape for the Scots, owing to the momentum of their charge, the gradient of the hill, and the concavity of the archers' formation sweeping around their flanks.

The penetrative power of the medieval arrow has been tested against armoured surfaces with impressive results. Those arrows used by the English archers at Homildon Hill probably fell into two categories: the bodkin type of varying lengths, shapes and weights, and the barbed type incorporating a swept-back tail, obviously more difficult to remove in the heat of combat. The arrows which punctured the armour of Archibald Douglas were probably of the former type, shot at an angle of approximately 90 degrees to the surface of the metal at a range of about 70 yards. Heavy war arrows in this category would have impacted on Douglas's body with some considerable force, probably catapulting him out of his saddle. They would have pierced his armour and his body beneath, again depending on the angle of trajectory; the greater the angle of incidence, the less chance of penetration. Douglas also lost an eye in the charge, which might have been attributed to an arrow ploughing through the sight hole of his helmet and into his eye-socket beneath, although this of course is hard to confirm.

However, the outcome for all those knights who charged down the slopes of Homildon Hill would have been the same: confusion, disarray or death. There was no escape from the barrage of arrows. Even if an individual was not hit directly, at point-blank range, or by ricocheting arrows, there was always a chance that his practically unarmoured horse would be, resulting in the same degree of confusion and death from broken backs and necks. Incapacitation in such a horrific situation clearly led to eventual capture, and Douglas, lying stunned and bleeding in the heather, was about to succumb to the privilege of his class.

According to Thomas Walsingham, at this point in the battle the rest of the Scots army fled the field, 'but flight did not avail them, for the archers followed them, so that the Scots were forced to give themselves up, for fear of the death-dealing arrows'.[122] No doubt Hotspur and the English men-at-arms, seeing the rout was on, had already spurred down the slopes of Harehope Hill to take advantage of the situation. However, they would have been disappointed by what they eventually saw in the dale below.

Admittedly, they may have taken great joy in hunting down and rounding up Scottish fugitives in the area known later as Red Riggs, but the English war bow had already done its deadly work by literally sweeping the field of Scottish resistance. Walsingham recounts that 'no [English] lord or knight received a blow from the enemy; but God Almighty gave the victory miraculously to the English archers alone and the magnates and men-at-arms remained idle spectators of the battle'.[123] In fact, casualties were almost non-existent on the English side. Six days after the battle, when Henry IV's council received news of the English victory, the unbelievable incidence of casualties proved that the Percys had not only won a great victory, but that they had also captured 'the earl Douglas, Murdoch of Fife, the earls of Moray, Angus and Orkney, lord Montgomery, Thomas de Herskyn, John Steward of Ernermeth, lord Seton, William Grame, and other knights and esquires amounting to 1,000 persons, Scots and French. Lord Gordon, John Swynton, knight, and other Scots and French were killed, with a loss of only five killed on our side.'[124]

Considering the confusion and uncertainty that existed on the medieval battlefield, this seemingly ridiculous English casualty figure illustrates quite graphically that the battle of Homildon Hill was particularly one-sided – almost a massacre. In no more than an hour nearly all the principal Scottish leaders had either been mown down by arrows or had been captured by their enemies. Moreover, the nucleus of Douglas's 'militant' Scottish army had almost ceased to exist, or been allowed to fall into enemy hands. The impact of the battle on the Scottish host as a whole was, to say the least, traumatic.

It is said that 500 Scots were drowned in the River Tweed when they were harassed by the English to their deaths, while Thomas Walsingham, in his closing description of the battle, confirms the death toll and lists those who were captured, along 'with many other knights to the number of eighty, in addition to the squires and yeomen, whose names are unknown'.[125] In short, Homildon Hill was hailed as a resounding victory for the Percys in the north. They had at last achieved a substantial victory over the Scots that could be celebrated as their own. But were these facts all true? After all, did the glory not belong to George Dunbar? What did Hotspur, for example, make of Dunbar's curt decision not to allow him to charge the enemy with chivalric honour? In fact, how did Hotspur respond to the whole idea of being overruled by his Scottish partner?

Although we cannot confirm Hotspur's actual feelings at this time, he must have acknowledged with explosive (and hesitant) speech that the English arrow storm had been a great success. The arrow-riddled battlefield, won exclusively by the lowly English border archer in his humble peasant garb and iron hat, was proof yet again, if further proof were needed, that the power of the longbow and the cloth-yard arrow was an unbeatable force if used against massed targets from defensible positions. The Scottish close-order *schiltrons* had provided the perfect archery 'butt' for well-aimed arrows, while the English knights, probably with increasing frustration, had been restrained from achieving what was exclusively theirs 'by right' on the field of honour. With no option open to Hotspur but to stand and watch an object lesson in troop harassment, tactical retreat in the face of the enemy, and brilliant point-blank marksmanship, here was confirmation once more that medieval cavalry actions were fast becoming a thing of the past. Although Hotspur and his followers no doubt took part in the pursuit from the field, it is extremely unlikely that any English knight or man-at-arms was happy with the situation. Apart from personally capturing the wounded Douglas, who Hotspur was later to hold for ransom, the battle of Homildon Hill had been quite simply a non-event as far as chivalry was concerned.

We can almost see the fiery Hotspur in our mind's eye, straining forward in his saddle, considering every detail of the battle unfolding below him, fingering the hilt of his favourite sword feverously and flashing an eager eye at his father, hoping to see some sign of weakness that might allow him to charge 'the Douglas' and his serried ranks before the lowly English archers finally stole his thunder. Hotspur possibly felt cheated by all the pent-up frustrations brought on by inaction. He probably knew that French knights at the battle of Crécy had ridden down their own archers in order to get to grips with the enemy. He also knew from experience that as support troops, archers were indispensable on the battlefield, but as far as *real* battle was concerned, the bow was certainly not a chivalrous tool of the trade, nor was it bold enough to match honour with honour on the battlefield. How wrong he was!

As the residue of the flower of the Lothians melted away into the Cheviots and their tenants floundered and drowned in the fast-flowing

River Tweed, John Hardyng, a witness to Homildon Hill, recounted his version of what fate befell many Scotsmen soon after the battle was over:

> Six earles taken and xl, thousande plainly,
> Some fled, some died, some maimed there for ever,
> That to Scotlande agayne than came they never.[126]

NINE

Westminster: 1402

On the very same day that Hotspur fought at Nesbit Moor, another far more significant battle was being fought near the village of Pilleth in Wales. Previously, in April 1402, not far from the town of Ruthin, Owain Glyndwr had managed to ambush and capture his arch-rival, Lord Grey, spiriting him away into the Welsh hills to await his ransom. With Grey in close custody, Glyndwr was now more self-assured than ever and directed his attention to Radnorshire and the valley of the River Lugg. This was Mortimer country, and it was here that one of Owain's captains, Rees Gethin, capitalised on his master's recent success by bringing another of Henry's chief marcher lords to battle on 22 June. With almost all the militia of Herefordshire, Sir Edmund Mortimer had advanced steadily into Wales, confident that he would not meet with any formidable resistance. However, he did not bargain on the dogged determination of Gethin's Welsh contingents advancing on Pilleth, a village long noted for a wondrous statue of the Virgin located in a small church near a flat-topped hill called Bryn Glas.

Bryn Glas, or the 'Green Hill' on which the battle of Pilleth was fought, was to provide the perfect platform for Welsh archery – a salient fact that many may have overlooked in the English army at the time. In a situation almost the reverse of Homildon Hill, Gethin's men were to position themselves ideally on a hill to take advantage of Mortimer's English border levies who were following the course of the River Lugg below. Using the very weapon that the English were to employ so effectively at Homildon a few months later, at the battle of Pilleth the Welsh were destined to seal the fate of Hotspur's brother-in-law after only a brief one-sided archery duel. Several well-aimed volleys of Welsh arrows were devastating enough to force the ambitious Mortimer to launch a foolish uphill assault, and the rest is firmly entrenched in the history of the bow. According to various reports received after the battle, treachery also played an important part in the English defeat, but this is hard to substantiate given that propaganda, as always, played a major role in adjudicating how Welsh victory was achieved on this and many other similar occasions.

Various chroniclers record that English casualties were between 200 and 1,000 men. However, Mortimer, undoubtedly Gethin and Glyndwr's main target, was spared from the horror that followed the English rout from the field. Indeed, it is said that a band of women who accompanied the Welsh army 'obscenely mutilated' many bodies of the slain in revenge for past ravages inflicted by the English. Although this battlefield mutilation is again difficult to confirm – bearing in mind that almost anything Welsh at this time was being given an extremely bad press in England – there is no doubt that the English defeat was bad enough without resorting to scaremongering as a means to exacerbate anti-Welsh feelings. Sustaining such a crushing physical defeat was a severe blow to English pride, but the subsequent capture of Edmund Mortimer, the most powerful of Henry's marcher lords, was a psychological blunder that somehow had to be justified in England. It is therefore no accident that the debacle at Pilleth was blamed exclusively on the treachery of Mortimer's 'fickle' marchmen and not onto the power of the Welsh archer.

However, the news of Mortimer's capture was to be far less upsetting for the house of Lancaster. Henry IV knew that here was the perfect opportunity to protect his throne from further danger. As previously explained, the Mortimers had always presented a threat to the Lancastrian dynasty and their claim to the thone, so what better way of making one of their number disappear than to leave Edmund Mortimer to his fate in the Welsh hills? As far as Henry was concerned his ransom would never be paid. It was to be the final solution to a dynastic problem that had haunted him ever since John of Gaunt had opposed parliament's choice of Roger Mortimer as Richard's heir. As for the present Earl of March, still only a minor, he was safe within the confines of Berkhamsted Castle with Henry's own children, Philippa and John, and so presented no immediate threat – that is, providing no one was allowed to champion his cause. With the earl's uncle, Edmund, in perpetual exile in Wales, Henry could not fail to recognise that Glyndwr had provided him with an extremely useful loophole of fate that craved to be exploited to the full. The house of

Mortimer could, at last, be finally put to rest as far as real kingship was concerned. All Henry had to do was to continue to appease the Percys and all would be well.

Henry, though, did not reckon with Hotspur's resolve to plead for his brother-in-law's release, and the king's final confrontation with his northern border commander was to prove so disastrous that it not only shattered his relationship with the Percys, but it also nearly lost him his crown.

But how can we be sure that King Henry intended to obstruct Mortimer's ransom payment? Certainly there was no sign of royal inactivity soon after Mortimer's capture at Pilleth. In fact, Henry promptly set about organising another Welsh invasion, this time involving three separate armies provisioned for fifteen days, the object being to enter the principality simultaneously and strike as much terror as possible by a fortnight's rapid and ruinous raiding. Urgent orders were issued to the sheriffs of twenty-one English counties to array their forces immediately and meet the king at Lichfield by 7 July, only two weeks after Mortimer's capture. The king's letter to his council highlights the urgency of this planned invasion:

25 June 1402. Berkhamstead Castle. To the Council. The Welsh rebels have captured Edmund Mortimer and several other knights, and the king wishes to proceed against the rebels himself. Warrant for orders under the privy seal to all the lords, knights and squires of his retinue, and to all those who have annuities from him, to be at Lichfield on 7 July, armed and ready to make war in Wales.[127]

It was intended that one of these armies was to assemble at Hereford under the command of the earls of Arundel, Stafford and Warwick; a second was to muster at Shrewsbury, under the king in person; while a third would march from Chester, under the command of the young Prince of Wales, now aged fifteen and quite capable of commanding one of his father's armies without tutelage. However, it was not until the beginning of September 1402 that the three armies finally entered the principality, the reason being that King Henry had now to deal with two hostile armies, due to the Scottish threat that had already made its presence felt in the north.

Hotspur and his father were awaiting Douglas's army to show itself in Berwickshire when King Henry's contingents made their entrance into

Wales. However, like so many other invasions before it, the king's bold offensive was doomed to failure almost before it began. The year had proved exceptionally stormy, and almost immediately the weather in Wales became Henry's greatest adversary. The Welsh, on the other hand, took shelter in the mountains, woods and caves and managed to avoid all contact with their main body. Indeed, only a few days after the king entered Wales he narrowly escaped death. The king's camp was almost washed away by a combination of rain, sleet and snow, apparently unheard of in Wales at that time of year. Henry's own tent was blown down, and it was said that but for the fact that he was sleeping in his armour he would have been killed instantly by its fall. Worse still, many of his men were dying from exposure in the bleak and barren hills; therefore, it was not for want of trying that Henry failed to recapture Mortimer and Grey from Glyndwr. However, by 22 September the king was in London, 'sent bootless home and weather-beaten back',[129] with no nobler trophies of war than some herds of inoffensive cattle which his men had managed to drive off the Welsh mountainsides.

Henry probably took his defeat in Wales very badly indeed, as given the right opportunity he might have been able to secure the releases of Grey and Mortimer by means other than being forced to part with a great deal of money, which he did not have. But what must Henry have felt when he received news of the Percy victory at Homildon Hill? Jealousy, contempt, maybe, for his northern march wardens? It was no accident that the king's letter, giving orders that no Scottish prisoners should be ransomed, was written soon after Nothumberland's squire, Merbury, brought news of the Percys' victory to the king at Daventry on 20 September. Indeed, Henry's explicit orders regarding the surrender of Scottish captives might have been considered not only vital to the security of the kingdom, but also to his pocket. In short, the king was probably thinking of ransoming the Scottish prisoners himself as, due to his latest military blunder in Wales, he was in a great deal of financial trouble.

Meanwhile, the Percy household was also in some disagreement over the prisoners captured at Homildon. By all accounts the Earl of Northumberland had already consented to obey the king's orders to deliver up all those captured at the battle. However, Hotspur refused point-blank to surrender Archibald Douglas, probably because he had captured him personally, or perhaps because the earl had been too badly wounded at Homildon to be removed from the north without endangering his life. Both excuses seem plausible enough given the circumstances, although the former is more likely and in keeping with Hotspur's stubborn but chivalrous character. In fact, the laws of chivalry dictated that all prisoners captured in battle were to be ransomed personally by their captors. No doubt due to the recent impoverishment of his soldiers in Wales and the north, Hotspur thought that Douglas's ransom might bring him a great deal of ready money that would in some way compensate him for his ill-treatment at the hands of Henry's thrifty council. Yet when Hotspur received news that his brother-in-law, Mortimer, had also been captured at Pilleth, he must have had his own unique reasons for keeping Douglas for himself. Suspicions that the king might not act honourably towards his brother-in-law must have also rankled with Hotspur's chivalric principles, especially since Henry had previously acted so indifferently towards the Mortimer family and their claim to the throne. Given that Hotspur had recently left the Welsh and Glyndwr on fairly cordial terms, there was perhaps only one way to deal with his king's request and this is probably the real reason behind Hotspur's stubbornness towards Henry IV – namely that if Douglas's ransom could be achieved, then this might pay for his own brother-in-law's release.

Whatever the reason for Hotspur's protection of Archibald Douglas, it was to cause, on the one hand, a major rift between the Percys and Henry IV, and on the other, a noticeable dissociation between Hotspur and his father. Probably indebted to Hotspur for his protection against an enemy that might, given the opportunity, make an excellent example of him 'in quarters', Archibald Douglas was to prove a staunch ally of Hotspur's cause in the coming months, despite his more recent brush with English archery at Homildon Hill. However, the captivity of Douglas was also to cause the Earl of Northumberland a great deal of trouble, especially when he was summoned before parliament in the autumn of 1402. The meeting in the White Hall at Westminster was an early indication that the king was not pleased with Hotspur's imperious behaviour, but above all, the heated arguments that followed were a sure sign also that all was not well in the Percy household.

Henry's third parliament sat on Saturday 30 September 1402, and the Earl of Northumberland, along with other members of the nobility, formally answered their names in the presence of the chancellor, the keeper of the privy seal, and other members of the council in Westminster Hall. Edmund Stafford, the Chancellor, made the opening speech on 2 October by claiming that the King of the Romans, the Emperor Rupert, had recently written to King Henry calling him 'the most powerful King in the world', and requesting him to do his utmost to heal the schism in the Church by which means there might be again 'one Fold and one Shepherd'. Stafford, then Bishop of Exeter, also reported the recent victory of the Percys over the Scots at Homildon Hill, but apart from these two highlights the outlook was not bright. There was the usual or, rather, worse than usual, shortage of money, and the troubles in Wales and Ireland continued to haunt the proceedings, so much so that the king asked for the urgent advice of parliament. The commons also thanked Henry for his great labours against the Scots and the Welsh, and applauded the young prince for his service in Wales. They also asked that the Lords Roos and Willoughby might be allowed to raise a loan of 10,000 marks[129] for Lord Grey's ransom, a request that probably caused a considerable stir in the house, considering that money, and how it was being apportioned, was a problem that had yet to be debated.

Four days later on 20 October the Earl of Northumberland came before the king and parliament in the White Hall, bringing with him some of his Scottish prisoners. These were Murdoch, Earl of Fife, son of the Regent Albany, three other Scots, Lord Montgomery, Sir William Graham and Sir Adam Forster, and three Frenchmen, Sir John de Heley, Sir Piers Hazars and John Dormy. Preceded by a triumphant parade of pageantry and trumpets, the prisoners knelt firstly at the entrance to Westminster Hall, secondly in the middle of the hall, and finally in front of Henry seated on his throne.

Casting an enquiring eye over the assembly before him, Henry cannot have failed to notice that the Earl of Douglas was not present, a fact that must have annoyed him intensely considering that Douglas had been the chief instigator of all the more recent ravaging in the north. Henry must have also observed that Hotspur, too, was conspicuous by his absence, although Percy's non-attendance cannot be confirmed considering that both his father and George Dunbar were present at Westminster and that the victory at Homildon Hill was, after all, a crowning Percy achievement.

However, at this point in the proceedings nothing was said on either subject by the king, and Henry bid the Scottish prisoners to speak. Their spokesman, Sir Adam Forster, prayed that the king might grant them favourable treatment since they had been taken on the field of honour. The king replied graciously that as a true knight he would respect the laws of chivalry, whereupon Forster, still on his knees, said that he hoped that soon a peace treaty might be concluded between England and Scotland, to which the king replied curtly that he had not forgotten Forster's 'white' words and promises when he had met him two years before. In fact, Henry rebuked Forster severely for his conciliatory behaviour and said that had he known then what he knew now, he would never have trusted him. Forster begged Henry for his forgiveness, after which all were bidden to rise to be entertained at the king's table in the Painted Chamber, proof, if any were needed, that the ostentatious imitations of chivalry were still alive and well at the English court.

It is said that during this recess the king had a stormy interview with the Earl of Northumberland regarding the prisoners still not accounted for. The resulting disagreement may well have stemmed from the monies still owing to the Percys for their involvement in the north and Wales, although this is difficult to confirm. E.B. de Fonblanque, the Percy historian, asserts that 'The earl, having urgently demanded payment for the custody of the marches, said "My son and I have spent our all in your service." The king replied, "I have no money, and money you shall not have." The earl said, "When you entered the kingdom you promised to rule according to your council; you have now year by year received large sums from the country, and yet you say that you have nothing, and pay nothing, which irritates your commons. God grant you better council!"'[130]

Despite the more personal opinions of the Percy historian, what is apparent from the above interview is that King Henry took immediate offence because – contrary to his demands immediately after Homildon Hill – Hotspur had deliberately disobeyed his orders. Harry Percy's refusal to release Archibald Douglas to the king obviously reflected directly upon his father, who immediately bore the brunt of all Henry's anger despite his own compliance with the king's commands. As a result, the deteriorating situation that had at first centred on purely financial problems with Henry's council was fast becoming a more personal matter of whether the

Percys were purposely undermining the king's authority. As for Hotspur, he obviously felt that he was in a good position to dictate what should be done with at least part of the money that could be achieved from Douglas's ransom. If the king and his council could not account for the cash and 'bad tallies' that were still owing to him, then the Scottish ransom money would. Unfortunately for Hotspur the king was also in great need of financial help himself and this was to be the major subject debated the next day in parliament.

Apart from the usual grants of money made for the next three years, fixed at an unusually high rate on wool exports, it was suspected by the commons that the king had accumulated a vast reserve of money independent of that normally required to support his household. Henry made a statement denying this, and asserted that he had nothing laid by. The king was then asked to account for the treasure that he had appropriated from King Richard's coffers, and Henry replied that the Earl of Northumberland had received it after his landing at Ravenspur. In answer to this the commons requested that the responsible officials should be questioned, but the request was refused. Henry was well aware that his commons knew that he had made an exceptionally large number of grants to his own supporters, as well as to those of Richard, by confirming their grants without the consent of the council; therefore the question was passed over. However, by refusing to comply with any further investigation Henry had to promise that henceforth he would only make grants of land and annuities with the advice of his council. Thus the king got his money – and got it without the prolonged discussion that usually accompanied such proceedings.

Before parliament closed on 25 November, George Dunbar rose and asked that he might be rewarded for his services against his countrymen – a liberty that was not without some justification, given that his military skill at both Nesbit Moor and Homildon Hill had helped secure the borders of Henry's kingdom. No doubt Dunbar's request was accompanied by much grinding of teeth on the part of every Englishmen present. However, his claim received some attention, although not the kind that Dunbar might have expected. Parliament promised that any estate or castle formerly his, but now seized by the Scottish king, would be restored to him – as and when it was captured by the English. This was undoubtedly a slight on

Dunbar's recent achievements, given that conquering these lands in the first instance was beset with infinite problems. Indeed, if Dunbar was hoping to claim a major share of the northern spoils wrought from his recent victories over the Scots, then he was sadly mistaken; and here possibly is the first sign that the former Scottish earl was feeling dissatisfied with his lot. Indeed, there is some evidence to suggest that the convulsions that were to follow in 1403 were derived from two very different internal rivalries: 'and especially the two principal lords who encouraged that evil work, men who could have extinguished all these bitter thoughts at the beginning and even almost at the end of the business, to wit, the earls of Dunbar and Worcester: since one of them, Dunbar, desired the death of Henry Percy that he might dominate more easily in parts of Northumbria, and the earl of Worcester desired the death of the king, that with him out of the way he might be more easily the principal power under his cousin'.[131]

It was strong stuff, from an author known to have been a staunch Percy supporter, but perhaps not so unbelievable if we consider whose side Dunbar took in the Percy rebellion and how Thomas Percy, Earl of Worcester, the so-called 'instigator of all the troubles', later reacted to King Henry once the die was firmly cast against his family. As for Dunbar, it is highly likely that he 'thought' that he might become one step closer to becoming King Henry's chief lieutenant in the north if the Earl of Northumberland could be ousted from office. With Hotspur also out of favour with the king, and with the promise of further lands to conquer in Scotland a distinct possibility, it was no accident that a man like Dunbar had everything to gain from a closer affiliation with his adopted king rather than siding with the Percys who were, after all, his former blood enemies. Either way, when parliament was dissolved in late November 1402, it seems that at least three men were dissatisfied with how they had been treated by the king. Northumberland, no doubt still stinging from his interview with Henry, probably rode back to Alnwick with the intention of persuading his son to give up his valuable prisoner. Dunbar, with his own grandiose territorial problems to solve in Scotland, was not slow in following the earl's lead, as both nobles were now indisputably in competition for the same Scottish territory.

Since both men hoped to capitalise on their joint victory at Homildon Hill, the way was now open for a rapid English advance into southern

Scotland; therefore the stress laid by the pro-Percy chronicler upon the opposition between Henry Percy senior and George Dunbar should not go unnoticed. Much like John Neville had been the Percy 'buffer' of John of Gaunt, Dunbar was fast becoming a new and disturbing element inserted into the Percy sphere of influence. As to whether the king intended this all along is open to question, considering that Henry IV knew all too well that Dunbar was a former enemy and a Scot of some considerable military ability. However, the Percys had now entered a new and dangerous phase of their ascendancy in the north, so there may be some element of truth in the suggestion that the king forced Dunbar and Percy together to create an impasse. Henry's design to emulate his father by appointing his brother-in-law Ralph Neville, Earl of Westmorland to the captaincy of Roxburgh Castle, a post formerly granted to Hotspur for ten years, is further proof of his determination to curb his northern warden's independence and recent impudence. It is particularly ironic that the king's memory had not served him well with regard to this more acidic appointment to office – the loss of Roxburgh and the east march had been one of the chief reasons why the Percys had betrayed Richard II in 1399.

Thus, this gradual history of deteriorating personal relationships was one of the many factors that forced the Percys to rebel against their king the following year. Coupled with the money that was still 'owed' to them as wardens of the marches, allegedly some £20,000 in the form of cash and 'bad tallies', plus the more recent issues regarding prisoners, and we may wonder at what else the Percys could bear without resorting to some form of action. Further anger and disagreement must have been heard in the Percy household when the Earl of Northumberland returned from London bearing the unwelcome tidings that Lord Grey was about to be ransomed over Hotspur's kinsman Sir Edmund Mortimer. It is hard to believe that Hotspur's suspicions would not have increased against his king at this time over the fate of his brother-in-law. Indeed, secretly Hotspur must have railed against Henry from what he thought was a safe distance in much the same way as he is said to have done in 1399 against Richard II. However, above all Hotspur was now certain that he must face the king as soon as possible in order to explain the reasons behind his obstinacy.

Contemporary English and French chroniclers suggest that Hotspur rode to London primarily at the king's request, and as a direct result of his father's stormy interview with Henry in November. But it must be said that the date of the interview is open to question, due in part to what was allegedly said when the two men met, and it is more likely that Hotspur arrived in London sometime after Edmund Mortimer declared his open treason against the crown on 13 December 1402. On this date Mortimer wrote to his tenantry from Mellenyth in Wales regarding his decision to side with Owain Glyndwr, and also to marry his daughter: 'Very dear and well beloved, I greet you well, and make known to you that Owain Glyndwr has raised a quarrel of which the object is, that if King Richard be alive, he be restored to his crown, and if not, that my honoured nephew, who is the rightful heir to the said crown shall be King of England, and that the said Owain will have his right in Wales. And I, seeing and considering the said quarrel is good and reasonable, have consented to join in it, and to aid and maintain it, and by the grace of God to bring it to a good end, Amen!'[132]

After he read this letter the king had no hesitation in declaring Mortimer a traitor. In fact, Mortimer had played right into the king's hands – he could now be labelled a rebel with treasonable ambitions on the crown. Taking up the cause of the 'deceased' Richard, lately a thorn in Henry's side due to a number of rumours that were circulating declaring that he was still alive, Mortimer had raised an issue that others could immediately associate with. If former Ricardians could not identify with a resurrected Richard, then physically a pretender to the throne could instantly be realised in Mortimer's young nephew, still an extremely dangerous if diminutive figure imprisoned in Henry's own household. Therefore, with much wider issues to discuss than merely those regarding Scottish prisoners, the whole question of rebellion, treason and usurpation was ripe for debate when Hotspur met Henry at Westminster that fateful autumn. All the tensions that had built up during the previous years over the Mortimer claim, perjury and financial deficit, were most likely festering within the two men like an infectious disease just waiting to break out.

The actual words spoken by both men may remain apocryphal, but it is alleged that after evading his father's demand to release Douglas into the king's custody, Hotspur rode to London with the intention of forcing Henry's hand. When Percy entered the king's chamber, Henry abruptly asked him whether he had brought Archibald Douglas with him. Harsh words were immediately exchanged, after which Hotspur requested that his brother-in-law, Mortimer, should be allowed to ransom himself as Lord Grey had done. Henry angrily refused Hotspur's demands, saying that he would not have money going out of the country to help his enemies (that is, the Welsh). 'Shall a man expose himself to danger for your sake,' said Hotspur, probably lapsing into a stammer, 'and you refuse to help him in his captivity?' The king replied that Mortimer was a traitor, who had yielded himself, 'by his consent and treason', to the Welsh, namely at the battle of Pilleth. 'And you are a traitor!' said the king, taunting Hotspur with the lame excuse that he had not captured Glyndwr when he had the opportunity. This accusation probably referred to the time when Hotspur had been conducting reasonable negotiations with Owain in an effort to resolve the rebellion by more conciliatory means. However, when the king struck Hotspur on the cheek and drew his dagger on him Percy reacted with characteristic impudence: 'Not here, but in the field!' he railed, shocked by the 'buffet' from his former friend. They did not speak again. Indeed, they did not see each other until their armies finally met at Shrewsbury in the following year.[133]

According to the *Brut Chronicle*, the interview between Hotspur and the king was particularly one-sided, and the highly dramatic conclusion was the fault of Hotspur's blunt and impetuous nature regarding the monies still owing to him: 'And anon after, fell a debate between the king and Sir Henry Percy, that was called by the Scots Henry *Hotespurre*. This Sir Henry came unto the king and asked of him certain wages that he was behind, for the keeping and wardenship of the marches, and the king him gave but a light answer.'[134] When the king, 'sore aggrieved' by Hotspur's persistence, struck him on the cheek the *Brut* claims that Percy retorted, 'by my faith this shall be the dearest-bought buffet that ever was in England!'

Evidently, Hotspur immediately returned to the north, although he may have first sped into Wales to consult with Glyndwr and Mortimer. It is known that John Morys (Morris), a messenger in the service of the Earl of Worcester, was still with Owain Glyndwr as late as 3 October 1403, and although Hotspur may not have directly consulted with his brother-in-law and Glyndwr at this time, there is every reason to believe that some form of communication was set up between the two camps. More than likely this was the work of Thomas Percy, Earl of Worcester, who until then seems to have managed to steer clear of all the internal politics that were once more galling his family. But some event changed Worcester's mind to such an extent that contemporaries later called him 'the instigator of all the troubles', and the man who 'desired the death of the king, so that with him out of the way he might be more easily the principal power under his cousin [the Earl of March]'. What had occurred between the king and his former confidant to warrant such an unscrupulous change of loyalty? The reasons behind the Earl of Worcester's defection are not so easy to fathom, although by Christmas 1402 Hotspur's uncle was probably aware only that there had been some slight disagreement between his family and the king, and that the severest of these arguments had been caused largely by the hot-headedness of his hyperactive nephew, Hotspur.

As for the general opinion of the common people of England in the last few months of 1402, the nation could hardly have failed to notice the contrast between the brilliant victories of the Percys in the north and the miserable defeat of King Henry in Wales. The captives taken at Homildon Hill were 'true' trophies of war that proclaimed to the entire kingdom that the Percys were once again 'kings of the north'. Owain Glyndwr, despite the warlike advances of the young Prince of Wales, was still proving to be a formidable opponent who refused to succumb to the yoke of English overlordship. Indeed, the English Prince of Wales was now directly in competition with his Welsh counterpart, a situation that would prove the making of the former when he faced the Welsh rebellion alone in the latter years of his father's reign. Still a force to be reckoned with in 1402, Glyndwr, despite his magical charisma, had lately been confined to guerrilla activities in his own land and in the marches; therefore, as most people saw it, England was safe for the moment. The king had sent for his new bride, Joan of Navarre, to be brought over from Brittany by his commissioners and this at least was a blessing that Henry, and indeed the country, might look forward to in contrast with the more recent troubles of his reign.

As for the chronicler Adam of Usk, who had lately reported the plight of the Welsh, he had fled to Rome in an effort to escape conviction for horse theft. However, his temporary exile did not stop him declaring that the Percys had lately become 'too much puffed up'[135] by their recent victories over the Scots at Homildon Hill. Indeed, he claimed that this was the cause of their ruin the following year, although, as will be seen, the Percy rebellion of 1403 was a far more covert and complex operation than even

Adam could have fictionalised. The spark of rebellion may have had its origins on the slopes of Homildon Hill, as Adam suggests, especially with regard to the Percys' pressing financial issues, but Hotspur's part in the rebellion was all about making amends for Richard's demise. By placing a new king on the English throne he hoped to put an end to the charade that had begun in 1399. As far as his uncle, Worcester, was concerned he too was interested in kingmaking – but for other, more personal, reasons.

TEN

Shrewsbury: 1403

'In this year there was a star seen in the firmament that showed itself in all the world for divers marvels that should fall by the token of this star. The which star was called Stella Commata. And in this same year on Saint Mary Magdalene day was the battle of Shrewsbury, and there did come Sir Harry Percy, the Earl of Northumberland's son, with a great multitude of men-at-arms and archers and gave battle to the king.'[136]

Such was the report made by the author of the *Great Chronicle of London* for the year 1403, a year in which the Percy family would see one of its brightest 'stars' extinguished for ever, a second fall under the headsman's axe, and a third witness many of his hard-won estates sequestrated by the crown.

What befell Hotspur in his last year of life is perhaps worthy of the influence attributed to the 'Stella Commata' in more ways than one if we take into account that a further cosmic occurrence was to feature immediately after Hotspur's death in battle. Perhaps both events might be considered coincidence today, but in the fifteenth and sixteenth centuries such celestial episodes were taken very seriously indeed by those who sought to explain the historical significance of major events. Shakespeare, even in his time, saw the significance of Hotspur's fate as a new beginning for Henry IV and his illustrious son and placed the fall of Percy at the very epicentre of his two-part drama *Henry IV*, it being a tragedy worthy of all the great tragedies of Shakespearian theatre. In short, the Bard incorporated Percy's death not only for dramatic effect, but also as a kind of personal soliloquy and warning to others who might harbour thoughts of rebellion in any age. Hotspur's death in battle also marked the end of an era for Shakespeare – not the end of Henry IV's troubles by any means, but the beginning of a far greater conflict that 'rained blood' later that century. Thus the battles of the Wars of the Roses were begun, according to

Shakespearian myth, on the field of Shrewsbury in 1403, rather than some fifty years later in the many squabbles and feuds that produced carbon-copy usurpations of the English throne aided by kingmakers who ultimately put the Percys to shame.

But how true are the myths attached to Hotspur's final ride into medieval legend? Was the fight at Shrewsbury really the first battle of the Wars of the Roses? What caused the Percys to finally rebel against their king? What influence, if any, did the Earl of Worcester have on the battle? And, lastly, why was Henry IV so ignorant of the Percy rebellion until the last moment? Many more such important questions need to be answered, but first it is vital to document the events leading up to Hotspur's final and irrevocable split with Lancaster; only if this path is traced will Percy's true character come into much sharper focus and prove that his famous impetuosity had in fact been inherently moulded by members of his own immediate family.

Following the thinking of J.M.W. Bean in his 1959 study, 'Henry IV and the Percies', the conclusions drawn hardly indicate that rebellion was anticipated, even after the high drama of Hotspur's so-called violent rebuke by the king:

> By the end of 1402 the situation that existed between Henry IV and the Percies was in marked contrast to that of three years earlier. They remained his most powerful subjects; but the atmosphere of personal friendship had disappeared, they could no longer be sure that they could wield influence over the king, and open quarrels had occurred. Does this situation in itself explain the Percies' rebellion of July 1403? There are good reasons for believing that it cannot be explained in these terms alone. Despite the quarrels, there is no evidence that Henry IV was actively hostile; and their disagreements with him had not inflicted any real damage on their family fortunes. There are clear indications that their rebellion, when it broke out, took the king completely by surprise.[137]

Indeed, once the 1402 Christmas festivities were over, the royal household left Windsor, and on 28 January it was at Clarendon in Wiltshire, leisurely preparing for the arrival of Henry's new queen. On 3 February the king moved to Winchester and it was here on 7 February that

Henry formally married Joan of Navarre in the cathedral amid much pomp and lavish feasting. That the king could ill afford such luxury was not apparent, judging by the extravagant nature of the celebrations that followed. Despite the promise made by the November parliament to levy funds from the laity and the clergy, half already paid on 2 February and the rest to follow on 24 June 1403, the king seemed determined to follow English tradition no matter what the cost. Prenuptial extravagance would be expected, even of an impoverished king, and Henry had already experienced enough impoverishment and embarrassment in bringing Joan to England not to be parsimonious with his hospitality.

After the sumptuous wedding celebrations the king and queen journeyed to London, then to Westminster, where Joan was crowned and given an equally expensive coronation banquet. Jousts also accompanied the festivities, the young Earl of Warwick being appointed the queen's champion, an occasion that was illustrated in the extremely detailed *Beauchamp Pageant*, drawn later in the fifteenth century. In March 1403 the king was to lavish even more expense on his new queen by granting her an annual income of 10,000 marks, dating from the day of her marriage, a princely gift which again the royal finances could ill afford. All this, and more, disadvantaged Henry's treasury to such an extent that when the campaigning season began in March 1403 the contents of his war chest were practically non-existent.

Meanwhile, in the north, trouble was brewing between the Percys and the Nevilles. No settlement had been made after Homildon Hill with regard to the payment of the Earl of Westmorland's troops who, despite their leader's absence on the actual battlefield, had taken a full and active part in the conflict. Disputes had already begun to arise between both their bands of retainers over their respective claims on the captives still held in the Percys' northern strongholds, and this argument prompted the king to intervene by appointing a commission to arbitrate and decide upon the various claims of the two houses. However, by March 1403 the rival claimants could not help but take note of certain other messages that were arriving from London. Now that the annexation of Teviotdale was possible, whereby the English border could be further extended into Scottish territory as far as the River Tweed, new territorial gains were anticipated. King Henry, no doubt eager to quell the northern dispute over prisoners, and to further increase his own influence in the north, now acted with preposterous gratitude – he declared that the whole of the Douglas territory, along with the valleys of Teviotdale, Eskdale, Liddesdale, Lauderdale, Selkirk and Ettrick Forest, Annandale and Galloway, were to be conquered by the Percys.

On 2 March 1403 a proclamation was issued granting the entire newly annexed region to the Earl of Northumberland and his heirs forever – that is, providing he could capture it. Henry further reserved to the Earl of Westmorland all his existing possessions in the north, and he appropriated for himself the castles and towns of Roxburgh and Annan, together with general overlordship over the whole. The king's decision must have wounded Ralph Neville to the core, but it was not long before Hotspur was crossing the border to take possession of the newly annexed districts in his father's name. George Dunbar, Earl of March rode with him, as it is said that King Henry's ambitions extended even further north to 'the Scottish Sea' (the Firth of Forth) and that all lands formerly belonging to George Dunbar were fair game – again, if they could be conquered by the English. Anglo-Scottish peace treaties were fast becoming a thing of the past, and the Tower of Cocklaw, whose owner, James Gladstone, promptly refused to recognise English authority, became Hotspur's first target in his quest for fame.

The Percy chronicler, John Hardyng, was present at Cocklaw with Hotspur, as he was at Shrewsbury later that year. However, he makes no mention in his chronicle of the grim siege that ensued, probably because it was a dismal failure due to the staunch efforts of Gladstone who, it seems, had firmly put his faith in the efficiencies of stone and mortar rather than that of valour in the open field. Showers of arrows rained down on Cocklaw's walls, siege engines were brought up and mines dug, but all to no avail; the small garrison held out and Hotspur, caught in a similar situation to that experienced at Conway against the Tudor brothers, was forced into suspending the assault. In keeping with all the chivalrous nuances of the era, a six-week truce was offered to the Scots, providing that all the English siege works at Cocklaw remained in place. In the meantime, the besieged could apply to their king for help, but if this was not forthcoming by the following August, the tower, with all its contents, was ordered to be surrendered to the English. It was a similar story at the castle of Ormiston near Hawick – the Earl of Northumberland took hostages, but again it was agreed that the stronghold should be held to ransom. As far as the English were concerned it was hoped that all this might force the Scots to face them in 'open' battle, and that by this the Percys might extend their fame by forcing a second Homildon Hill. With such great possessions in Scotland just waiting to be conquered, it was the only possible solution open to the Percys, considering the enormity of the task in hand.

Unfortunately it was to be a long wait for all concerned, and the increasing financial burden on the Percys' already impoverished war effort would ultimately mean that further petitioning of the king's council would be required. In fact, on 30 May 1403 the Earl of Northumberland was forced to write a formal letter from Newcastle asking the council urgently for money. Meanwhile, Hotspur, no doubt finding the present situation increasingly frustrating, ravaged Teviotdale with George Dunbar close on his heels. Between them they drove off flocks of sheep and herds of cattle and captured those Scots who put up little resistance. However, despite their persistent efforts, it was destined that Hotspur would never see Cocklaw fall to the English; the tide was turning fast and Hotspur, judging by his present mood, was the man most likely to ride the first wave.

In Wales the spring brought with it news of further advances made by young Prince Henry. On 8 March he had been made the king's lieutenant in Wales, an appointment that to all intents and purposes superseded that of Hotspur made on 31 March the previous year. The prince had made Shrewsbury his headquarters and the counties of Shropshire, Worcester, Hereford and Gloucester supported him in a new offensive against Glyndwr. Soon the prince was able to report to his father that he had marched through Denbighshire with little resistance and that he had burnt to the ground Glyndwr's principal residence at Sycharth. After continuing to burn and plunder in Merioneth and Montgomery, the prince returned to Shrewsbury on 15 May; but Glyndwr was biding his time and, in fact, was about to go on the offensive.

On 30 May the Prince of Wales wrote to the king's council asking for payment for his men and pointing out the urgent need for relieving and provisioning the garrisons of Aberystwyth and Harlech which the Welsh had been long besieging. However, in much the same way as Hotspur had been given short shrift by Henry's council the previous year, the prince also found that Henry's government was not prepared to take any immediate action with regard to financial backing. On 6 June the castle and town of Carmarthen fell to Glyndwr, which prompted the king's former treasurer, Richard Kingston, now Archdeacon of Hereford, to write to the king in haste about the deteriorating situation in the marches of Wales: 'And for God's love, my liege Lord, think on your self and your estate, or by my troth all is lost; but ye come yourself with all haste and others with follow after. And on Friday last Carmarthen town was taken and burnt . . . and slain in the town of Carmarthen more than 100 persons . . . and I cry your mercy and put me in your high grace that I write so shortly; for by my troth that I owe to you, it is needful.'[138]

Despite the worries of the archdeacon, and the fact that Glyndwr was now moving freely about the principality, King Henry failed to show any outward signs of panic. On 16 June he sent orders to the sheriffs of Shropshire, Worcester, Gloucester and Hereford warning them to prepare to face the Welsh threat, but apart from these measures Henry demonstrated that he was in no mood to act foolishly by leading another abortive campaign against Glyndwr; he was, as always, short of money. With Prince Henry unable to move at Shrewsbury also due to lack of funds, Glyndwr saw his chance, and his dream of nationalism was suddenly realised as never before. However, the rising tide of Welsh patriotism was hindered by ambitions on the crown. While King Henry's leisurely itinerary was followed to the letter – Easter at Eltham, May and June at Windsor, Easthamstead and Henley, then London by way of Sutton and Kennington – Edmund Mortimer was receiving interesting messages in Wales from the Percys.

It is known that the Earl of Northumberland had been allowed to communicate with Mortimer and Glyndwr since the capture of his kinsman the previous year, and it is possible that John Morys, Worcester's servant, was the go-between, as probably the only man the Percys could trust with such delicate information. Apart from a constant stream of letters informing Mortimer about the progress of his ransom, the opening correspondence from the Percys must have been primarily from Hotspur's wife, Elizabeth, to her brother. However, the tone of these messages was soon about to change, and as a forerunner to the so-called 'Tripartite Indenture', signed between Mortimer, Glyndwr and Northumberland in

February 1405, the probable contents of these later letters – although none exist today – must have been about matters much closer to all their hearts, namely who should rule if Henry was deposed. The 1405 indenture ruled that if the king could be ousted from his throne, then the country should be divided into three 'equal' parts: Glyndwr ruling Wales, Northumberland presiding over the north, and Mortimer controlling southern England. The three principals also contracted in 1405, in a pact of mutual loyalty, to defend the realm against all invaders. But contrary to what history tells us was foreseen two years after Hotspur's death, it is possible that this treaty was at least mooted in 1403, hence the Percy rebellion of that year and the personalities involved. Evidently, this pre-contract of kingship left Hotspur out in the cold, but the inclusion and compliance of all the Percys was no doubt assured, considering the fact that they would all benefit from the fall of Henry IV and the final autonomy of their family in the north. All that had to be done was to plan the workings of usurpation, and it is likely that in 1403 this fateful conversion was stage-managed by none other than Thomas Percy, Earl of Worcester.

Logistically speaking, the Earl of Worcester had been extremely adept at provisioning and organising all civil and military expeditions for the last two monarchs. He had been Admiral of the Fleet, Captain of Calais, Justiciary of South Wales and, more importantly, Steward of the King's Household in the reign of Richard II. More recently, apart from having all his appointments under Richard confirmed by Henry IV, he had been Treasurer, Keeper of the Privy Seal and Governor of Aquitaine. In 1402 he had been the king's lieutenant in South Wales, had organised the return of Richard's queen to her father and had assisted in the transfer of Joan of Navarre to England at no small risk to his own life. In short, the Earl of Worcester had a proven track record of large-scale administration; he knew the workings of Henry's council, and he was the perfect insider to infiltrate Henry's government offices.

However, none of this explains why Thomas Percy deserted his king at the last moment. The Earl of Worcester had not taken sides previously against the king and it appears that, despite his close connections with Hotspur, he had not as yet taken offence at any of Henry's rebuffs aimed at curbing the financial and personal ambitions of his family. So what changed a once loyal and chivalrous man into a hated rebel? Thomas was much like his nephew Hotspur, although not as impetuous, but the answer to Thomas's treachery seems to lie in a measure of discontentment and unrewarded service, although this can be overruled by the fact that he was, before all this, a Percy, and would no doubt face his own blood in battle if he sided with the king.

Worcester was no doubt aware of what his elder brother was planning in the north and presumably acted according to his wishes, but what event (or sequence of events) forced the Earl of Northumberland over the edge in July 1403? Everything the earl had worked for over the years was to be committed to the hazard if he acted against the king. He had, after all, been instrumental in placing Henry on the throne. Could he trust Glyndwr and Mortimer implicitly? Would they keep to their side of the bargain when it finally came to blows? All this and more must have been coursing through the earl's mind at this time. Perhaps one more application for funds could be made to King Henry before it was too late. On 26 June the Earl of Northumberland wrote to his king personally from Healaugh in Yorkshire.

It was a strong letter, but in no way disrespectful or disloyal to the king. The earl even styled himself 'Your Mathathias', a pet name used by him in his correspondence to denote a close affinity with his king and hinting that the bond between them was still as resolute as ever. The king had already told the earl that some money would be sent to him, but he had not specified the amount – proof, if any were needed, that now something more fundamental had to be done to seize the money he was owed. On the other hand, Northumberland may have had no thoughts of rebellion in his mind when he wrote to Henry and, but for his impetuous son, all might have gone on as before. However, it is more likely that the aged earl was also frustrated with the king, although perhaps not as likely to act so impulsively as his son.

As for Hotspur, the shining star of all the aforementioned rebels, the temperature was steadily rising. Cooled momentarily in the shadow of the Cocklaw peel, he had already decided to give George Dunbar the slip with his personal retinue of trusted men-at-arms. John Hardyng accompanied the 'four score horse' that rode to Chester where Hotspur, 'purposed had Mortimer his coronoment'.[139] But as to the intentions of Hotspur at this point, we must briefly pause to take stock of Hardyng's poignant words regarding his master's intentions. According to Hardyng's own evidence, there was in fact no so-called 'Tripartite Indenture' in force; Hotspur's intention all along was that young Edmund, Earl of March should wear the 'coronoment'. From the very beginning of Henry's rule he had championed the Mortimer cause like a loyal subject, and as he saw it the workings of succession had not changed in the slightest. The Earl of March had been deprived of his right and he alone was to be the next king, something that was to be reiterated in the Percy manifesto presented to Henry immediately before the battle of Shrewsbury in July of that year. But what had Hotspur been told by his manipulative father? Was the kingdom to be shared between three men, or was it that only the young Earl of March should rule under Percy guidance? It seems that Hotspur was convinced of the latter – the question was, had Hotspur's father deceived him into believing that Mortimer would be king while a more covert plan of action was formulating, aided and abetted by the Earl of Worcester?

Meanwhile, Henry had no suspicions that anything was planned against his throne. He had set out from Kennington at the beginning of July, apparently on a normal summer itinerary, and on 10 July he wrote to the council that 'Master William Feriby, his chancellor, and John Waterton, esquire, have brought news of the successes of the prince which has given the king great pleasure. He orders the council to pay the Prince £1,000 as quickly as possible so that he may continue his campaign, because his men are about to desert for want of payment. The king himself proposes to go towards Scotland to assist the Earl of Northumberland and his son. Then he will go to Wales to suppress the rebellion.'[140]

The king, in accordance with his desire to help the Percys in the north, then continued to Leicester, where he dispatched another, more urgent, letter on 12 July to his council, ordering them not to issue any licences to leave the country. Henry also sent writs to the keepers of all English ports forbidding them to allow anyone to leave the country, and except for the officers of Calais and the march no one was to board a ship without the king's special leave. Further orders were put in place to prevent 'ill-words from reaching the king's enemies',[141] although who the king's enemies were at this time is open to question, considering that Hotspur had thrown off the mask and was already mustering an army.

After sidestepping the watchful Dunbar at Cocklaw, Hotspur had released Archibald Douglas and twenty other Scottish prisoners with the promise that the important border town of Berwick would be handed over to them if they supported his cause. All these men accompanied Percy through Yorkshire, where it is said that the Archbishop of York and many of the clergy favoured his movement. Hotspur's route through Percy territory may have provided him with more willing recruits to swell the ranks of his army; however, when Cheshire was reached there was only one way to increase his numbers substantially. Aided by a noted hermit, who was more than willing to do his duty where Hotspur had previously wielded great influence, the small rebel column was soon preceded by shouts and prophecies that Richard II was still alive. Championing the cause of Richard opened the floodgates to Chester, which Hotspur reached on Monday 9 July. No doubt he applauded the sight of the famous Cheshire archers as they swelled his ranks. Rummaging in their secret hiding places, the dead king's faithful servants soon donned Richard's white hart badge as a sign of fealty to their resurrected king – a miracle which Hotspur now had somehow to deliver.

Resurrecting the starved-to-death Richard was, of course, impossible. Many men knew that the former king was dead and that he had been reburied at Langley in 1400 after having been exposed to public gaze at St Paul's in February or March of the same year. However, since his death there had been a number of risings in his name and it was rumoured that he was exiled in Scotland. Even as late as Henry's third parliament there had been speculation that one of the Scottish prisoners brought to London by the Earl of Northumberland knew of the pseudo-Richard's whereabouts and that he had lately been in his charge. Henry had Lord Montgomery transferred backwards and forwards from Windsor to the Tower for some inexplicable reason, until in September 1403 he was incarcerated in the Tower indefinitely because he knew something of Richard's whereabouts. Richard's exact double also existed at this time, and it was thought that he may have been buried in place of the real king; therefore no one knew for certain what to believe, especially those of Richard's Cheshire bodyguard who had previously revered their master as a god.

For the moment, at least, Hotspur had the support of the region, but could he count on others to join his cause? The Percy chronicler, John Hardyng, briefly alludes to certain letters 'that were bounde to theim by their seales, except thele of Stafford; which letters I sawe in the castell of

Werkeworth, when I was constable of it under my lord, sir Robert Umfreuile, who had that castell of kyng Henry his gift, by forfeture of therle of Northumberland'.[142]

The authenticity of these letters of allegiance is dubious, but the fact that they once existed is proof of Hotspur's determination to gather all support available to him in England. According to Thomas Walsingham in his *Annals Ricardi Secundi et Henry Quarti*, the seals belonged to the Percys. In defence of their conspiracy, Hotspur and Thomas Percy had written 'to various nobles of the realm, as well as the people of the land, letters sealed with their own seals, asserting that the plan which they had put forward was not contrary to the allegiance or fealty which they had done to the king, and that they had not assembled an army for any other end, than to secure the enjoyment of personal safety, the reform of government, and the appointment of wise counsellors for the good of the king and the realm'.[143]

Indeed, many Englishmen may have sympathised with Hotspur and Worcester's intentions and instead of condemning the rebellion out of hand, one of Hardyng's stanzas provides an interesting story, substantiated by official accounts, that at Shrewsbury Hotspur and his uncle were betrayed by treacherous men:

> The lordes all of England had hym hight,
> And Owayn also on Severn hym to meet,
> Except therle of Stafford too young to fight,
> By their letters under their seales mete;
> But in the point they brake all their behete,
> And he was slain, and all the cause conselid
> Why he the field tooke and the kyng appelid.[144]

Hardyng's damning evidence features prominently later in our story. However, it is doubtful that any other leading nobles were involved in the rebellion at this point, apart from the Earl of Worcester, who soon arrived at Chester from Shrewsbury along with a contingent of Welsh archers sequestrated from the Prince of Wales.

In a show of independence similar to that displayed against Richard in 1399, Thomas Percy would now play a prominent role in the rebellion. He undoubtedly knew of his brother's probable plan to divide the nation into three, but it seems that now the die was cast there could only be one course of action open to him. He had already removed his treasure from London, and although not dismissed from office, as Shakespeare would have us believe, he had openly declared his intentions against the crown by deserting his post. If he did not act decisively alongside his family, all would be lost. He therefore decided to champion Hotspur's cause, even though he knew that there was another more grandiose plan afoot in the north and in Wales.

Thus, Hotspur's army rested in Chester on the night of 9 July 1403, waiting for more recruits to come in from the surrounding countryside. Percy lodged at the house of Petronilla Clark, whose son, John Kyngesley, was among the most devoted of his supporters. Many recruits paraded through Chester's gates in the following days – archers from Wales and Cheshire with their great bows of yew, and men from Rostherne, Hawarden, Pulford, Doddlestone, Hanley and Davenham, besides many Beestons, Leighs and Wenningtons and other great Cheshire names. They were all promised that they would see King Richard within a few days, surrounded by a great army led by the Earl of Northumberland. How wrong they were. In a few days the muster was complete and all pretence as to the real nature of the rebellion was cast aside in favour of immediate action. Richard was pronounced dead, and Hotspur proclaimed that he now meant to set England to rights. He declared that he had made a terrible mistake by helping Henry to the throne and now this would be rectified in blood. Edmund, Earl of March was the rightful king and Hotspur had the formal defiance in his mailed fist ready to deliver to 'Henry of Lancaster', renouncing his allegiance and charging him with perjury. Henry had lied on the sacred relics of Bridlington Priory and now Hotspur vowed with God's help to make good his words, in extremis if necessary.

Entrapped as they were by the feudal obligations they owed to their lords, and not knowing what service would be required until it was too late, some of Hotspur's levies no doubt felt betrayed by what had been said. John Kynaston, for example, had summoned the tenants of Lord Lestrange to attend their lord and the king. The men from the hundred of Ellesmere and the townships of Hampton Culmere and Hampton Wode followed their steward without question, but when Lestrange failed to show up at the promised muster point his men decided that they wished to return home. Under threats that they would be hanged, drawn or beheaded, Hotspur detained them and they were bullied into staying with the rebel army – such were the desperate measures of the final days before battle.

Meanwhile, the king had received the shock news that Hotspur was up in arms. He was at Derby on 13 and 14 July and the next day he was at Burton-upon-Trent, by coincidence ideally placed in the Midlands to deal with any military threat to his kingdom. Judging by Henry's diversion from Nottingham to Derby, he had probably received news of Hotspur's insurrection at either Leicester or Nottingham. However, on 17 July he sent an urgent message to London from Burton-upon-Trent:

> To the Council. The king encloses a letter drafted with the advice of the lords, knights and esquires at present in his company, to be sent to the Archbishop of Canterbury, all the prelates and lords temporal, to tell them of his plans, and let the council not fail in this. Henry Percy has risen against the king, calling him 'Henry of Lancaster', and has proclaimed that Richard is still alive. The king wants all members of the council wherever they may be to hasten to him, except the treasurer, who is to remain behind and raise all the loans he can.[145]

Attached to this letter was a note explaining that a member of the council, unnamed, had met the king's messenger hastening south on the Wednesday, the day after the letter was dispatched. The note explained that the anonymous councillor had opened the letter and read it before sending it on its way. On the same day Henry, then only accompanied by a small force of men-at-arms, ordered all the sheriffs of the Midland shires to raise their forces. He had to act swiftly, and in this respect he exceeded all his captains' expectations.

Sometime after the king had left Leicester, George Dunbar had arrived with a small force from the north. Dunbar probably warned Henry of the seriousness of the Percy threat and no doubt informed him that the Earl of Northumberland was party to the rebellion against him; after all, it would have been in Dunbar's interests to do so considering his rivalry with the Percys and the ultimate proportioning of their claims in Scotland. The crafty Scot may have also told the king that the Earl of Northumberland was gathering forces in Yorkshire, hoping to join his son, and that if Henry could act swiftly before both Percys united then he could crush them piecemeal. According to contemporary chroniclers this course of action was urged upon the king in the strongest terms for purely unselfish reasons; however, Dunbar must have gloried in telling the king of Percy treachery and his own loyalty to the English crown. Regardless of the vehemence that Dunbar displayed against his border counterparts, Henry only had two choices. He could wait until his army was fully mustered, or he could advance quickly in the hope of defeating Hotspur before the Percys were in a position to concentrate their army. Henry, it seems, had no hesitation in taking Dunbar's advice; he moved his contingents to Lichfield, now realising that he must link up with his son at Shrewsbury as soon as possible.

Now isolated and dispossessed of some of his soldiers seized by the Earl of Worcester, the Prince of Wales was in no position to venture out of Shrewsbury to join his father. However, he knew that his chosen headquarters would provide the ideal defensive bulwark against Hotspur's army if it chose to attack him – Shrewsbury being, in 1403, a comparatively large market town surrounded, as it is today, on three sides by a great meander in the River Severn. As a border outpost, the town was possessed of a strong castle that covered the only landward gate into England; it also had a fine network of walls breached only by two other gates that led to bridges over the river. Aptly described by John Leland in his Tudor *Itinerary* as standing 'on a rokky hill of stone of a sadde redd earth', Shrewsbury was in essence 'savinge a little pece . . . as it wer an isle'.[146] With its 'English Bridge' situated to the east of the town, and its 'Welsh Bridge', originally located to the west, forming the principal crossing place over the River Severn into Wales, the town was the main supply depot for English armies in the marches; therefore the prince might have been well pleased with his chance location against the gathering forces of Hotspur in the north and Glyndwr in the west.

It is assumed that by at least 19 July, Prince Henry would have been informed by his 'scourers' (scouts) that Hotspur's army was marching towards him. Setting his own standard immediately on the fly above Shrewsbury Castle, directly facing the only possible landward route that the rebels could take towards the town, the prince ordered the walls promptly manned by his troops. Gazing apprehensively across the flatlands of ridge and furrow that criss-crossed the outlying villages to the north, he could now only wait. Perhaps the prince hoped to see his father's standard advancing out of the early morning mist to aid him, but it soon became apparent that burning farms and houses heralded the approach of the rebel army and its fearless leader. Presently the man who had once been the prince's friend, mentor and comrade-in-arms would stand before him as a rebel and a traitor. What must the prince have thought of the situation? What possible explanation could Hotspur have for rebelling against the king? How could a man who embodied the very essence of chivalric honour turn his back on the hand that fed him? It is unfortunate that of the two men who had been most kind to him in his youth, and who had become to some extent the heroes of his boyhood, Hotspur should now have become Prince Hal's most dangerous enemy. The Prince of Wales had lost a father figure in the melée of 1399 in the guise of Richard the true, anointed King of England; now his warlike mentor was a declared rebel craving admittance to feed his army. What should he do?

It is difficult to fathom the clash of personalities that undoubtedly existed in the Shrewsbury campaign of 1403, but Prince Henry was by no means a witless pawn in the events that were ultimately to climax in battle the next day. After all, he was sixteen years old and quite recently he had shown that he was well capable of military command, independent of his father. As a leader of men the prince was a charismatic figure by all accounts: he had proved himself against the Welsh and was already a warrior quite capable of leading his men 'unto the breach' without a second thought. His scouts had almost certainly informed him that he would be reinforced by his father very soon, and he probably knew the position in Wales with regard to Owain Glyndwr's movements better than most. However, despite all his innermost feelings for the famous Hotspur, he knew the seriousness of the situation: his adviser the Earl of Worcester had, after all, deserted him to join the rebels and both he and Hotspur had to be dealt with or the prince's authority would always be questioned when he finally became king. In short, he had to act like a prince; he had to bar the gates against his former mentor and sit tight.

As for Hotspur, he was determined to achieve a meeting with Glyndwr. By capturing Shrewsbury from the prince, the Welsh might cross the River Severn, and thereby his strength would be dramatically increased against the king. As probably promised by his uncle, Worcester, the meeting of the two forces had been planned for weeks. Mortimer would lead the way, in the name of the young Earl of March, and with Glyndwr in support, the White Lion of Mortimer would stake his all in the coming fight for the throne. Worcester probably failed to mention that a prophecy had been submitted with regard to their bold venture, and that according to the Welsh bards, the 'lion', despite its reference to the Percy badge, was not Hotspur:

> And now after these shall come out of the north a Dragon [Glyndwr] and a Wolf [Mortimer], the which shall be the help of the Lion [Percy], and bring the realm great rest with peace and glory, with the most joy and triumph that the like was never seen this many years before. . . . These three shall rise against the Moldewarpe [Henry IV], which is accursed of God. . . . Also, they shall thrust him forth from the realm, and the Moldewarpe shall flee and take ship to save himself, for he shall have no more power over this realm; and after that he shall be glad to give the third part of his realm to have the fourth in peace, but he shall not get it, for the will of God is that no man shall have mercy but he that is merciful.[147]

Considering the ambiguities of the phrasing, it is nonetheless astounding that the prophecy is so accurate in determining the intended course of action of the leading protagonists in 1403. However, whatever Worcester knew of its real or prophetic symbolism, it was apparent from the Percy manifesto delivered to King Henry before the battle of Shrewsbury that Hotspur never intended to adopt the tripartite idea. As far as he was concerned there could only be one rightful king of England, and that was young Edmund, Earl of March.

As the evening sun grazed the salient crenellations of Shrewsbury Castle, Hotspur may have seen his young apprentice, the prince, organising his troops against him. The men from Cheshire were already looting the suburbs and firing its houses; however, little did Hotspur know that at that

172

very moment the king's army was ominously crossing the English bridge into Shrewsbury on the opposite side of the 'gentle Severn's sedgy bank'. Soon the prince's feathers would be replaced by the king's royal standard, leaving Hotspur little choice but to beat the retreat northward and seek a better place to stand and fight.

ELEVEN

Bull Field: 21 July 1403

Medieval battlefields are notoriously difficult to pinpoint with any accuracy. What occurred on them is equally hard to analyse, given the appalling lack of tactical evidence contained in some of the chronicles. Add to this the truth that any landscape is constantly changing with the passage of time, and the military historian is left feeling decidedly let down by the sheer weight of problems at hand.

For a few fleeting hours battlefields bore witness to the maximum amount of human activity, pursued at the greatest risk, at the highest possible price. The fact that medieval battles were fought in comparatively small areas also frustrates the chances of finding them, and even leads to making mistakes as to their location. Given that terrain features, field names and even whole areas have changed since the Enclosure Acts of the eighteenth and nineteenth centuries, what remains to research is perhaps best expressed as the 'ghost' of a battle: a fleeting glimpse of history outlined in the shadow of a hill, in the humped ridges of an ancient field system, in the weather-beaten stones of a extant medieval building, or even perhaps in the shallow depressions in the land that mark the position of medieval war graves.

In some cases a battlefield memorial or cross may have been erected to denote where the fighting took place; indeed, such monuments dot the topography of Britain like symbolic drops of blood in the ever-changing landscape. Essentially, a battlefield memorial is a poignant epitaph to the men who fought and died at a specific place, and even if their 'headstone' has not been erected in exactly the right spot, these latter-day cenotaphs to fallen comrades have invariably become the only reminders of our military heritage – a heritage that is best not forgotten lest we overlook the fact that invasion, civil war and terrorism were as prevalent then as they are today. Erected by individuals who may have known of the fighting first hand, or

174

by curious Victorian antiquarians, historical societies, and even forward-thinking modern-day borough councils, battlefield memorials undoubtedly aim to help preserve the memory of an undeniably grim moment in history. However, despite the controversy surrounding their erection, they are our only link with the past, and hence we need to preserve them in context with the land they commemorate.

To pinpoint battlefields with even greater accuracy is an ongoing challenge. The contest is fierce, the results conflicting and open to endless criticism, but consistently there has been no lack of interest in the search, or the resulting erudition. Like the greatest case of mass murder, a battlefield can be compared to a cordoned-off crime scene and thus the historian must sift through the evidence, follow every clue in the pursuit of his passion, formulate an opinion as to what occurred there, and ultimately put his theory on the line. The 'personal' memorial he creates is a permanent reminder of the event he expounds, and therefore it is as solid and as lasting as any stone obelisk or battle stone erected in an open field. Subsequent evidence may point to a different location and in some cases the debate might bring the carefully constructed theory crashing down around the historian's ears, but this is the nature of battlefield detective work, and thankfully the work goes on, surely the true memorial to those who fought in any given engagement.

The essential history of Shrewsbury battlefield is much like any other, but its uniqueness lies in the fact that the actual site was identified only a few years after the dead were cleared from the field. Unlike the battles of Otterburn and Homildon Hill, fought on the far-flung borders of medieval England, Hotspur's last pitched battle was fought just outside a Shropshire market town; therefore, it was accessible to the curious right from the start. Consequently, it was soon decided that a lasting memorial needed to be built where the battle took place, and in the case of Shrewsbury this was a church, a place where the faithful could pray for the king and the souls of the dead who had died in the fighting. Today this grand memorial stands in quiet meadows three and a half miles north of the town and it has the honour of pinpointing at least part of the site where the battle took place. However, to get closer to the actual area (or areas) of conflict we have to dig much deeper into recorded history; only by establishing why the church was built in the first place can we proceed to analyse the opening positions of both armies and hence their movements on the afternoon of 21 August 1403. In order to do this it is necessary to briefly leap forward in time to after the battle of Shrewsbury, with the clearing of the dead from the field, and the digging of war graves.

Contemporary chroniclers tell us that after the battle the surrounding countryside was littered with thousands of bloated corpses covering an area of about three miles. Considering that the battle and its subsequent rout had lasted until nightfall, it is highly likely that the clearing-up operation would have taken place the following day, the main concentrations of dead being in the vicinity of the fiercest action. Once the dead were enclosed in the clay soil, the once-peaceful meadows bordering the road from Shrewsbury to Whitchurch would have returned to normal almost immediately, apart from the more physical scars of battle: a series of shallow mounds that many locals may have hailed as the place where their king had so very nearly lost his crown.

Chief among the individuals who may have taken an interest in the site were those who had fought there, those who lived adjacent to the field, and almost certainly those of a chivalric class who understood the significance of the events that had taken place there. By coincidence, in 1403 there was a large manor house situated just over half a mile west of the battlefield, owned by the Hussey family, and hence the present name, Albright Hussey, has a direct link with not only the locale, but also with the medieval family who probably witnessed the battle first hand, virtually in their own back yard. The Hussey manor had a small chantry chapel attached to it dedicated to St John the Baptist, and in 1403 the rector was Roger Ive of Seaton, who had held this parochial position since about 1398. Ive, or his master Richard Hussey, seems to have taken a distinct interest in the battlefield for reasons that remain somewhat blurred. Maybe Hussey fought for the king, or perhaps he had purely humane reasons for his subsequent actions. However, soon after the battle, Richard Hussey as '*domini de Adbrigton-Hussee*' signed over to Roger Ive a portion of his land so that a memorial chapel could be erected to the dead. A royal licence, issued by Henry IV on 28 October 1406, granting two acres of Hussey land, 'situated in the field called *Bateleyfield* [now Battlefield] in which a battle had lately been fought between the king and Henry Percy deceased and other rebels',[148] was therefore set aside, and building work started on a lasting memorial to the fallen. The subsequent chapel, built on the recognised battle site, was dedicated to St Mary Magdalene, due to the fact that the conflict was fought on 21 July (the feast of St Praxedes, or the eve of St Mary Magdalene). Hence a permanent memorial to the battle was founded in the quaintly named Bateleyfield and its war graves marked quite precisely in the two-acre rectangular field some three and a half miles north of Shrewsbury.

Oddly enough this parcel of land may have been partially moated, as according to a later charter, granted by Henry IV in 1410, the ground was then 'enclosed by a ditch, containing in length and breadth two acres of land, together with two inlets and outlets, one extending along the lands of Richard Hussee twenty feet, and the other containing in breadth fifteen feet',[149] a curious statement to make if Bateleyfield was just another nondescript field previously used for arable farming. The inlets and outlets over the ditch quite clearly indicate that at least by 1410 the original field had been enclosed. Indeed, by this date there were other buildings on the site, namely a small secular college run by its principal or master, Roger Ive, along with five chaplains, together with a hospital for the poor, of which Henry IV was the benefactor.

Roger Ive was the first of seven successive masters of what became known as Battlefield College, the last of these being John Hussey, a member of the original founding family. Sadly, in the reign of Edward VI the Hussey family lost control of the college, and after being granted back to the king by parliament, the school was promptly closed down. John Leland, the great Tudor traveller and topographer, was probably the last English antiquarian to see the battlefield 'complex' in its heyday when he visited Shrewsbury sometime between 1535 and 1543. He recorded in his *Itinerary* that 'Batelfild chapel is a mile out of Shrobbesbyri by north. Kinge Henry the 4 foundyd this litle colledge, and endowed it. A gentleman called . . . [Hussey] . . . who was owner of the ground whereon it was builded had the patronage thereof geven to him and his heires.'[150]

Today, no vestige of Leland's 'litle' college remains, but it probably occupied a portion of land immediately to the south or west of Battlefield church, where today various undulations in the ground indicate that medieval buildings may once have stood there. However, the moat or ditch that surrounded both college and church and enclosed the site can still be traced, and hence the area once known as Bateleyfield can be positioned on a map with great accuracy. Richard Brooke, the great battlefield antiquarian, identified the moat's existence in the 1850s, 'as straight as a canal', and with 'an abrupt angle at each end',[151] although he was not able to trace its course on the west side of the enclosure due to the fact that here the ditch had been filled in. As for the inlets and outlets traversing the enclosure, these were clearly the entrance and exit points of a track that once extended across the Hussey lands from the main Whitchurch road in the east to Albright Hussey in the west.

Other field names connected with the battle of Shrewsbury also give us a much clearer picture of the ground over which the two armies fought. These are Hateley Field (undoubtedly a corruption of Bateleyfield), Old Field, Husifield, King's Croft, and more interestingly an area known as Bull Field in the township of Harlescott. Nineteenth-century maps of Shrewsbury show Old Heath, Old Farm, and various other permutations on the name 'old', located to the south of Battlefield church, and this has given rise to theories of alternative battle sites not consistent with the traditional area of conflict.

John Speed's map of Shropshire, dated between 1596 and 1610, states clearly that the battle of Shrewsbury took place in an area then known as Olfeilde, which at first glance might suggest that the name 'Old Field' was intended. However, the possible omission of a capital 'B' may denote that Olfeilde was in fact a corruption of Boleffyld (that is, Bull Field in 1403) and hence the names have simply been misinterpreted. Similarly, Husifield was a large field to the west or south-west of Battlefield church, it then being owned, like Bateleyfield, by the Hussey family (Richard Hussey in 1403), before being transferred to the Corbet family in 1638. However, the name King's Croft is undeniably a name given to a field sometime after the battle was fought, it being situated to the south-east of Battlefield church and bordering the Whitchurch road. Known as the 'traditional' position of King Henry's right 'battle', King's Croft was almost certainly part of a much more extensive field system that, in all likelihood, was called Bull Field in 1403. Bull Field is therefore the more accurate medieval field name associated with the battle, given the fact that most official sources used this name to pinpoint where the battle of Shrewsbury had taken place.

In the *Great Chronicle of London*, for example, where notes by successive authors provide elucidatory or supplementary remarks to more important yearly entries, a paragraph in faded red ink indicates that the 'Batayll of Shroysbery' was fought 'in a ffyeld then namyd Boleffyeld and now Batayll ffeyld wheryn stanyth a chapel ffoundid In worship of seynt Mary Magdaleyn by a Revelacion made to kyng Henry the iiii'.[152] This addition clearly indicates that Boleffyeld and Bateleyfield were one and the same, as was Olfeilde and 'a field called Hayteleyfeld',[153] where Hotspur's army took up position prior to the conflict.

Considering that vast quantities of human bones were discovered sometime prior to 1857, when a drain was dug to carry off water from the Corbet vault located in Battlefield church, it may be assumed that it was here, and in the aforementioned 'corrupted' field name location, that the heaviest fighting took place in 1403. This premise is based on the fact that, if practicable, medieval battlefield graves were dug very close to the main action (or actions), soil levels not deterring local labourers from interring the dead in even the shallowest or hardest of ground if the need was great. The fact that a manuscript states that a pit was made for the slain, 160 feet long by 68 feet wide to the north of Battlefield church, also adds weight to the theory that this building was erected extremely close to – if not actually on – the original mass graves of 1403. Admittedly, some of the Shrewsbury dead were buried elsewhere if the scale of the rout is to be believed, but on the whole documentary evidence proves quite conclusively that the church site is the most important link to the area once known as Bolefield (Bull Field) – that is, a field once owned by Richard Hussey and partitioned off to Roger Ive in 1406. The building of a lasting memorial on, or near, relatively fresh mass war graves, and the fact that Battlefield church was originally built some distance from the main Whitchurch road, also adds considerable weight to the traditional site being the most authentic one.

The name Bolefield is our most direct link with Hotspur's last battle even though the manoeuvres during the day, and more evidently, after the fight, certainly encompassed a much wider area generally referred to in official accounts as simply 'a plain near Shrewsbury'. However, apart from this generalisation, can we take our investigations one stage further by saying that Bolefield was an actual medieval field name synonymous with an open space used for grazing cattle? Certainly the name 'Bull Field' suggests that it was, and the mention of a ditched enclosure may indicate that this was a place where bulls were kept apart from the rest of the herd. If nothing else, the most likely explanation certainly brings the battlefield into much sharper focus, given that Bolefield was also situated at the base of a more arable medieval field system that, according to contemporary sources, climbed the northern slopes away from the present church, and was filled with crops.

Bull Field, by its association with Bateleyfield, was therefore not only the scene of the fiercest action on 21 July 1403, but also the most likely place where the battle ended. However, where did Hotspur embattle his forces to face the royal army? What was the extent of his position, and what advantages, if any, did the ground offer him against an army similarly equipped with the most formidable weapon of the day – the bow? It is clear that in order to clarify these and other related problems we must return to the events of 1403 and Hotspur's shock discovery that the king's army had entered Shrewsbury before him.

By this time it must have become abundantly clear to both Hotspur and his uncle, the Earl of Worcester, that the king now held a distinct advantage over them. Henry, by entering Shrewsbury over the English Bridge, had managed to block the Percys' path across the Severn and consequently there was now only one choice left open to them. If they were ever to increase their own strength against the king's forces then their only hope was to find a crossing over the Severn elsewhere. That the Percys were outnumbered, in the open, and vulnerable to attack was bad enough, but if Glyndwr's Welsh contingents did not reinforce them as promised, then some form of advantage must be sought elsewhere, preferably north of Shrewsbury in order to redress the balance. It was imperative that the rebel army retired to a more defensible position where they could make a stand while still retaining their vital lines of communication with the north.

But what ground was available to Hotspur? Should he retreat north to link up with his father who, it is said, was then mustering his forces in Yorkshire, or should he wait at the agreed meeting place for Glyndwr's Welsh contingents to cross the Severn at some other point? There was no question of retreat as far as Hotspur was concerned, but where could he use the skill of his Cheshire archers to maximum effect? Unfortunately, contrary to what is popularly believed to have taken place the following day, Hotspur's last battlefield was found more by accident than design.

It is generally accepted that the battle of Shrewsbury was fought on the eve of St Mary Magdalene's day, that is, Saturday 21 July 1403, but alternative scenarios have been put forward to explain the movements of the armies prior to the engagement. These opinions are mainly based on two local traditions: firstly, that on the night before the battle the rebel army was encamped in the vicinity of Berwick, a small hamlet situated on the eastern bank of the Severn about two miles north-west of Shrewsbury; and secondly, that on the same night the king's forces are said to have been positioned at Haughmond Abbey, three and a half miles north-east of the town.

Scenario one, the accepted version, specifies that after taking the road from Chester to Sandiway, the rebels' muster point, Hotspur first marched his army south to Whitchurch, and passing through Wem arrived at the Castle Foregate before Shrewsbury on 19/20 July. Finding that the king had reinforced the prince's garrison only a few hours before, Hotspur then decided to retreat to more favourable ground north-west of Shrewsbury, namely the village of Berwick, where he spent the night in a house owned by the Betton family. The following day, apprised that the king's forces were close at hand, Hotspur marched his army due east to Harlescott, then due north to the position later called Battlefield, where he decided to make a stand on sloping ground north of the present church.

But what caused this rapid change of direction from Shrewsbury to Berwick and then to Battlefield in the face of the enemy? Why was Berwick village chosen as a suitable place to spend the night, it being barely a mile from the king's forces and in a position where Hotspur had his back to the River Severn? If we believe that Hotspur could have made such a simple error of judgement in the heat of the moment, are we to believe that his uncle, Thomas Percy, the veteran of so many battles in France, could have also made the same basic mistake? Perhaps the rebels were planning to cross the Severn elsewhere to make contact with Glyndwr, but to what end? Surely the royal forces would have been immediately informed of their position and would have marched swiftly across the Welsh Bridge at Shrewsbury to cut off Hotspur's advance. Therefore, at face value at least, the Berwick manoeuvre is highly suspect, apart from the intriguing story of a soothsayer's prophecy and the whereabouts of a lost sword.

According to Thomas Walsingham, on the day of battle (21 July) Hotspur bid his page gird him with the sword he had worn at Homildon Hill, and on being informed that the weapon had been left overnight at 'little Berwick', Hotspur changed colour, exclaiming, 'Now I see that my ploughshare is drawing to its last furrow, for a soothsayer once told me in my own country that I should perish at Berwick. Alas! he deceived me by that name, which I believed to mean Berwick in the north!'[154]

E.B. de Fonblanque in his *Annals of the House of Percy* notes the incredible coincidence that Hotspur's first and last feat of arms should be associated with the border town of his youth. However, if the infamous soothsayer's prophecy can be dismissed as a fantastic flight of fancy then the ill omen of a lost sword is perhaps more worthy of belief if only to place Hotspur (and his army) at the village of Berwick the night before the battle. The reason for this change of location can only be attributed to one possible detail – that Hotspur was unsure of Glyndwr's position and was desperate to make contact with him before the king's army could bring him to battle. To do this a messenger had to be sent across the River Severn in the hope that Glyndwr and Mortimer could be located somewhere on the other side. Unfortunately for Hotspur, Glyndwr was at that moment some 100 miles away at Carmarthen consulting with a well-known seer. There would be no reinforcement of the rebel army due to widespread flooding in the Welsh valleys, and contrary to what had been planned so meticulously in the weeks preceding their rebellion, Hotspur and his uncle were now well and truly on their own.

As for the preliminary movements of the king's army before the battle, they can be traced up to a point by official documents. Henry was at Burton upon Trent between 15 and 17 July mustering his forces, Stafford or Lichfield on 18 and 19 July and finally at Shrewsbury on 20 and 21 July, the royal army covering the last thirty-two miles from Stafford to Shrewsbury in a single day's march. According to some sources the king was at Haughmond Abbey the night before the battle, and on Saturday 21 July he marched his forces due west to Battlefield, where Hotspur had taken up position in Hateley Field. Presumably, according to this scenario, Henry had previously linked up with his son's forces somewhere outside Shrewsbury on the morning of the battle, but again these later movements by the royal army are conjectural, the last march from Stafford to Haughmond Abbey and Battlefield lacking any firm evidence. The notion that Hotspur's army was in the vicinity of Lichfield on or about 17 July can also be discredited, chiefly due to the fact that the rebels were undoubtedly trying to link up with Glyndwr in Wales via the Severn crossing at Shrewsbury; and also that the king's army was actually at Lichfield between 16 and 17 July, making any such approach march by Hotspur decidedly foolish, given that his intention at this point was reinforcement, not actual engagement.

Scenario two, supported by official documents, including Henry's Household Accounts, asserts that after the king had got word of Hotspur's rebellion at either Leicester or Nottingham, he immediately changed direction and marched to Derby. A letter dated 14 July was sent to the mayor and citizens of Coventry from Nottingham indicating that he intended to march to Chester and Wales, 'to meet Henry Percy who has risen in rebellion'. However, on 15 July Henry had reached Burton upon Trent where again an official letter, dated 17 July, was dispatched to Henry's council informing them that, with the exception of the treasurer, all of its members were 'to hasten to him' as quickly as possible. According to Henry's Household Accounts, the king had already reached Lichfield on 16 July, giving credence to the possibility that all these royal dispatches were probably sent the day after the king had moved on to his next muster point. To arrive at Shrewsbury on 20 July, therefore, the royal army had only to march fifty miles from Lichfield in three days. Even allowing for the possibility that Henry was still at Burton on 17 July, the added sixteen miles from the latter to Lichfield was still well within the capabilities of a medieval army – that is, provided that Henry did not march to Haughmond Abbey by way of Stafford, and instead crossed the River Severn at Atcham before marching on Shrewsbury.

The truth about both approach marches will perhaps never be fully known, but it is clear that when Henry crossed the Severn into Shrewsbury, Hotspur had little choice but to fall back to more favourable ground. According to some chronicles, a degree of skirmishing had already occurred in the suburbs of Shrewsbury, and preserving what was left of his extremely fickle army was no doubt Hotspur's main concern at this time. With the terrible prospect of being caught in an unprepared position, the rebels marched first to Berwick, in order to try to locate the whereabouts of Glyndwr and Mortimer by means of the Shelton ford, and then at first light turned north-east to try to gain the Whitchurch road so that the army might not be cut off with its back to the river. Hotspur now realised that speed would be of the essence. He presumably also knew that rising ground was to be found north of Shrewsbury; however, the fact that he came across the perfect position for his archers was probably owed to one of Hotspur's eagle-eyed scourers who, due to the close proximity of the king, were presumably sent out ahead of his army to reconnoitre the ground.

Passing through the village of Harlescott in the hope of finding more favourable terrain to the north, the rebels could only hope that they had enough time to gain the more advantageous escarpment that rose gently from the Shrewsbury plain like a great sleeping animal. It was not long before the Percys saw the distinctive ridge of ground running east–west between the Whitchurch road and Albright Hussey that would soon become the battlefield of Shrewsbury. It was by incredible luck that the slope on which the rebel army chose to make a stand was running at right angles to their intended line of march; more incredible still was the fact that the slopes above Bull Field were planted with a tangle of mature crops that might also protect their contingents of archers from a cavalry attack.

Saturday afternoon must have seemed like a black day to Hotspur, even though the weather was probably fair and temperate for the time of year. In all probability Percy had been apprised privately that Glyndwr was in no position to aid his cause and that help from his father was totally out of the question. All memories of Otterburn could hardly have slipped Hotspur's mind as the advancing hours heralded an afternoon of dreadful uncertainty. Once again he was isolated and in an extremely vulnerable position. He probably felt let down by everyone except those who now stood by him under their respective banners. John Hardyng, who was present at Shrewsbury with his master, later wrote that he felt that Percy was not only deceived by his supporters, but also by his father, who 'came not out of Northumberland, but failed hym foule without witte or rede'.[155] However, as Hotspur waited for the king's banners to appear out of the afternoon haze he paid no heed to those whom he thought might desert him. His impetuosity was goading him; something was driving him on to deliver his manifesto to the king, or the Lancastrian dynasty would completely eradicate the Mortimer claim to the throne without a single drop of blood being shed in its defence.

According to John Hardyng, Hotspur considered that Henry IV was guilty of perjury; he was a usurper, and as a true knight, his former friend and comrade of St Inglevert had failed to honour the workings of ransom. Despite a few faint hearts in Hotspur's ranks, his Welsh and Cheshire archers were renowned for being the best shots in the kingdom, and they also had something else to prove. Most of them knew that their precious Richard was now dead, but they cherished his memory and no doubt many of them vowed to bring his murderer to justice at the end of their cloth-yard arrows. Even the redoubtable Earl of Douglas was eager for battle with the English king, and especially with George Dunbar, whose severed head might solve a great many problems in lowland Scotland. As for Thomas Percy, the veteran of so many similar 'finest hours' in France, he knew the situation all too well. Like his nephew, he accepted that rebellion was a terrible crime, but his needs were great and he was determined to see it through now that he had nothing left to lose. Already he could see the tell-tale signs that Hotspur was spoiling for a fight. Kingmaking was a game that required guts and nerve, and the Percys had acquired plenty of both in the revolution of 1399. On the other hand, Hotspur's need to prove himself was even greater than that of his ambitious uncle. He could almost hear the parental chains and manacles of his youth falling from his body like great leaden weights to the ground. Now, like a true and chivalrous knight, he was free to right the wrongs of 1399 in blood; now he could lift the personal guilt of Richard's demise from his armoured shoulders and assert his claim to greatness on the field of honour, if not with words then with feats of arms. The supreme test of strength that all true knights yearned for was imminent. In truth, Hotspur had no greater wish than to fulfil his destiny in a battle royal for the prize of the crown of England.

ARMIES AND PARLEYS

By mid-afternoon both armies were in sight of each other. The royal army had at last showed itself, and it was steadily progressing up the Whitchurch road in the usual three 'battle' formations that most medieval armies adopted for both marching towards the enemy and for attacking it in the field. The van, the middle and the rear of Henry's force had most likely 'peeled off' the main road quite early that morning in anticipation of a pre-emptive cavalry charge by the rebel army; the flat meadows below Hotspur's position provided a clear advantage to horsemen if they could catch their victims unawares, exposed and out of formation. However, the battle of Shrewsbury was to be far from a hit-and-run border action involving cavalry, and the manoeuvres necessary to embattle the king's army in line abreast were probably carried out at a leisurely pace in the fields later known as King's Croft, Battlefield and Hussey Field with all the pomp and extravagance of a royal pageant.

Hotspur, encouraging his army on the slopes known later as Hateley Field, would have had an excellent view of the masses of men and horses now forming up below him. Taking in the appearance of three irregular, but well-ordered blocks of soldiery, there would have been no indication at first that any violent action was intended until, at about 300 yards distant, flashes of protruding steel and burnished helmets warned that this was to be no mere ceremonial procession. Fluttering banners and standards of war flaunted the ranks of Henry's loyal nobility, while ancient badges and family mottoes told of many years of military service on more distant fields in France. Lesser knights, some only dubbed earlier that morning by the king, sported the very latest designs in plate armour, while their local captains in composite layers of protection commanded local contingents gaudily clad in coloured liveries and corporate insignia. Leather jerkins brushed against silk-covered jupons sporting heraldic devices of fabulous beasts, while bits of rusty old armour acquired on numerous other battlefields identified the veterans of Henry's army who knew the paths of glory like the backs of their scarred and once-bloody hands.

Town levies with jackets stuffed with tow, iron and mail shared the same space as yeomen archers wearing aketons, close-fitting metal caps and camail hoods. Other lesser archers, wearing little more than the traditional garb of the day, had already rolled their leggings down to their knees due to the summer heat. Practically defenceless, and lacking in any plate armour, they stood with their comrades at the forefront of the royal army where they set about inspecting their arrow bags and sturdy bows with meticulous pride. Some of their number had already hammered sharpened wooden stakes into the ground to protect themselves against possible cavalry attack while others were busy checking their hand weapons so that that they might better defend themselves when their trusty bow had done its deadly work.

It was a sight to snap the nerves of many a raw recruit or unsure rebel soldier stationed on the slopes of Hateley Field, but all of Hotspur's men were mesmerised by the hypnotic ordering of ranks and the rhythmic beat of the drum. It was only when the king's army finally halted, motionless before them, that the reality of the situation drew sharply into focus. When the trumpets sounded the arrival of the king and his son, each rebel knew his crime intimately. Clad in a fabulous jupon bearing the arms of England, the king was an awesome sight, intended to shock his enemies to the bone, so much so that a contingent of Hotspur's men, captained by Richard Horkesley (know sometimes as Richard Ramkyn), decided to desert Hotspur's army by immediately rushing forward to find safety among the king's men. The royal vaward, to the forefront of King Henry's army, opened up to receive Ramkyn and his contingent with a huge cheer of self-satisfaction.

Probably extending some 1,000 yards in length between the Whitchurch road and Albright Hussey in the west, the royal front line was most probably positioned parallel to the modern edifice of Battlefield church and was wholly composed of archers under the command of Edmund, Earl of Stafford, then twenty-five years of age and only that day named Constable of England. The middle ward, under the king's direct command, probably took up its final position behind Stafford's archers to the right of the army covering the area later known as King's Croft and part of the field soon to be given the celebrated name of Bateleyfield. The Prince of Wales, to the left of his father, would have naturally commanded the rearward 'battle' stationed to some extent in Bateleyfield, but extending westward into the fields bordering Hussey Field.

It is not known for certain exactly where Henry's main captains were positioned when the battle began, but it is clear from what occurred later in the day that most of the king's household men were eventually found fighting in an extremely restricted area around the royal standard. George Dunbar, for example, figures significantly in the final phase of the battle, as do men like Sir Walter Blount and three other unnamed persons, armed in all respects like the king and acting as decoys, dressed in the king's livery. The men who were killed in this final act of confusion all probably fell in Bateleyfield, although it is possible that the Earl of Stafford was killed quite early on in the fighting, chiefly due to the carnage caused by the opening archery duel on the tangled slopes of Hateley Field.

As for the rebel position, it is known that at least part of Hotspur's line stood behind a large field of ripening crops. The chroniclers Otterbourne and Walsingham vividly describe this field as being planted with *pisis adultis* (mature peas)[156] which apparently severely hampered the royal assault and to a greater extent enabled Hotspur's Cheshire and Welsh archers to rain a terrible slaughter on their enemies advancing up the slope to meet them. However, apart from this piece of vital horticultural evidence we have no actual information as to the battle formation adopted by the rebel army except to say that Hotspur's troops were most probably similarly deployed in three independent battles under local knights or captains each commanding locally raised contingents. In Hotspur's army were northerners, Welsh archers and contingents from Chester, Derby and Flint, along with a host of other provincial militias who either sympathised with Hotspur's cause or were pressed into service because of it. No doubt Thomas Percy commanded the body of men he had appropriated from the Prince of Wales at Shrewsbury, and as for the Earl of Douglas and the twenty Scots who had accompanied him out of captivity, they were probably given free rein of the field, provided that the Douglas strategy fell well within the bounds of reason. It is recorded that notable captains such as Sir Richard Venables and Sir Richard Vernon were also present in Hotspur's ranks, and due to widespread recruitment, the county of Cheshire was well represented by men who commanded large followings in Richard's former principality. However, the focus of rebel attention surely must have been on the men whose county had raised the best archers in the land – the 'White Hart' contingents of Cheshire archers – who no doubt would be tasked with breaking up the enemy advance prior to an all-arms assault on King Henry's vulnerable position.

Most of the Cheshiremen who had accompanied Hotspur to Shrewsbury had previously served Richard II in his notorious corps of archers. Their sole purpose had been to guard the king against his enemies, but it is clear that from 1397 the Cheshire archers had also become a law unto themselves, owing allegiance to nothing and no one, save their royal master. Regularly and highly paid by the king (a rare luxury for medieval soldiers in any era), they had gained a fearsome reputation for terrorising the countryside with their unruly and disreputable behaviour. The 'corps' was even permitted to treat the king with great familiarity, to the extent of addressing him to his face by the affectionate nickname of 'Dickon' (Dick) whenever they saw fit.

Wherever Richard went, day or night, his infamous Cheshire archers went with him. Various accounts list their strength, their numbers fluctuating from 200 to 300 men to over 760 men in times of particular need. In 1397 Adam of Usk records that 4,000 of Richard's Cheshire archers surrounded Parliament House, while the Monk of Evesham records that 2,000 archers 'thought that some quarrel or dissension had broken out there, and, bending their bows, drew their arrows back to their ears and, to the terror of everyone present, began to shoot'.[157] Adam of Usk goes on to say that Richard's archers only drew back their bows as if to shoot, but it is clear from what contemporary chroniclers said about them that the Cheshiremen were feared even by the bravest of the king's own household servants. In fact, many chroniclers blamed Richard's bodyguard of archers for his downfall. Thomas Walsingham gives a lasting impression of the kind of men that fronted Hotspur's army in Hateley Field on the afternoon of 21 July 1403:

These Cheshiremen were ready to commit every sort of crime, and their shamelessness soon increased to the point where they regarded only the king as their equal, treating everybody else, however powerful or noble he was, with contempt. Yet they themselves were by no means gentle-born, but rustics, or shoemakers and suchlike, people who within their own localities were scarcely regarded as worthy to pull off their masters' boots; here, however, they thought themselves to be peers and equal of lords. And so greatly did their unwarranted pride, distain, and cruel insolence grow, that before long, when travelling through the realm with the king, either within the royal household or apart from it, they began to beat and wound with impunity the king's faithful subjects; some indeed, with extraordinary cruelty, they even killed. They also seized people's goods, paying nothing for their provisions, and raped and ravished both married and unmarried women, for no one dared to stand up to them.[158]

Although Hotspur's combined contingent of archers probably amounted to 7,000 or 8,000 in 1403, at least half of these were men from Cheshire (probably from 2,000 to 3,000 is perhaps nearer the mark, given that 2,000 men figure in two official manuscripts regarding wages, the named archers being divided into 7 squadrons of 44 to 46 men under 7 leaders called Masters of the Watches).[159] Sporting silver brooches of their former king's livery, the white hart, they were humbly born but highly paid marksmen well acquainted with the rigours and hardships of medieval life. Their experience with the bow was certainly beyond the norm as it was then understood, so they were used to drawing the very heaviest war bows available, making this 'secret weapon' of the rebel army feared by almost every man facing them in the royal army. Their use of the bow and their cold-blooded reputation for cruelty had made the men of Cheshire invulnerable while Richard lived. In death, they were remembered as his elite force, their permanence and notoriety being recognised as a chilling reminder of any official bodyguard linked to a tyrant whose rule was built on fear and oppression.

Somehow, Hotspur had tamed the insolence of the Cheshiremen with a clever combination of discipline and understanding. By punishing their audacity in 1339 when they harassed Bolingbroke's baggage train en route to London, he had asserted a measure of power over them that has never been fully acknowledged by historians. By repaying their boldness in kind, an alliance had been forged and this greatly aided Hotspur's cause in 1403, to the extent that some of the more belligerent Cheshire archers were probably prepared to die for him and the memory of their former paymaster without a second thought. This respect and self-sacrifice is hard to explain, other than to say that Hotspur empathised with their feelings against Henry IV. It is almost as if he knew that he would need Richard's archers in years to come and was in fact paving the way for rebellion as early as 1399. However, now that the Cheshire archers were facing the usurper who had murdered their beloved king, what feelings of intense hatred flowed through their minds as the hour came to exact their vengeance?

Viewing their enemy from the slightly elevated position of Hateley Field, the rebels knew that tactically the royal position was vulnerable to attack, especially from a downhill charge by determined troops. But contrary to what is asserted by J.H. Ramsay in *Lancaster and York*, it is extremely unlikely that Henry's army (positioned as it was at the base of the slope) was restricted from movement in any appreciable way. The grouping of three small ponds, which were no doubt dug a very long time after the battle was fought, caused Ramsay to mistake another topographical feature in Andrew Wyntoun's chronicle, and spread the much-misinterpreted idea that the royal army was divided into two battles instead of the more usual three, common to medieval armies of the period. A.H. Burne, writing in the early 1950s, and R. Brooke, writing in 1957, both mention the presence of water in the place later known as Bateleyfield (that is, the area where the battlefield 'complex' was built). Therefore we can safely assume, given the unusual position of the ponds, that these are the remnants of a later age, and certainly not obstacles that pre-date the battle. It is clear that these hazards did not hinder movement in 1403, nor did they obstruct the progress of the royal army by splitting their array into two or even three separate divisions.

However, it is possible that there was a feature in 1403 that hampered the movement of both armies to a certain degree, and this may have been a slight bank or ditch extending east–west at the base of the slope bordering Hateley Field and Bull Field. According to A.H. Burne, 'The probable explanation of Ramsay's theory of the ponds is a passage in the *Scottichroniconi* that the king's army has to pass through a *strictum passum*. . . . Wyntoun, writing far away in Scotland, may have pictured the Shropshire terrain as similar to his own mountainous country; but it is more likely that the word was used in the usual medieval sense of a temporary narrowing in the approach, such as a ford, bridge or sunken road.'[160]

Although Burne's ideas are far from conclusive, the *strictum passum* (restricted way) mentioned in Wyntoun's text is interesting if it is taken to mean the road or the field of peas that fronted Hotspur's army. However, another meaning gives us cause to question whether a slight bank or trench ran parallel to the north side of the present lane leading to the church. Brooke saw this entrenchment in the 1950s bordering the extremities of King's Croft (in 1403, Bull Field), but he took it to be the remains of entrenchments made by Hotspur's army prior to the battle. Ditches and banks were intended to divide livestock from crops in the medieval period; therefore it is possible that some form of obstruction did indeed exist at the time of the battle and that it ran at the base of the slope separating Bull Field from Hateley Field, the latter, according to chroniclers, being sown with mature peas. These twin obstacles of crops and ditches would have undoubtedly hindered both armies if they chose to advance first; therefore, if battle could not be avoided then it was clearly up to the king to initiate the attack on the enemy position before any forms of impetuosity by Hotspur could lead to a clear advantage in this distinctly unfavourable ground.

Although there was a minority of faint hearts that had betrayed the rebel army while the armies faced each other that afternoon, John Hardyng's claim that Hotspur commanded a well-disciplined army has stood the test of time. As an independent eyewitness to the battle that followed, there is every reason to believe that the Percy chronicler also knew the approximate composition and strength of the rebel army first hand as he claims that:

> With Percy was the erle of Worcester,
> With nyne thousonde of gentyls all that wer,
> Of knyghtes, squyers, and chosen yomanry,
> And archers fyne, withouten Raskaldry.[161]

It is likely then that the combined strength of the rebel army was probably somewhere in the region of 9,000 to 10,000 men, with the king's forces slightly larger in comparison. Although most medieval chroniclers tended to exaggerate numbers of combatants to fulfil the needs of personal or propagandist issues, Thomas Walsingham's conservative estimate of 14,000 men for the royal army comes closer than most. Other estimates vary from 30,000 to 60,000 for Henry's army, while the Scots chronicler, Andrew Wyntoun, gives Hotspur 'twenty thousand Ynglis men, at Schrewis-bery gadryte then', and estimates that 'thretty thousand or ma than, wes with ye King of Inglendis men',[162] both extremely large armies that, given the urgency and time allowed for mustering, may be discarded as pure embellishment.

With regard to numbers of men in the king's army, we may also take into account that on 17 July 1403 Henry IV made payments to 4 barons, 20 knights, 476 esquires, and 2,500 archers (3000 men in all) who had recently enrolled in the royal army. The payments, presumably made at Burton upon Trent on 17 July, amounted to £8,108, a figure that at face value gives us some idea of the size of King Henry's army at this time. However, these wages do not include payments made to men who had already accompanied the king from Nottingham to Burton, nor does it account for any levies liable to enlist in the royal army at Lichfield or on the final march towards Shrewsbury. Given that the Prince of Wales commanded a much-depleted force of garrison troops at Shrewsbury, we may be sure that any calculation over 14,000 for the king's army is excessive, this being one of the main reasons why Henry chose to close with his adversaries as soon as possible, before they could be reinforced by their allies.

To the last, however, the king shrank from accepting battle. His army was prepared for action, his archers ready to attack the rebel position, his men-at-arms willing to die for him if need be, but something else was preventing Henry from advancing his banner and committing his cause and quarrel to Almighty God. Deciding to parley with the rebels first, probably against the wishes of men like George Dunbar who had everything to gain from crushing the Percys, he sent forward two notaries to try to avert the shedding of 'Christian blood'. These two illustrious messengers were Thomas Prestbury, the Abbot of Shrewsbury, and Henry's clerk of the privy seal who, Walsingham says, 'served as a delegation on behalf of the king, to offer Henry [Percy] peace and pardon, if he would desist from his adventure'.[163]

Hotspur was probably very surprised to hear that the king wished to parley with him, given the obvious disparity in numbers and that both armies had just witnessed an unruly desertion in Hotspur's ranks. However, after receiving the king's men, there seems to have been a certain willingness to negotiate on behalf of the rebels, although Hotspur refused to confer with the king in person. Instead, Walsingham states that Hotspur's uncle was sent to deliver the Percy manifesto to Henry and explain the reasons for their rebellion. It was to be Hotspur's greatest and, as it turned out, most fatal mistake according to historians, although at the time, due to the friction that no doubt still existed between him and the king, it was thought the best thing to do under the circumstances.

As previously explained, Thomas Percy was the most capable administrator in England and had been well known for his diplomatic missions abroad, as well as for his way with words, his courtesy, his chivalry, and, above all, his political acumen in very delicate matters of state. In short, the famous Earl of Worcester was the perfect man to have on your side in a tight corner. The most pertinent question, though, remains far from conclusive or proven and that is, what actually occurred in the king's presence late that afternoon to make the honourable Earl of Worcester spin a pack of lies to his impetuous nephew so that he yearned and thirsted for battle? Why did the most able and honourable of Henry's ex-officials want the king misrepresented at the eleventh hour? Was this an attempt at further kingmaking by Worcester, or was it perhaps that Thomas Percy was not involved in the mediations at all and became a scapegoat for Hotspur's notable impetuosity?

It is clear that the battle of Shrewsbury began after several hours of waiting and protracted negotiation. Thomas Walsingham stated in his chronicle that the Percy manifesto had been previously dispatched to various nobles of the realm in order to try to win their support, and that it was not delivered to King Henry on the battlefield in any formal way. However, after Henry's delegation had said their piece in Hateley Field under a flag of truce, the chronicler Walsingham reports that Thomas Percy was sent to explain the causes of the rebellion and to demand a real reformation of Henry's government. Walsingham claims that the earl was in a particularly autocratic frame of mind at the time and, 'when the king had condescended as far as reason would allow and had humiliated himself otherwise than became a king, Thomas Percy returned to his nephew and reported the contrary of the royal replies; thus he inflamed the mind of the young man [Hotspur] and impelled him to battle, even though he was reluctant to fight'.[164]

In effect, Walsingham was chiefly responsible for blackening the Earl of Worcester's good name and for causing Hotspur's famous reaction, claiming that his uncle had been 'the originator of all the evil and the cause of the present misfortune'.[165] Later historians such as Raphael Holinshed followed Walsingham's lead to add to the confusion and hence Shakespeare perpetrated the legend. However, another chronicler has a different story to tell. John Hardyng was insistent that he saw the Percy manifesto dispatched to King Henry 'in the felde'[166] by two of Hotspur's squires, Thomas Knayton and Roger Salvayn, and that Hotspur's uncle played no further part in the negotiations prior to the battle. In fact, Hardyng does not mention Worcester's name at all in connection with any of the preliminary talks; he simply states that, 'after long trete the prince began to fight',[167] which if nothing else betrays the fact that Hotspur did not begin the battle of Shrewsbury falsely egged on by Worcester, but that the king, or more precisely, the Prince of Wales, made the first move.

Why did the king instigate his son's advance up the slope? Quite simply he had read the wording of the Percy manifesto delivered by Hotspur's esquires, charging him with perjury. The Percys claimed vehemently:

. . . that when thou after thine exile diddest enter England thou madest an oath to us upon the Holy Gospels, boldly touched and kissed by thee at Doncaster, that thou wouldest never claim the crown, kingdom or state royal, but only thine own proper inheritance and the inheritance of thy wife in England; and that Richard our sovereign lord the king and thine, should reign during his term of life, governed by the good council of the lords spiritual and temporal . . . WHEREFORE THOU ART FORSWORNE AND FALSE.

. . . that where thou sworest upon the same Gospels in the same place and time to us that thou wouldest not suffer any monies to be levied of the clergy, nor fifteenths on the people, nor any other tallies and taxes to be levied on the realm of England on behalf of the realm during thy life, but by the consideration of the three estates of the realm, except for great need in causes of importance . . . WHEREFORE THOU ART PERJURED AND FALSE.

. . . that thou hast caused the same our Sovereign Lord and thine, King Richard, traitorously within the Castle of Pomfret, without the consent or judgement of the Lords of the Realm, by the space of fifteen days and so many nights (which is horrible among Christian people to be heard) with hunger thirst and cold to perish, to be murdered. WHEREFORE THOU ART PERJURED AND FALSE.

. . . that thou at that time, when our Sovereign Lord and thine, King Richard, was horribly murdered as above said, thou by extorted power, diddest usurp and take the kingdom of England, and the name and the honour of kingdom of France, unjustly and wrongfully, contrary to thine oath, from Edmund Mortimer, Earl of March and of Ulster, then next direct heir of England and of France immediately by due course of inheritance after the decease of the aforesaid Richard. WHEREFORE THOU ART PERJURED AND FALSE.

. . . that thou fraudulently and contrary to the law of England and thy council, have written almost through every shire in England to choose such knights for to hold a parliament as shall be for thy pleasure and purpose, so that in thy parliaments no justice should be ministered against thy mind, in these our complaints now moved.

Also we do allege, say and intend to prove, that when Edmund Mortimer, Earl of March and Ulster, was taken prisoner by Owen Glendor in a pitched and foughten field, and cast into prison and laid with iron fetters, for thy matter and cause, whom falsely thou hast proclaimed willingly to yield himself prisoner to the said Owen Glendor, and neither wouldest deliver him thyself, nor yet suffer us, his kinsmen, to ransom and deliver him, yet notwithstanding we have not only concluded and agreed with the same Owen for his ransom at our proper charges and expenses, but also for a peace between thee and the said Owen. Why hast thou then not only published and declared us traitors, but also craftily and deceitfully imagined purposed and conspired the utter destruction and confusion of our persons. For the which cause we defy thee, thy supporters and accomplices as common traitors and destroyers of the realm, and the invaders, oppressors and confounders of the very true and right heirs of the crown of England, which thing we intend with our hands to prove this day, Almighty God helping us.[168]

It was a challenge that demanded no further words of mediation between the two sides. It is extremely doubtful that the Earl of Worcester ever negotiated with the king prior to, or even after, the Percy manifesto was delivered; worded in the strongest possible terms, there was clearly nothing else to explain or deliberate about. The rebels had stated their quarrel quite plainly to the king, and now Henry had to act quickly in order to crush Hotspur's forces before the combined armies of Percy, Mortimer and Glyndwr could arrive on the field.

Probably the young Prince of Wales had already asked his father if he might lead the first wave of attack on the enemy position. However, as he sped back to his waiting 'battle' and dismounted from his warhorse, sword in hand, the future Henry V must have wondered what it would be like to face his former mentor in battle. When it finally came to blows and Hotspur was before him, would he slay him without a second thought?

Would all his respect for Hotspur fade when the drums beat the advance? Indeed, would all resemblance of friendship and memory blur in the melee of clashing steel? Nothing was certain any more, but at least Prince Henry was about to learn an extremely valuable lesson that Hotspur could never have taught him in Wales – for once in his life the victor of Agincourt was about to feel what it was like to be on the receiving end of an English arrow storm.

ENGLISHMEN AGAINST ENGLISHMEN

There is no doubt that the battle of Shrewsbury was fought in a very similar fashion to a battle in the Wars of the Roses, both armies being similarly equipped with bows, hand weapons and armour; both commanders having similar tactical ideas practised in France and on the borders of the kingdom; and both with previous knowledge that unsupported cavalry charges were useless against massed ranks of archery. Incredible disarray and casualties could be perpetrated by the bow in the opening few minutes of battle, but still the tactic, even by the end of the Wars of the Roses, was for commanders to line up their men in three divisions, bows to the fore, and face the terrible archery duel that ultimately preceded, and to some extent dictated, the initial moves of a battle. The hard slog and indiscriminate slaughter of the resulting free-for-all was a contest of stamina that beggars description, but modern research and chronicled evidence has consistently shown that (especially during the Wars of the Roses) it was the side that advanced first that very often lost the resulting hand-to-hand phase of the battle.

Any major movement of medieval battles during the Wars of the Roses was dictated by the use of massed archery. The side that was getting the worst of the arrow storm invariably had to move forward or simply retreat in disarray – there was no other course of action open to dense formations of infantry struck by a withering hail of plummeting arrow shafts arriving in successive volleys on their position. It was the task of massed archery to somehow win this shooting match, but the vawards of both armies had first to move into range in order to compete with the other. This forward movement of men, gauged by the draw weight of the bow and the type and weight of arrows used, more often than not determined what the no-man's-land between the two armies would be, and this killing zone was especially marked out at the battle of Shrewsbury by the importance of the aforementioned field of peas.

This tangle of vegetation must have severely hampered the progress of the royal archers, more noticeably so as the first silhouetted arrow shafts hailed down on them from Hotspur's serried ranks. As the range between the two armies narrowed, so the confusion in the royal ranks increased, forcing Henry's men to make a stand or be shot to pieces where they stood. No doubt up to their ankles in a veritable quagmire of roots and tendrils, Stafford's archers now had to unleash a number of successive volleys of their own. It was a terrible position to be in, but somehow the rebel shooting had to be matched until either side had either run out of arrows or had yielded to a greater weight of casualties. Thomas Walsingham vividly describes how devastatingly effective, and fatally destructive, this continuous arrow storm was to the king's side: 'Therefore the archers of Henry Percy began the fight and the place for the arrows was not on the ground . . . for men fell on the king's side as fast as leaves fall in autumn after hoar frost. Nor did the king's archers fail to do their work, but sent a shower of sharp points against their adversaries.'[169]

Contests between bodies of massed archers never lasted for a long period of time. Apart from the logistical problem of arrow supplies being exhausted after only a few minutes of continuous shooting, the resulting carnage perpetrated by the bow was too difficult for any body of men to bear indefinitely. In only about five to ten minutes of shooting, for example, the forty-eight arrows carried by the royal archers would have been expended, each archer being able to draw his bow an average of about eight times in one minute under ideal conditions. Situated much closer to their own supplies than the royal army, Hotspur's archers may have been able to command a more substantial arrow supply than their opponents; however, it is clear that under no circumstances was this phase of the battle a long-drawn-out affair dictated by skill at the archery butt. The medieval archery duel was a test of endurance, experience, luck, and more than anything else, the will to survive under incredibly disorientating conditions.

Modern ballistic research has shown that heavy war arrows falling at angles of 45 to 90 degrees would easily pierce medieval leather jerkins, mail, and the more partial armour of the period. Medieval arrowheads of

4 ounces in weight would easily shatter human bone and damage plate armour to the point of penetrating the metal and entering the flesh beneath. Once an individual was hit, the force of the arrow would immediately disable and shock him; it would render him useless further shooting and, if unprotected by more substantial plate armour, it would probably kill him where he stood. Many men in the royal army would have been fatally wounded in the face, head or arms. Legs and feet would also have been exposed to the arrow storm, making the resulting 'dance of death' an appalling sight to behold and a terrible ordeal to endure without respite. Most men would have been hit by more than one arrow, some may have even tried to remove them from their bloody wounds, so that they might be able to return fire, or ultimately escape the killing zone. But all, whether wounded or still shooting, would not have experienced anything like it on an English battlefield – indeed, the scene of terrible mayhem had never been seen before on English soil.

In the Wars of the Roses the medieval arrow storm was expected and dealt with accordingly by both soldiers and commanders alike. At the battle of Shrewsbury it is no wonder that part of the royal vaward collapsed under the increasing pressure dealt by the bow and arrow. Due to their unenviable position in the field of peas, coupled with the undoubted skill of Hotspur's Cheshire archers, Henry's men were in no position to advance in any concerted way. They began to fall back in some disorder.

Whether any enemy arrows struck the Earl of Stafford, or indeed the Prince of Wales, during the opening archery duel is open to debate, but if either man was disabled by falling arrows then this would explain why part of the royal vaward chose to retreat down the slope, their commander's presence being imperative both for coordinating shooting and for keeping morale high among their men. However, it is said that at some point during the battle of Shrewsbury 4,000 of the king's men actually fled the field, something that might be accounted for after the devastating effect of losing a commander under such disorientating conditions.

As for the Prince of Wales, it is known with some certainty that he was hit in the face by an arrow, even though the timing of this injury is not known precisely. Both Thomas Walsingham and Thomas Elmham later referred to the prince's wound in their chronicles, and that in spite of this injury he managed to fight on. But can we believe that this statement is true, given the power of the bow and the penetrative force of a 30-inch arrow shaft? If Prince Henry was wounded in the face, then surely it was by a ricocheting or splintering arrow rather than a direct hit. A glancing blow would have been bad enough under the circumstances, but nothing compared to the damage that would have been inflicted by a direct hit. The fact that Prince Henry was not killed outright implies that he was left with a severe wound that did not impair his fighting ability nor, as it transpired, his quick thinking. In fact, shortly after this, contrary to those who would have Prince Hal fighting with an arrow protruding from his face, Henry was to lead the most significant manoeuvre of the whole battle.

Meanwhile, the excitable rebel archers cheered and edged forward when they saw their adversaries retreating down the hill. Even though Hotspur knew that his own ranks had been severely depleted by the ferociousness of the archery duel, he was now determined to use the terrain to his advantage. To the cry of 'Esperance Percy!' the rebel army was ordered to advance en masse, and Hotspur, free from all the restrictions previously placed on him by his family, immediately launched an all-arms assault on the king's standard. It was no accident that the resulting headlong charge broke into the royal line in the field that was later called Bateleyfield. According to Thomas Walsingham, 'Henry Percy, leader of the opposite army, and the Earl of Douglas, than whom no one was ever more spirited, in spite of the rain of arrows and the dense bodies of horsemen, urged their men against the king's person alone, and concentrated all their arms on him.'[170]

Evidently, while the rebels were executing this impetuous charge, the Prince of Wales was regrouping some of Stafford's routing archers who were trying desperately to escape the field. Consolidating his position, along with his own men-at-arms on his father's left, the prince now had to wipe all memories from his mind and turn the tables on his former mentor, using the only tactic that was now open to him. Advancing against Hotspur's right, which was by then fully committed to fighting with the king's militia, the wounded prince led his men yet again across the arrow-and-body-strewn slopes of Hateley Field. According to Edward Hall, 'The prince Henry that daie holpe muche his father, for although he wer sore wounded in the face with an arow, yet he never ceased ether to fight where the battail was moste strongest, or to courage his men when their hertes was moste danted.'[171]

The highly intelligent manoeuvre by the sixteen-year-old prince certainly had the desired effect. Soon, he and his men were pushing back Hotspur's right, and forcing the rebel flank upon its centre, resulting in what can only be described as a domino effect in the rebel army. Hotspur's men were now enclosed on two sides, and as a result of the terrible crush, both armies became so packed together that falling men were not only dying of their wounds, but also from the effects of suffocation.

Apart from the fact that now most men were fighting with hand weapons, it is also apparent that at least some of the prince's archers may have been able to shoot discarded arrows into confused masses of men that were now being pushed back. Groups of horsemen, according to Thomas Walsingham, towered over the sea of foot soldiers to add to the chaos, and apart from the butchery and horror that always accompanied the later stages of a medieval battle, the vulnerability of those who remained mounted, including possibly Hotspur, must now have been called into question. Most knights, by the Wars of the Roses, would choose to fight on foot rather than risk exposure to the lowly archer and his bow. However, Shrewsbury was a transitional battle in many ways, the like of which had not been seen since Evesham in 1265, and consequently there was a considerable lack of civil war experience on both sides to counteract the arrogance of the mounted medieval knight. Englishmen had yet to deal with the very weapon they had developed so effectively and had employed so dramatically in France, but at Shrewsbury there was no precedent and the real power of the bow was most effective when aimed at masses of men drawn together in a crowd.

Through all this mayhem, it is clear that Hotspur had his eyes fixed on the king's standard, wavering above the packed ranks of steel, and as luck would have it Henry appeared to be fighting, in true medieval fashion, at the forefront of his men; his standard pinpointed his exact location like a multicoloured sail in a stormy sea. The prince's flank attack was still pushing the rebels back and Hotspur, determined to end the battle quickly by killing the king, immediately saw his chance to prove his worth. In a fit of determined recklessness it is said that he gathered thirty of his best men to cut a pathway through the thicket of weapon-points that churned before him. Along with Archibald Douglas, his detachment eased a furrow through their own men until they ploughed into the royal troops, hacking and slashing at everything before them. Hotspur's last act of impetuosity was to have a strange and tragic outcome, and it was ironic that George Dunbar, Percy's old adversary at Otterburn, was instrumental in his final downfall. Thomas Walsingham again takes up the story: 'When the Earl of Dunbar had guessed their designs, he withdrew the king from his position at the front. This deed saved the king's life, for the royal standard bearer was felled by the fury of the enemy, and his banner thrown down, and those who stood round him were killed.'[172]

Among those who were killed by Hotspur and Douglas at this point were the Earl of Stafford, 'undir the kynges baner',[173] and Sir Walter Blount, a knight of the king's household. With the royal standard-bearer butchered and his priceless trophy torn and trampled under foot by the advancing rebels, it was not long before cries of 'The king is dead!' rose from Hotspur's ranks. However, when the reality of the situation revealed that a trick had been played on Hotspur, elation quickly turned to desperation when another 'king' was spotted fighting close by him. Adam of Usk recorded what he heard of the clever deception perpetrated by the royal army: 'There fell also two noble knights in the king's armour, each made conspicuous as though a second king, having been placed for the king's safety in the rear line of battle. Whereat the earl of Douglas of Scotland, then being in the field with the said lord Henry [Percy], as his captive, when he heard victory shouted for king Henry, cried in wonder: "Have I not slain two king Henries (meaning the said knights) with mine own hand? Tis an evil hour for us that a third yet lives to be our victor."'[174]

Edward Hall, writing in the Tudor period, affirms the curious legend that a number of decoy kings were used at Shrewsbury in order to confuse the rebels, a possibility that might be construed as contrary to what we might expect of a medieval king who was fighting to protect his throne. Indeed, was this unchivalrous act actually arranged before the battle commenced? Can we believe that Henry IV, one of the most chivalrous knights of his age, stooped so low as to favour deception over valour? How would the king explain this fraud afterwards? Might he not be taken for a coward who preferred that other knights might die in his place while he directed his army from the rear? In short, what are we to make of this outrageous behaviour that some later chroniclers state was such a salient feature of the battle?

Thomas Walsingham makes no mention of decoy kings, only that George Dunbar managed to remove the king from the melee for his own safety. Henry had apparently slain thirty-six men with his own hand and was in great danger not only of being surrounded by his enemies, but also of being overcome by exhaustion. However, more interesting are the claims of Adam of Usk and the author of the *Scotichroniconi* who maintain the decoy story. Usk had recently been exiled from England and was no advocate of King Henry's rule, and the *Scotichroniconi* was obviously biased against the English side in more ways than one. Indeed, at face value, both decoy stories smack of propaganda against Henry and his Scottish adviser George Dunbar; that is, however, unless we look at the deception from a different angle: namely that just one man was wearing a duplicate of the royal jupon over his armour.

The author of *Gregory's Chronicle* heard that 'the Earle of Stafforde was slayne in the kyngys cote armure undyr his baner and many mo lordys and knyghtes loste thre lyvys',[175] a clear indication that Stafford was the only man to adopt this changed role. By swapping his own livery for the king's royal jupon while Henry was being extracted from the fiercest fighting, the pretence of majesty could be maintained at the forefront of the royal battle line, but for how long? Evidently, it was long enough to enable George Dunbar to remove Henry from danger without any appreciable loss of morale. However, with the Earl Stafford now dead and the king's banner no longer visible above the metallic mayhem of battle, some royalists in Stafford's immediate retinue must have faltered, the rebels once again gaining the upper hand in the gathering gloom of Bateleyfield.

As the sun gradually began to set in the west and an eerie black shadow edged silently across the face of a ghostly moon, the hoarse cry from the rebels of 'Henry Percy king!' probably caused King Henry some concern, and he immediately decided to rejoin the fight. Accompanied by his household men, and no doubt his saviour George Dunbar, the king would have known that the battle would now be a test of sheer strength and endurance. Most men would not have recognised that it was gradually becoming darker, but those non-combatants who saw the total eclipse of the moon on 21 July 1403 probably took it for a bad omen. Those men in the rear ranks of both armies who were not fighting must have stood aghast at what they saw in the cloudless sky. It was barely eight-thirty and the hot July evening was ending prematurely with an atmospheric phenomenon that was guaranteed to induce extreme foreboding in those of both sides.

The battle was finely balanced when the bright evening sunlight was abruptly snuffed out and a sombre half-light replaced the certainty of day. A great many of Henry's chief supporters had already been killed and trampled under foot, but to Hotspur and some of his loyal followers the one-to-one carnage must have seemed reminiscent of the night battle at Otterburn. Archibald Douglas, like many of his illustrious forebears, was still smashing his great axe or 'clava' against anything that stood in his path. There was no question of giving up the fight, but the rebels were frantically trying to slice their way out of being totally surrounded by the prince's men, and the rest of Henry's beleaguered army were gradually retreating due to the confusion surrounding his apparent death. However, because of his impetuous attack on the king's person, Hotspur and his thirty loyal men-at-arms had now become isolated from the rest of the rebel host and Henry soon capitalised on this situation as the deadly wavering struggle entered its final bloody phase.

THE DEATH OF THE CRESCENT MOON

The death of Harry Hotspur is portrayed in Shakespeare's *Henry IV Part I* as the tragic end to a reckless life, founded, in part, on the pursuit of fame and fired by the insatiable need to right the wrongs that had been committed against his house and the Mortimer family. However, Shakespeare's 'Hotspur Mars in swaddling clothes . . . robbed of his youth' cannot be taken too literally. As previously stated, Henry Percy was no 'infant warrior' but a battle-hardened veteran of some thirty-six years old when he died at Shrewsbury in 1403, and despite Shakespeare's dramatic rendering of Hotspur's death at the hands of Prince Hal, the truth of Percy's demise remains far from conclusive. Even contemporary chroniclers were uncertain who was actually responsible for killing him, while Thomas Walsingham concluded that 'while he led his men in the fight rashly penetrating the enemy hosts, [Henry Percy] was unexpectedly cut down, by whose hand it is not known'.[176] Adam of Usk stated that 'In this battle the said lord Percy, the flower and glory of the chivalry of Christendom, fell, alas! and with him his uncle. Whereby is the prophecy fulfilled: "The cast-off beast shall carry away the two horns of the moon."'[177] But whatever the circumstances of Hotspur's death, it is clear that no one knew exactly who killed him, something that is wholly in keeping with all the confused and disorientating aspects of medieval hand-to-hand combat.

However, following popular belief, it is highly likely that when the battle was at its height Hotspur, sweating profusely from the sheer physical exertion of fighting, removed his helmet and was struck in the head by either a hand weapon or possibly an arrow shot from the ranks of Prince Henry's enveloping archers. At this point in the battle most men would have been fighting on foot, pressed together, neither side yielding more than a few yards of ground to the other. Still, it will be remembered that, according to Thomas Walsingham, some knights had managed to retain their mounts during the battle, and if Hotspur was one of these more exposed targets, fighting above the multitude, then surely he would have been singled out for execution more than any other, his heraldic banner pinpointing his whereabouts in his overzealous push towards the king.

As the full moon began to enter the earth's umbral cone towards the phenomenon known to later astronomers as 'totality', cries of 'Henry Percy dead!' began to echo from the royal ranks. The lunar face had by now turned blood red, and as Hotspur's last impetuous charge faltered he was completely surrounded and dragged from his battered horse. In a mass of falling bodies and weapons Percy's final gasps of life were probably expelled beneath the advancing hoard of royalist troops trampling over him and his fallen banner. After their leader had fallen in the crush, shouts of 'Esperance Percy!' were heard no more in Bateleyfield. It was now up to the rebels to make their escape into the night, and according to Walsingham this they were allowed to do, as a result of the uncertainty posed by the advance of night.

Under such disorientating circumstances the rout would have been an uncertain scramble for cover, and many wounded soldiers would have been massacred purely for what they carried with them. The hunt for plunder would be a frenzied affair and exacerbated by the need to be repaid in some way for the ordeal the royalists had just been through. A squire of the Duchess of Norfolk, weighed down by his armour, was forced to crawl on his hands and knees under a hedge. Panting for air and trying to staunch the flow of blood from an injury, he could only wait for the rout to end. Unlike others, trapped in far worse predicaments, the duchess's squire was one of only a few who would see the light of day again. Surviving the 'pilours' or strippers who prowled among the bodies, dispatching the wounded and looting the dead was one thing, but later to write his account of the battle in the *Annals of Richard II and Henry IV* was nothing short of miraculous. However, many more of the rebel host were to be captured almost immediately, although the threat of arrest became less of a reality as the last remnants of Hotspur's renegade army cleared Bateleyfield and continued their flight up the Whitchurch road.

The king's men had already apprehended some of the main instigators of the rebellion, and the Earl of Worcester and a number of Cheshire lords were tied to their horses and led to the rear. The Earl of Douglas too had been tracked down. Having fallen from a nearby rock he had sustained yet another wound, this time to one of his 'cullions' (testicles). However, despite the fall of Hotspur it was still not clear which side had gained the field, and many men, according to the chroniclers, collapsed in mixed heaps, weary, beaten and bleeding. In accepting the possibility of either victory or defeat, those who had endured approximately three hours of fighting were in no position to continue. The dreadful battle had taken its toll on both sides. The dead could neither be counted nor buried under such impossible circumstances. Even the wandering heralds were uncertain how to fulfil their usual task of identifying the nobles from the common man. Such was the end of a bloody day – 'one of the wyrste bataylys that ever came to Inglonde, and [the] unkyndyst',[178] according to *Gregory's Chronicle*; a day, 'rather to be celebrated with tears than triumphs',[179] as Speed would later write.

TWELVE

Yorkshire: 1403–8

When the corpse of Hotspur was eventually found in Bateleyfield it is said that the king shed tears over it, grieving for the death of his erstwhile friend. However, with hindsight (and according to some contemporary chronicles) it is perhaps more likely that this mourning was done by the Earl of Worcester who, having survived the battle of Shrewsbury, may have felt some degree of guilt for bringing his nephew thus far, only to be let down by allies who had failed to support him at the crucial moment.

Thomas Percy may have also shed some tears for himself as he beheld the more personal results of failed rebellion lying prostrate and bloody at his feet. He knew that soon he too would be dealt with in a similar manner. As a despised rebel who, only a few hours before, had been given a chance to surrender, Worcester understood his crime, and the punishment he would receive, all too well. As Hotspur's battered corpse was borne away by Thomas Neville, Lord Furnival, to be solemnly buried in the neighbouring chapel of Whitchurch, the elder Percy was bound to his horse like a common criminal and taken to Shrewsbury Castle, there to await his fate.

It is estimated that 1,600 men were killed in Bull Field on 21 July 1403, while Thomas Walsingham recorded that 3,000 men were wounded, many of these later dying of their injuries as a result of sub-standard medical treatment and lingering infection. The Scottish chronicler, Andrew Wyntoun, put the number of dead on both sides at as many as 7,000 to 8,000 men, their bloated corpses scattered within a three-mile radius of the battlefield. Some of these bodies would undoubtedly have been left to decompose of their own accord; however, as stated by the charter of Battlefield College, the more concentrated patches of dead were heaped together in a great pit, close to (or actually on) the spot where the church now stands, a legacy of death and a permanent memorial to those who fell on St Mary Magdalene's Eve six hundred years ago.

But even if we take all these figures into account, it is apparent that many more than 1,600 died as a result of the battle, and that this number only denotes the number of men actually buried in Bateleyfield – the bloodiest meadow of the Shrewsbury conflict. The confusion caused by the rout and the lateness of the hour must have also delayed proper identification of the dead until the following day, so that bodies were still being gathered and interred for some considerable time after the battle had ended. Indeed, it is possible that Hotspur's body was not found until Sunday 22 July, despite the capture of his uncle the previous night.

Of the named dead on the king's side, the Earl of Stafford and nine other knights had been slain in the battle. These were Sir Walter Blount, Sir Hugh Stanley, Sir John Clifton, Sir John Cokayne, Sir Nicholas Gansell, Sir John Calverley, Sir John Massey of Pontington, Sir Hugh Mortimer and Sir Robert Gonsill, most of these receiving the honour of knighthood on the morning before the battle. As for the rebel leaders, Hotspur and 200 knights and gentlemen of Cheshire had been killed, according to Walsingham, 'beyond the gentlemen and footmen whose numbers we do not know'.[180]

Another manuscript records that precisely 2,291 men were killed in 'Bellum Salopia in campo vocato Haitlefeld alias Berwykefeld'[181] and the fact that Battlefield church was built over the remains of the slain is confirmed by its dimensions: namely, 126 feet in length and 65 feet in breadth (including the cemetery). That Sir Richard Venables and Sir Richard Vernon were taken prisoner, along with the Earl of Worcester, when the fighting was over is well documented, a clear indication that the king aimed to make an example of at least some of the rebel leaders who had fought against him. Indeed, on Monday 23 July Worcester, Venables and Vernon were summarily convicted of treason and formally beheaded in Shrewsbury market place. The head of Worcester was immediately dispatched to London, where it was set up on London Bridge as a warning to all of Henry's wavering subjects that rebellion would not be tolerated in any part of his realm. It was not until 18 December that the head of Thomas Percy was taken down and buried alongside his body in the abbey church of St Peter at Shrewsbury – it was a sad end to such a promising political and knightly career.

But of all the rebels who had been either executed or interred in Bateleyfield, the worst fate of all was reserved for the already decomposing body of Hotspur. A day or two after its burial at Whitchurch, the king ordered it exhumed from its resting place, rubbed in salt, and placed upright between two great millstones at the High Cross in Shrewsbury. And here Hotspur's once hyperactive body sat inertly on public view, guarded by armed sentries, until it was further decreed that other parts of the realm needed to be reminded of Hotspur's intransigence. Removed from public exhibition at Shrewsbury, Percy's head was cut off and sent to York so that it might be spiked over one of its gates. In keeping with the policy followed at the time, the rest of Hotspur's corpse was similarly dealt with – butchered into quarters and dispatched to hang above the gates of London, Bristol, Newcastle and Chester for all to marvel at. In order to prevent further rumours circulating that Hotspur might be still alive, the king also sent a number of messengers to proclaim his death all over the kingdom and these orders were soon followed up by another set of couriers who were sent out to warn people against speaking ill of the king's government. Every effort was made to ensure that duplicates of Hotspur would not plague King Henry's reign, and the victor of Shrewsbury made doubly sure of this worry by immediately riding into the north to deal personally with those 'rebels' who were still at large.

With his valiant son, the Prince of Wales, tasked to deal with another threatened incursion by Glyndwr and Mortimer in Wales, Henry's next problem centred on Yorkshire where, according to popular report, the Earl of Northumberland had remained 'crafty sick' while his son and brother had perished in battle. However, the Earl of Westmorland and Sir Robert Waterton had already dealt with Percy's show of strength near the town of Tadcaster. Seizing the golden opportunity to thwart his rival's plans by gathering substantial forces of his own in the rear of Northumberland's army, Neville not only managed to block Percy's advance to Shrewsbury, but also succeeded in proving his loyalty to King Henry at a time when he needed it most. By forcing Percy to withdraw on Newcastle, the stage was set for a final reckoning between the two northern families. It is ironic that on the very same day that Thomas Percy had perished at the block, the Earl of Westmorland could confidently report to Henry that he had managed to restrain the power of the lion in the north.

Meanwhile, the friendly northern castle of Warkworth provided a welcome refuge to the broken Earl of Northumberland until he finally agreed to submit to Henry at York. On Saturday 11 August 1403 the once-proud earl rode into the city to beg his king for forgiveness, but the fact that he had to view the ghastly sight of his son's head above the gate must have completely crushed what was left of his famous northern pride. He alone had been responsible for placing Henry Bolingbroke on the English throne; now he had come to yield himself to his mercy. In a welter of apologies and excuses the poor old man stooped so low as to lay the blame for the rebellion wholly upon his son, who, he said, had acted without his consent. John Hardyng, who survived the battle of Shrewsbury, was so scathing of the great earl's degrading statement about Hotspur that one cannot help but sympathise with his feelings both immediately after the battle, and also in later years when Hardyng had time to consider how his readers might view the Percy achievement. Speaking of Hotspur's plight at Shrewsbury, the Percy chronicler maintains that,

> His uncle dere was with hym there dedde,
> His father came not out of Northumberland,
> But failed hym foule without witte or rede;
> But to the kyng he came I understand,
> Holy submitting hym unto his royall hand.[182]

Why did Henry Percy fail his impulsive son at the eleventh hour? Was he indeed sick in some remote part of Yorkshire? Or had Hotspur acted without his father's consent in the heat of the moment? Whatever the real explanation for the apparent split in Percy loyalties, one common element seems to run ahead of all the rest, and this centres on how the Earl of Northumberland viewed his son after being reprimanded by the king during the parliament of 1402. Hotspur's reluctance to give up his share of the Scottish prisoners captured at Homildon Hill was undoubtedly an issue that was bound to cause an amount of friction in the Percy household. But how entrenched was this ill feeling? Plainly Hotspur's disagreements with the king suggest that he could no longer rely on Henry's friendship, despite the king's willingness, within four months of the rebellion, to further increase Percy gains in the north. So did King Henry intend to distance the Earl of Northumberland from his fiery son by bribing him with territory that he had lusted after for years? Again, nothing can be certain, but there is evidence to suggest that Northumberland may have been the instrument of Henry's will to curb Hotspur's further ambitions with his brother-in-law Mortimer. The various contentious issues over unpaid wages for his men, Hotspur's request for the king's help to pay for Mortimer's ransom, his refusal to surrender Douglas because of this, and the final bitter quarrel between the king and Hotspur, when the former rebuked Percy for his defiance, could only have caused acute embarrassment to the Earl of Northumberland.

But was this humiliation serious enough to turn father against son? John Hardyng, despite his pro-Percy viewpoint, seemed to think so, although there is some element of truth in the idea that the rebellion was badly planned right from the start. Northumberland and Glyndwr's movements were certainly flawed at every turn by 'mitigating' circumstances, but was this disparity of aim due to Hotspur's unbridled impetuosity or was it that both parties wanted to strike independently when the king had been 'bruised' by Hotspur at Shrewsbury? Whatever the real reason, it is clear that Hotspur's fate was sealed by his own chivalrous impetus brought on by the king's unwillingness to surrender to his demands. However, it is also apparent that others whose politics ran separate to the precepts of honour and chivalry must also share the blame.

As for the victor of Shrewsbury, all that remained was to apportion the spoils of victory. Soon after Northumberland's meeting with Henry at York, the earl consented to a formal agreement that the castles of Berwick, Cockermouth, Alnwick, Warkworth, Prudhoe and Langlee should be kept and governed by officers appointed by the king. Henry Percy senior was, in effect, about to be supplanted by others more worthy of the king's trust. Deprived of his office as constable and brought before parliament to answer for the rebellion in person, Percy once more found that his fate and that of the house of Percy hung in the balance. However, as we have seen, the Earl of Northumberland was the perennial survivor of his age and the lords in parliament held that his actions, serious as they were, did not amount to treason and that he might be only punished with a large fine.

No doubt still protesting that Hotspur was wholly to blame for the rebellion, the lion was released not before too long back into the north – but what manner of gilded cage awaited him in his kingdom? Certainly all Percy's northern castles had been surrendered to the crown. Letters had also been dispatched to bring before all the knights and esquires of Northumberland an oath binding them to the king and his heirs, and urging them to renounce the company and the service of the earl on pain of death. As for those who had remained loyal to the king through his most difficult time, the rest of the Percy estates seemed ripe for an early harvest.

King Henry had won his only full-scale battle by the very narrowest of margins, but he had many men to thank for his success in the field despite the fact that Hotspur may have been killed at Shrewsbury by a chance arrow shot from an unknown royal bowstave. Among those who benefited from suppressing the Percy rebellion, George Dunbar, Earl of March may have been considered the most worthy to receive Henry's thanks, being deemed the king's rescuer in the heat and uncertainty of battle. However, apart from acquiring Hotspur's forfeited possessions in the fens of Lincolnshire and some of the many estates and properties that had once been owned by the Earl of Worcester, Dunbar failed in his attempt to secure a substantial foothold in northern England, ostensibly his preferred area of influence.

All manors, castles and lands formerly belonging to Henry Percy in Cumberland were subsequently granted to the king's third son, Prince John, then aged fourteen, while other more prestigious northern appointments were reserved for those who had English rather than Scottish roots in the marches. The keeping of the west march, for instance, was predictably given over to John Neville, Earl of Westmorland, although the post was not formally conferred upon him until March 1404, while Dunbar's grandiose ambitions were further frustrated by the appointment of Prince John to Hotspur's former post of warden of Berwick-upon-Tweed. The east march was also given to Prince John when the king decided that Westmorland's appointment to both marches was far too dangerous, considering recent history. However, with the border region secure and largely in royal hands for the moment, the king felt that it was safe to once more turn his attention to Wales where Owain Glyndwr, as elusive as ever, was still at large.

The main threat to Henry's reign had been put down in Bull Field with the death of Hotspur, but it is clear from what transpired after the battle of Shrewsbury that the Earl of Northumberland would never be satisfied as long as he thought that there was a chance to regain his former power in the north. Evidently, in February 1405, Percy had signed the partition treaty with Glyndwr and Mortimer in North Wales that was later known as the Tripartite Indenture, but soon events much closer to home were providing the earl with another chance to further his cause. Archbishop Scrope's rebellion, centring on Yorkshire, was directed towards Northumberland's forces mustering at Berwick and Jedburgh, but unfortunately for the earl, Scrope's 'army' was promptly dealt with by the energetic Earl of Westmorland who, as loyal as ever, confounded the rebels at Shipton Moor six miles outside York. Scrope's petition, which had been posted on the doors of churches in York, was very similar to Hotspur's manifesto read before Henry prior to the battle of Shrewsbury, in that it accused the king of breaking his oath and falsely dethroning Richard II, an interesting statement to make if John Hardyng was responsible for fabricating the whole Doncaster 'oath' story years later. Scrope's petition also claimed that Hotspur had been wrongfully put to death without trial, that the rightful heir, carefully unnamed, should have been put on the throne, that peace should have been made with the Welsh and the Irish, and that the realm should be freed from all exactions, extortions and unjust payments forever. It is hardly surprising that soon after Scrope's capture, Henry ordered his archbishop's death; it was an act that he was to regret for the rest of his life.

The Earl of Northumberland, already marked by the royal headsman's axe for his part in Scrope's rebellion, was forced to flee into Scotland with only a few loyal supporters, and it was not until 1408 that he was ready to try his famous luck again. Thomas Walsingham recorded what took place when the proud Percy 'returned to England at an unfortunate hour', and arrived at the town of Tadcaster with a great crowd of people:

The sheriff [Sir Thomas Rokeby] pursued him through the town of Tadcaster, and placed sentinels round it, so that [the earl] could not escape without battle. When they saw this, the said lords promised that they would hazard their fortunes on the battlefield. Therefore at about two o'clock in the afternoon, the earl with his men rode to Bramham Moor near Hazelwood where he chose a place of battle. Without delay the sheriff and his men chose their ground, displaying the banner of St George, with the pennon of his arms spread out. On the other side the earl unfurled a pennon of his arms, and began with the sheriff a

213

desperate battle in which he preferred to die for his cause than to be captured; and so he was slain and fell. And there he was stripped and his head was cut off.[183]

Henry Percy was sixty-six years old when he died at the battle of Bramham Moor on 20 February 1408, but it seems that his severed head, allegedly full of silver hoary hairs, lasted longer than anyone could credit on a spike over London Bridge. Indeed, Thomas Walsingham states that the earl's head remained there in position until finally the king ordered it taken down, when it was found to be as fresh as ever, with the same appearance that it had when it had been living. However, despite the earl's 'preservation', along with his death came far greater problems for the remaining members of his family. With the house of Percy now in ruins, and Hotspur's only son an outcast, the very worst of all medieval holocausts seemed prey only to time and occasion.

All his life the Earl of Northumberland had been proud, selfish, crafty, unstable and faithless. His desertion of his son was shameful, but his power was all-consuming, especially when he was threatened with losing it. In the end his heart had become increasingly bitter when he saw his Neville rivals advancing in his place and this resulted in an incredible lack of wisdom and sound judgement. In his last mad bid to topple King Henry from an unstable throne, the earl stepped over the edge of reason and acted with a recklessness that cost him his life and his title. If Hotspur was guilty of chivalrous impetuosity, his father was undone by a trait bequeathed of his ancestors – the need to survive at all costs. As a result, he alone was responsible for demolishing the Percy achievement in one fateful generation. The succeeding ones would never be so powerful again, even though Henry V eventually restored Hotspur's son to his title and estates in 1416.

As for the rest of the 1403 rebels, Archibald Douglas was captured after Shrewsbury and eventually ransomed by the Scots in 1408. He continued to raid the English border from 1412 to 1422 in an effort to establish Scottish 'fay' in the absence of more rigorous action by his king. Archibald, true to his nickname 'the loser', went to his death fighting against the English at Verneuil in 1424, although his resilience as a fighter is to be marvelled at considering that his many wounds, especially by medieval standards of surgery, would have killed many lesser men outright, if not on the field of battle then after the event. By way of contrast, Henry IV only fought one major pitched battle in all his life. Admittedly it was one of the most important battles he could have ever conceived winning, but he never had to tempt fate again, despite further incursions by the Welsh.

During his turbulent reign King Henry failed to resolve the Scottish question, but he had succeeded in disposing of an anointed king, an impetuous rebel, an archbishop, and his most powerful northern earl. However, Glyndwr and Mortimer continued to threaten his reign like an incurable disease, a malady that would eventually kill him at Westminster in 1413. Owain Glyndwr, on the other hand, survived as a guerrilla leader until 1411, after which he disappeared from history, little being known of his death or his whereabouts after the Welsh submitted to Henry V in 1413. Sir Edmund Mortimer met with a less respectful end, although his house continued to remain a thorn in the Lancastrian side during the fifteenth century in the conflict of the Wars of the Roses. Defiant to the last, Sir Edmund died of starvation, besieged by the English in Harlech Castle in January 1409, a pitiable end that placed his family, and the earldom of March, forever in the shadow of the throne until Edward, Earl of March snatched the Lancastrian crown at the bloody battle of Towton in 1461.

Today, the broad fields that once bore grim witness to the battle of Shrewsbury are a peaceful haven of quiet contemplation. Battlefield church is a site of historical interest, much the same as it was when people visited the original chapel and college built there soon after the battle. That the battlefield complex was originally constructed is an enduring testament to those far-sighted individuals who sought to venerate the men who had died there only a few years prior to its foundation. However, one can hardly dismiss the possibility that Bateleyfield was also probably the first medieval visitor centre where commoners could pray and contemplate on the very spot where history could have turned out so differently.

Not much has changed with the passing of years, but if Shrewsbury had been won by the rebels, who would have been crowned king? Hotspur or Mortimer? Considering that the Earl of Northumberland and the Welsh had failed to arrive at Shrewsbury in time, and the fact that according to the chronicles Hotspur had already been acclaimed king by his followers in the heat of battle, would Thomas Percy have advocated Hotspur's usurpation of Henry's throne instead of Mortimer? Indeed, why was Hotspur so ready to die for what he believed in on that fateful day in July 1403? Was it the cause of 'revolted Mortimer' or was it actually his own? In short, what turned Hotspur from a renowned and much-loved English knight into a much-hated medieval rebel?

As already determined, the popular estimate of Hotspur is mainly derived from Shakespeare's picture of the impetuous hotheaded soldier; but this is not the whole story. Even in 1887 the real Henry Percy was regarded, in Fonblanque's own words, 'as a more interesting object to contemplate than the poet's brilliant creation, as we see him prepare to dive into the depths of the ocean to pluck up drowned honour by the locks, or soar into space to pluck bright honour from the pale-faced moon'.[184] Shakespeare's Hotspur was indeed a dramatic reconstruction of a man who probably defied all reasonable understanding by those who actually knew him. However, the historical Hotspur is perhaps more accessible to the curious. Cradled in war, and trained in all respects to deal with local border raiding, his main obligation was to hold by force that which his ancestors had previously won. Thus Hotspur's life ended as it had begun, with a mailed fist on the hilt of his sword. In his later years he was employed in civil duties under two kings, he had served as a defender of English borders and as an envoy to foreign lands. But Hotspur's diplomacy was essentially an armed one; the argument he best loved was that which placed him at the head of an armed retinue of mounted lances riding against his enemies with honour. Wherever the clash of arms was to be heard, Hotspur was certain to be in the thick of the fight. Free of his father's influence, he blundered against the Scots at Otterburn and hence his reputation for rash action was born out of a chivalrous need to prove himself in battle.

Honour followed him like a double-edged sword. On the one hand, he was the protector of kings and on the other he was their worst enemy. Determined to help dethrone Richard II in 1399, he became the instrument of kingmaking, first with Lancaster and then with Mortimer. It is highly unlikely that Hotspur wished to be king himself, contrary to the fact that some of his followers clearly thought him worthy of the crown in his last fateful moments of life. That he was constrained by an ambitious and selfish father may explain much about his decision to personally oppose Henry IV at Shrewsbury, but his real motives were clearly of a more personal nature. Certainly others had more ambitious plans for him, and may have intentionally used Hotspur's impetuosity in order to fulfil a much grander design. Above all, Hotspur was an uneasy spirit, a chivalrous man who from a very early age took up the code of arms and ran with it to his death. We may have some sympathy for his intentions to place a more legitimate heir on the English throne, but there is no doubting that he was a rebellious man at heart and that this was his ultimate failing.

In death Hotspur was very soon remembered as the quintessential knightly hero of 'Chevy Chase' whose involuntary outbreak of admiration for Douglas's bravery in battle reveals a bygone age of chivalry that, even through many corruptions and additions, resonates as clearly today as it did in the court of Henry VI where it was first heard. Ever since then writers have not strayed too far from the legend, and thus the real historical Hotspur has been lost in time, to be replaced by oral tradition:

> At last the Duglas and the Perse met,
> Lyk to captains of might and mayne,
> They swapte togethar tyll the both swat,
> With swords that wear of fyn myllan,
> . . . Holde the, Perse said the Duglas,
> And i'feth I shall the brynge,
> Wer thowe shalte have a yerl's wagis,
> Of Jamy our Scottish kynge.
> . . . Nay then, sayd the Lord Perse,
> I tolde it the beforne,
> That I wolde never yeldyde be,
> To no man of a woman borne.
> With that ther cam an arrowe hastely,
> For the off a mightie wane,
> Hit hath strekene the yerle Duglas,
> In at the brest bane.
> . . . The Perse leanyde on his brande,
> And sawe the Duglas de,
> He took the dede man be the hande,
> And sayd, 'Wo ys me for thee!'
> To have savyde thy lyffe I wolde have pertyd with

My landes for years thre,
For a better man of hart, nare of hande,
Was not in all the north countre.[185]

Sadly, no similar ballad was ever composed of Hotspur's death at Shrewsbury. However, soon after his corpse had been exposed, Hotspur's widow, Elizabeth Mortimer, was instrumental in performing the last act of her husband's worldly existence by requesting that his remains be removed from the gates of the various the towns where they had been displayed. The grisly orders of reclamation are given in E.B. de Fonblanque's *Annals of the House of Percy*:

For the Head and Quarters to be delivered.
Percy

Whereas of our special grace we have granted to our cousin, Elizabeth, who was the wife of Henry de Percy, knight, the head and quarters of the same Henry to be buried. We command you that the head aforesaid placed by our command upon the gate of the city [of York] aforesaid you deliver to the same Elizabeth to be buried according to our grant aforesaid.

By Writ of Privy Seal.

The King to the Mayor and Sheriff of the town of Newcastle upon Tyne, greeting. Whereas (as above) we command you that you deliver to the said Elizabeth a certain quarter of the said Henry placed upon the gate of the city aforesaid to be buried according to the grant aforesaid.[186]

Unfortunately, the place of Hotspur's final interment is not given in the roll. However, William Peeris in his *Metrical Chronicle of the Percye Family* stated that, once collected, all of Hotspur's remains were buried next to his father in York Minster, although this has always been open to some conjecture, given that the more prominent Percy tombs were then situated at Beverley and Alnwick. With hindsight, it is perhaps more appropriate to leave Hotspur's last resting place a mystery, seeing that his remains had previously suffered a great deal of displacement and deserved a more secure burial far away from those who considered his memory still a potential threat to the kingdom. Even Fonblanque failed to locate the exact place of Hotspur's grave, or to fathom the man behind the legend. Preferring instead to focus on his father, Fonblanque follows the theory that Hotspur's extreme impetuosity was actually a myth, misrepresented by Shakespeare and woven into the pages of history without a second thought as to how contemporary sources viewed his many 'chivalrous' actions. The truth is that a medieval knight was impetuous by nature; therefore Shakespeare was not entirely wrong in his assumptions that Hotspur was in fact a product of class, ostensibly a hothead with a hot spur. In agreeing with contemporary chroniclers such as Thomas Walsingham, who saw Hotspur as the greatest, bravest and most honourable soldier of his day, the story is therefore brought full circle. Indeed, Shakespeare's well-worn description of Harry Percy might have been written by Walsingham, although perhaps not as eloquently:

> . . . and by his light
> Did all the chivalry of England move
> To do brave acts. He was indeed the glass
> Wherein the noble youth did dress themselves.[186]

Hotspur's distinctive name has left an indelible imprint on the English consciousness that endures today in the works of Shakespeare and even in the traditions of a famous London football club whose ground still bears the name of the famous White Hart badge of Richard II. Hence the legend of Harry Percy changes from generation to generation, and becomes more fascinating with the passage of time.

The age of Hotspur is long gone, but his spirit can be resurrected by the faithful, in the ruins of Spofforth, in the halls of Alnwick, on the moors of Otterburn and Homildon, in the quiet acres of Bateleyfield, and in the wilds of the border country. He was the epitome of what a medieval knight strove to be, and it is this image of Hotspur that endures when in our imagination we see him 'heating his spurs' in the early dawn light and speeding to match his skill against those who thought him worthy of such a notorious nickname.

Notes

1. The author does not hold the opinion that Hotspur was born on 20 May 1366 at Alnwick Castle – see chapter 3.
2. E.B. de Fonblanque, *Annals of the House of Percy*, 1887. Pat. 2, Edward II, p. 2, m. 19.
3. 'Spawford' – 'the ford by the River Spaw'.
4. See R.L. Storey, 'The North of England', in S.B. Crimes, C.D. Ross and R.A. Griffiths (eds), *Fifteenth Century England 1399–1509*, 1995, p. 131.
5. Ibid., pp. 129–30.
6. J.A. Tuck, 'War and Society in the Medieval North', *Northern History*, 21 (1985), p. 42.
7. H. Ellis (ed.), *The Chronicle of John Hardyng*, 1812, p. 380.
8. The phrase was first coined by Lord Hunsden to William Cecil. See A. Pollard, 'Percies, Nevilles, and the Wars of the Roses', *History Today* (September 1993), p. 42.
9. L.T. Smith (ed.), *The Itinerary of John Leland 1535–1543*, 1910, vol. 1, pp. 45–6.
10. Fonblanque, *Annals*, p. xx.
11. A.R. Myers (ed.), *English Historical Documents, 1327–1485*, vol. 4, p. 82.
12. Ellis, *John Hardyng*, i–ii, MS Lands. 200, f. 204b.
13. Fonblanque, *Annals*, p. 111.
14. J.M.D. Meiklejohn, *History of England and Great Britain*, 1893, p. 192.
15. R. Barber (ed. and trans.), *The Life and Campaigns of the Black Prince*, The Folio Society, 1979, p. 136.
16. G.F. Beltz, *Memorials of the Most Noble Order of the Garter*, 1841, p. 315.
17. G.C. Macaulay (ed.), *The Chronicles of Froissart*, 1904, pp. 424–5.
18. Fonblanque, *Annals*, p. 111.
19. E. Maunde-Thompson (ed.), *Chronicon Angliae ab Anno Domini 1328 usque ad Annum 1388, auctore Monacho quodam Sncti Albani* 1874, p. 75.
20. See A. Tuck, *Border Warfare – A History of Conflict on the Anglo-Scottish Border*, 1979.
21. H.T. Riley (ed.), 'Thomas Walsingham', *Historia Anglicana*, vol. 1 (1863–4), pp. 387–8.
22. M.H. Keen, 'Chivalry, nobility and the man-at-arms', in C.T. Allmand (ed.), *War, Literature and Politics in the Late Middle Ages*, 1976, p. 45.
23. Riley, 'Thomas Walsingham', p. 144.
24. T. Rymer (ed.), *Foedera, Conventiones, Litterae . . .*, 1704–35, vol. vii, p. 353.
25. A mark was worth approximately 66p.

26. J.R. Lumby (ed.), *Chronicon Henry Knighton*, 1895, vol. ii, p. 210; T. Hearne (ed.), *Historia Vitae et Regni Rich. II*, by a monk of Evesham, 1729, p. 73.
27. Riley, 'Thomas Walsingham', p. 144.
28. Macaulay, *Chronicles of Froissart*, p. 174.
29. N.H. Nicholas, *The Scrope and Grosvenor Controversy*, vol. 1, 1832, p. 199.
30. See W. Dickson (ed.), 'Chronicles of Alnwick Abbey', *Archaeologia Aeliana*, 1844, vol. 3, p. 42. 'Henry was born of the said Lady Margaret the 13th of the Kalends of June, in the year of our Lord 1364'; the chronicle fails to mention where.
31. J. Speed, *History of Great Britain*, 1623, p. 534.
32. Fonblanque, *Annals*, p. 141.
33. Beltz, *Order of the Garter*, p. 315–16.
34. T. Hearne (ed.), *Johannis de Fordun Scotichroniconi Continuatio*, iv, 1722, p. 1075.
35. Macaulay, *Chronicles of Froissart*, p. 380.
36. Ibid., p. 374.
37. Probably at Southdean (Suden), lying between Hawick and Otterburn. The church is now in ruins.
38. *English Historical Documents*, vol. 4, p. 59.
39. Macaulay, *Chronicles of Froissart*, p. 370.
40. Ibid.
41. C.W.C. Oman, *The Art of War in the Middle Ages*, 1991, vol. 2, p. 108.
42. Macaulay, *Chronicles of Froissart*, p. 370.
43. Ibid.
44. H.L. Trevor Roper, 'The Bishopric of Durham and the Capitalist Reformation', *Durham University Journal*, 38 (1945–6), p. 47.
45. Macaulay, *Chronicles of Froissart*, p. 371.
46. Riley, 'Thomas Walsingham', p. 176.
47. Hearne, *Scotichroniconi*, p. 1075.
48. Fonblanque, *Annals*, p. 148. The Cavers standard may also be of later origin.
49. R. White, *The Battle of Otterburn*, 1857. Now a very rare book.
50. Inherent Military Probability. Burne employed this technique by starting with the 'undisputed' facts, then placing himself in the shoes of each commander in turn, asking himself in each case what *he* would have done in a similar situation.
51. A.H. Burne, *The Battlefields of England* (consolidated edition), 1996, p. 132.
52. Macaulay, *The Chronicles of Froissart*, p. 371.
53. Ibid.
54. Ibid., p. 373.
55. Ibid., p. 372.
56. Ibid.
57. Ibid., p. 373.
58. Hearne, *Scotichroniconi*, p. 1075.
59. Ibid.
60. Macaulay, *Chronicles of Froissart*, p. 373.
61. Hearne, *Scotichroniconi*, p. 1075.
62. H. Ellis, *John Hardyng*, p. 342.
63. Macaulay, *Chronicles of Froissart*, p. 374.
64. Hearne, *Scotichroniconi*, p. 1075.
65. Macaulay, *Chronicles of Froissart*, p. 373.
66. D. MacPherson, *Andrew Wyntoun's Orygynale Cronykil of Scotland*, vol. 2, 1795, p. 341.

67. Macaulay, *Chronicles of Froissart*, p. 373.
68. Ibid., p. 374.
69. Hearne, *Scotichroniconi*, p. 1075.
70. M. Brown, *The Black Douglases*, 1998, p. 143.
71. Macaulay, *Chronicles of Froissart*, p. 374.
72. Ibid., p. 375.
73. Ibid.
74. Ibid., p. 376.
75. J. Taylor (ed. and trans.), *The Kirkstall Abbey Chronicles*, Thoresby Society, xlii, 1952, p. 72.
76. MacPherson, *Cronykil of Scotland*, p. 341.
77. Macaulay, *Chronicles of Froissart*, p. 376.
78. 'The Battle of Otterbourne', British Library, Cotton MS, Cleopatra, C.IV.
79. Fonblanque, *House of Percy*, p. 151. Issue Rolls, 12 Richard II, 15 July 1389.
80. Riley, 'Thomas Walsingham', p. 181.
81. Ibid.
82. M.L. Bellaguet (ed.), *Chronique du religieux de Saint-Denys. . .*, vol. 1, 1839–52, pp. 673–83.
83. D. Wright (trans.), *The Canterbury Tales*, Oxford, 1986, p. 66.
84. J. Strachey (ed.), *Rotuli Parliamentorum*, vol. 3, 1783, p. 360.
85. G.B. Stow (ed.), *Historia Vitae et Regni Ricardi Secundi*, 1977, p. 51.
86. H.T. Riley (ed.), *Annales Ricardi Secoundi*, in *Johannis de Trokelowe et Anon Chronica et Annales*, Rolls Series, 1866, p. 238.
87. PRO E404 (Warrants under the Privy Seal), no. 46. See also R.L. Storey, 'The Wardens of the Marches of England towards Scotland, 1377–1489', *EHR*, vol. 72, 593–615.
88. Ellis, *John Hardyng*, p. 353.
89. M.V. Clarke and V.H. Galbraith, *The Dieulacres Chronicle*, Bulletin of the John Rylands Library, XIV, 1930, p. 179.
90. Ibid.
91. E. Maunde-Thompson (ed.), *The Chronicle of Adam of Usk*, 1990, p. 46.
92. Riley, *Annales Ricardi Secoundi*.
93. B. Williams (ed.), *Chronique de la traison et mort de Richard Deux*, English Historical Society, 1846, pp. 193 ff.
94. Maunde-Thompson, *Chronicle of Adam of Usk*, p. 48.
95. C. Given-Wilson (ed.), *Chronicles of the Revolution 1397–1400*, Manchester University Press, 1993, pp. 193–4.
96. Clarke and Galbraith, *Dieulacres Chronicle*.
97. Ellis, *John Hardyng*, p. 358.
98. T. Wright (ed.), *Political Poems and Songs . . . Edward III to Henry VIII*, Rolls Series, 2 vols, 1859–61.
99. Maunde-Thompson, *Chronicle of Adam of Usk*, p. 95.
100. Ibid.
101. *Archaeologia Aeliana*, vol. 4, 1860, p. 182.
102. F.C. Hingleston-Randolf (ed.), *Royal and Historical Letters of Henry IV* 1863–4, pp. 69–70.
103. Issue Rolls, 3 Hen. IV.
104. J.A. Giles (ed.), *Incerti Scriptoris Chronicon Angliae*, 1848, p. 31.
105. Ibid.
106. Fonblanque, *House of Percy*, p. 203.
107. Maunde-Thompson, *Chronicle of Adam of Usk*, p. 107.
108. J.M.W. Bean, 'Henry IV and the Percies', *History*, XLIV (1959), p. 222.

109. Ibid., p. 223.
110. See J. Ramsay, *Lancaster and York*, vol. 1, 1892, p. 45.
111. J.L. Kirby (ed.), *Calendar of Signet Letters of Henry IV and Henry V 1399–1422*, 1978, letter 77.
112. Brown, *Black Douglases*, p. 153.
113. Ellis, *John Hardyng*, p. 359.
114. Riley, 'Thomas Walsingham', p. 251.
115. Kirby, *Signet Letters*, letter 81.
116. Ibid.
117. Ellis, *John Hardyng*, p. 359.
118. Hearne, *Historia Vitae et Regni Rich. II*, p. 180.
119. Riley, 'Thomas Walsingham', p. 251.
120. Ibid.
121. Ibid.
122. Ibid.
123. Ibid.
124. Kirby, *Signet Letters*, letter 81.
125. Riley, 'Thomas Walsingham', p. 251.
126. Ellis, *John Hardyng*, p. 359.
127. Kirby, *Signet Letters*, letter 76.
128. J.H. Wylie, *History of England under Henry IV*, vol. 1, 1884, p. 287.
129. A mark was worth approximately 66p.
130. Fonblanque, *Annals*, p. 212.
131. Giles, *Chronicon Angliae*, p. 33.
132. H. Ellis (ed.), *Original Letters Illustrative of English History*, 2nd Series, vol. 1, 1827, p. 24.
133. The interview between the king and Hotspur can be found in various accounts, but more specifically in F.W.D. Brie (ed.), *The Brut Chronicle of England*, Early English Text Society, Original Series, 136, p. 548.
134. Ibid.
135. Maunde-Thompson, *Chronicle of Adam of Usk*, p. 126.
136. A.H. Thomas and I.D. Thornley (eds), *The Great Chronicle of London*, 1983, p. 85.
137. Bean, 'Henry IV and the Percies', p. 225.
138. Ellis, *Original Letters*, vol. 2, p. 19.
139. Ellis, *John Hardyng*, p. 361.
140. Kirby, *Signet Letters*, letter 153.
141. Ibid., letter 154.
142. Ellis, *John Hardyng*, p. 361.
143. Riley, 'Thomas Walsingham', p. 361.
144. Ellis, *John Hardyng*, p. 361.
145. Kirby, *Signet Letters*, letter 155.
146. L.T. Smith (ed.), *The Itineraray of John Leland 1535–1543*, vol. 4, 1910, pp. 81–2.
147. The prophecy is mentioned by a number of historical sources as being the major cause of the Percy rebellion, including Edward Hall, Raphael Holinshed and John Speed.
148. Dugdale's *Monasticon*, vol. 6, part 3, pp. 1426–7.
149. Ibid.
150. Smith, *Itineraray of John Leland*, p. 83.
151. R. Brooke, *Visits to Fields of Battle in England*, 1857, p. 17.
152. Thomas and Thornley, *Great Chronicle of London*, p. lviii.
153. H. Nicholas (ed.), *Acts and Proceedings of the Privy Council*, vol. 1, 1834, liii.
154. Riley, 'Thomas Walsingham', p. 396.
155. Ellis, *John Hardyng*, pp. 361–2.
156. H. Owen and J.B. Blakeway, *History of Shrewsbury*, vol. 1, 1825, pp. 187–8.
157. Hearne, *Historia Vitae*, p. 53.
158. Riley, 'Thomas Walsingham', p. 228.
159. British Library, Cotton MS Claudius B.IX, f. 296, and Cotton MS Tiberius C.IX, f. 27v.

160. Burne, *Battlefields of England*, p. 73.
161. Ellis, *John Hardyng*, p. iii.
162. MacPherson, *Cronykil of Scotland*, p. 407.
163. Riley, 'Thomas Walsingham', p. 257.
164. Ibid.
165. Ibid., p. 258.
166. Ellis, *John Hardyng*, p. 352.
167. Ibid., p. 361.
168. Ibid., pp. 352–3.
169. Riley, 'Thomas Walsingham', p. 257.
170. Ibid., pp. 257–8.
171. H. Ellis (ed.), *Edward Hall's Chronicle*, 1809, p. 51.
172. Riley, 'Thomas Walsingham', p. 258.
173. Thomas and Thornley, *Great Chronicle of London*, p. 85.
174. Maunde-Thompson, *Chronicle of Adam of Usk*, p. 123.
175. J. Gairdner (ed.), *The Historical Collections of a London Citizen*, 1876, p. 103.
176. Riley, 'Thomas Walsingham', p. 258.
177. Maunde-Thompson, *Chronicle of Adam of Usk*, p. 123. The application of the two horns of the moon to the two Percys is no doubt suggested by the Percy badge, a crescent, a livery that was worn by Percy retainers at this time. See Nicholas, *Acts of the Privy Council*, I, p. 209.
178. Gairdner, *London Citizen*, 1876, p. 103.
179. Speed, *History of Great Britain*, p. 629.
180. Riley, 'Thomas Walsingham', p. 258.
181. Owen and Blakeway, *History of Shrewsbury*, p. 194.
182. Ellis, *John Hardyng*, p. 362.
183. V.H. Galbraith (ed.), *The St Albans Chronicle*, 1937, p. 27.
184. Fonblanque, *Annals*, p. xx.
185. Ibid., p. 152.
186. Ibid., pp. 531–2.
187. *Henry IV Part 2*, Act 2, Scene 3.

Select Bibliography

C.T. Allmand, ed., *War, Literature and Politics in the Late Middle Ages*, 1976.

R. Barber, ed., trans., *The Life and Campaigns of the Black Prince*, The Folio Society, 1979.

J.M.W. Bean, 'Henry IV and the Percies', *History*, XLIV, 1959.

M.L. Bellaguet, ed., *Chronique du religieux de Saint-Denys*, vol. 1, 1839–52.

G.F. Beltz, *Memorials of the Most Noble Order of the Garter*, 1841.

R. Brooke, *Visits to Fields of Battle in England*, 1857.

M. Brown, *The Black Douglases*, 1998.

A.H. Burne, *The Battlefields of England* (consolidated edition), 1996.

M.V. Clarke and V.H. Galbraith, *The Dieulacres Chronicle*, Bulletin of the John Rylands Library, XIV, 1930.

S.B. Crimes, C.D. Ross, R.A. Griffiths, eds, *Fifteenth Century England 1399–1509*, 1995.

R.R. Davies, *The Revolt of Owain Glyn Dwr*, 1995.

W. Dickson, ed., 'Chronicles of Alnwick Abbey', in *Archaeologia Aeliana*, 1844.

H. Ellis, ed., *Edward Hall's Chronicle*, 1809.

H. Ellis, ed., *Original Letters Illustrative of English History*, 2nd Series, 1827.

H. Ellis, ed., *The Chronicle of John Hardyng*, 1812.

E.B. de Fonblanque, *Annals of the House of Percy*, 1887.

J. Gairdner, ed., *The Historical Collections of a London Citizen*, 1876.

V.H. Galbraith, ed., *The St Albans Chronicle*, 1937.

J.A. Giles, ed., *Incerti Scriptoris Chronicon Angliae*, 1848.

C. Given-Wilson, ed., *Chronicles of the Revolution 1397–1400*, 1993.

A. Goodman, *John of Gaunt*, 1992.

T. Hearne, ed., *Historia Vitae et Regni Rich. II*, by a monk of Evesham, 1729.

M. Keen, *Chivalry*, 1984.

J.L. Kirby, ed., *Calendar of Signet Letters of Henry IV and Henry V 1399–1422*, 1978.

R. Lomas, *A Power in the Land: The Percys*, 1999.

J.R. Lumby, ed., *Chronicon Henry Knighton*, 1895.

G.C. Macaulay, ed., *The Chronicles of Froissart*, 1904.

A.J. Macdonald, *Border Bloodshed: Scotland, England and France at War, 1369–1403*, 2000.

D. MacPherson, *Andrew Wyntoun's Orygynale Cronykil of Scotland*, 1795.

E. Maunde Thompson, ed., *Chronicon Angliae ab Anno Domini 1328 usque ad Annum 1388, auctore Monacho quodam Sncti Albani*, 1874.

Select Bibliography

E. Maunde-Thompson, ed., *The Chronicle of Adam of Usk*, 1990.

P. McNiven, *The Scottish Policy of the Percies and the Strategy of the Rebellion of 1403*, Bulletin of the John Rylands Library, 62.

J.M.D. Meiklejohn, *History of England and Great Britain*, 1893.

P.J. Morgan, *War and Society in Medieval Cheshire*, 1277–1403, Chetham Society, 1987.

C.J. Neville, *Violence, Custom and Law: The Anglo-Scottish Border Lands in the Later Middle Ages*, 1998.

N.H. Nicholas, *The Scrope and Grosvenor Controversy*, vol. 1, 1832.

N.H. Nicholas, ed., *Acts and Proceedings of the Privy Council*, vol. 1, 1834.

C.W.C. Oman, *The Art of War in the Middle Ages*, 1991.

H. Owen and J.B. Blakeway, *History of Shrewsbury*, vol. 1, 1825.

J. Ramsay, *Lancaster and York*, vol.1, 1892.

J. Reed, *The Border Ballads*, 1991.

H.T. Riley, ed., *Annales Ricardi Secoundi*, in *Johannis de Trokelowe et Anon Chronica et Annales*, Rolls Series 1866.

N. Saul, *Richard II*, 1997.

J.W. Sherborne, 'Perjury and the Lancastrian Revolution of 1399', *Welsh History Review*, 14, 1998.

L.T. Smith, ed., *The Itinerary of John Leland 1535–1543*, 1910.

J. Strachey, ed., *Rotuli Parliamentorum*, vol. 3, 1783.

H.L. Trevor Roper, 'The Bishopric of Durham and the Capitalist Reformation', *Durham University Journal*, 38, 1945–6.

J. Taylor, ed., and trans., *The Kirkstall Abbey Chronicles*,Thoresby Soc., xlii, 1952.

A.H. Thomas and I.D. Thornley, eds, *The Great Chronicle of London*, 1983.

J.A. Tuck, 'War and Society in the Medieval North', *Northern History*, 21, 1985.

J.A. Tuck, *Border Warfare – A History of Conflict on the Anglo Scottish Border*, 1979.

J.A. Tuck and A. Goodman, *War and Border Societies in the Middle Ages*, 1992.

R. White, *The Battle of Otterburn*, 1857.

B. Williams, ed., *Chronique de la traison et mort de Richard Deux*, English Historical Society, 1846.

D. Wright, trans., *The Canterbury Tales*, Oxford, 1986.

T. Wright, ed., *Political Poems and Songs . . . Edward III to Henry VIII*, Rolls Series, 2 vols, 1859–61.

J.H. Wylie, *History of England under Henry IV*, vol. 1, 1884.

Index

Index